MW01116405

Humans on the Move

# International Refugee Law Series

VOLUME 20

The titles published in this series are listed at *brill.com/irls*

# Humans on the Move

*Integrating an Adaptive Approach with a Rights-Based Approach to Climate Change Mobility*

*By*

Grant Dawson and Rachel Laut

**BRILL**

**NIJHOFF**

LEIDEN | BOSTON

The Library of Congress Cataloging-in-Publication Data is available online at https://catalog.loc.gov
LC record available at https://lccn.loc.gov/2021048915

Typeface for the Latin, Greek, and Cyrillic scripts: "Brill". See and download: brill.com/brill-typeface.

ISSN 2213-3836
ISBN 978-90-04-29760-9 (hardback)
ISBN 978-90-04-29888-0 (e-book)

*This book is dedicated to those amongst our ancestors who gazed upon the arc of the unknown horizon—and then dared to go there in search of a better life.*

⋱

Perhaps there is a kind of silver lining to these global environmental problems, because they are forcing us, willy-nilly, no matter how reluctant we may be, into a new kind of thinking—in which in some matters the well-being of the human species takes precedence over national and corporate interests. We are a resourceful species when push comes to shove. We know what to do. Out of the environmental crises of our time should come, unless we are much more foolish than I think we are, a binding up of the nations and the generations, and even the end of our long childhood.

— CARL SAGAN

# Contents

**PART 3**
*Implementing an Adaptive Approach to Climate Change Mobility*

# Foreword

When haven't we humans been on the move? The answer may be never. Unlike most of our closest primate relatives, to be human is to wander, to range far beyond that little patch of familiar forest, into the unknown. It's been the norm for us for at least several hundred thousand years. And even back at the beginning of human experience it may have had to do with climate change.

The very day that I finished reading this urgent and magisterial book, a new analysis was published concerning the earliest evidence we have yet found of indiscriminate violence against humans of all ages. Researchers from France and the United Kingdom, writing in Nature's Scientific Reports (27 May 2021), analyzed the remains of sixty-one of our ancestors who lived at least thirteen millennia ago. Their bones had been discovered in the 1960s at Jebel Sahaba, a cemetery of the late Pleistocene, in the Nile Valley. The new paper revealed a hundred wounds previously missed, both healed and unhealed, suggesting that the dead, male and female, children and adults, were not as was thought, the victims of a single battle, but the battered casualties of long periods of sustained conflict. Their skeletons were riddled with wounds caused by projectiles, blunt trauma, and stabbings with sharpened stone weapons. The researchers believe that this brutality was a result of the long-term stress on resources caused by the climate change at the end of the last glacial maximum.

We are still slaughtering each other. But some things have changed. We are no longer the clueless hostages to the fortunes of the Earth's natural cycles, but instigators of our own catastrophe. It is our fate to be citizens of the Anthropocene, the epoch of human-caused global environmental destruction and massive species extinction. We and our children, and theirs, live beneath the swiftly descending shadow of global catastrophe. There is hardly a place on Earth that will be left untouched, no nearby clement valley to pick up and move to for refuge from the deteriorating environment for the billions of us humans and our fellow Earthlings.

Science has given us unprecedented predictive powers. For more than a hundred years, the scientists have known that a reckoning over our planet-wide production of greenhouse gases was coming. Prophecies of the rising global mean temperature, made more than sixty years ago at the dawn of climate modeling, have proven to be surprisingly accurate. And yet, these early warnings could not seem to awaken us from our sleepwalking. In the 1970s when I first began writing about climate change, there was an impenetrable wall of fossil fuel economy propaganda buttressed by our natural tendency to deny and look away rather than face a daunting, and as it appeared back then, a largely abstract challenge.

Today, all but the most invested and benighted of us have joined the scientific consensus that we are in trouble. This dawning recognition was earned at the cost of countless scorched acres of land, evaporating glaciers, bleached reefs, inundated homes, and extinguished species. The marketplace has discovered a world-wide consumer appetite for the recycled, the renewable, and the sustainable. This critical first step towards change, the acceptance of reality, is a source of hope, one that has the potential to slow the rate of the warming of the world.

Though no matter what we do now, the worst impact of the agricultural and industrial revolution on our environment can only be blunted, not averted. For those consequences that are already built into our future, the question remains, how will we meet this challenge.

From the shattered bones of Jebel Sahaba through the broad cross-cultural surveys of human history, we know that scarcity and adverse change bring out the worst in us. The global novel coronavirus pandemic, itself possibly another symptom of climate change and habitat ruin, has exposed the vulnerabilities of our supply chains and the inadequacy of our health care infrastructure. For those of us who felt aggrieved by the restrictions and deprivations of the pandemic lockdown, rest assured this was but the mildest foretaste of what the full effects of even mitigated climate change hold in store for us. Recently, in the United States we have seen how civil and legal norms deemed solidly established for a couple of centuries can rapidly disintegrate under the assault from a single anti-democratic politician in power.

That's why this book is so important to me. Dawson and Laut are unflinching in their grasp of our blood-stained history and the grave trepidations of climate science. Their response is to propose a detailed, well-argued legal and social framework for navigating unprecedented dislocations without repeating the heinous sins of our violent and greedy past.

One of the most encouraging passages concerns the great wall being built across the entire Sahel, from coast to coast, where Africa is at its broadest. Not a wall to keep out desperate and starving humans on the move, but something much more promising. A natural wall of forest that can prevent the Sahara Desert from encroaching farther. Dawson and Laut encourage human self-confidence with their account of the Great Green Wall, a collaborative initiative of twenty-one African nations, begun in 2007, to transform a million square kilometers of desert into lush and fecund forest. A fifth of this epic goal has already been accomplished.

The authors take the longest, grandest possible view of a virtually infinite human future. They're not afraid to think in the lavish timescales of science and even to imagine a time when the human diaspora ventures on to the worlds of other stars.

But first things first. Earth is where we make our stand now. Our world is in need of loving, conscientious restoration. Read this book and become inspired by our ability to break the ancient spell of Jebel Sahaba. We don't have to slaughter each other in a hopeless struggle for resources; we can act constructively to redeem our future. *Humans on the Move* is a survival manual for our humanity just when it is likely to be tested as never before.

*Ann Druyan*
Ithaca, NY
1 June 2021

# Acknowledgements

Grant wishes to express his gratitude to his wife, for her boundless support in all things and at all times—and for being the calm stone in the raging river. He also wishes to thank his children for the many discussions about the environmental problems of the world and the sound and creative solutions they offered.

Rachel wishes to express her profound thanks to her husband for his steadfast belief in the value of her work and his unfaltering efforts to support all her endeavors. She is also deeply grateful to her two children for their infinite creativity and inspiration, and for their commitment to being part of a generation that will make a positive impact on the environment.

We would like to thank Professor Clara Bosak-Schroeder and her colleagues for pointing us in the direction of ancient examples of environmental displacement.

We are also grateful for the wise feedback and unwavering support of our publisher, Ms. Lindy Melman, who encouraged us to expand our previous law review article into a book.

Finally, words cannot describe our profound appreciation to Ms. Ann Druyan. Amidst all her other critical work, she generously devoted her academic acumen and precious time to reviewing the manuscript and crafting a timely, poignant, and eloquent Foreword. We are honored that Ms. Druyan has shared her acutely stirring perspective on the challenges facing our civilization at this crucial time in history. Her intellect, wisdom, and exquisite prose are admonitions to be heeded and treasures to be cherished.

# Introduction

The future is not what will happen, but what we will do.
— HENRI BERGSON

∴

Law is the beginning of wisdom, not the end. This book analyses the law governing the movement of humans within States and across international boundaries due to climate change. But it also seeks to transcend present legal frameworks and engage with the crescent movement towards non-normative approaches to the problem of human movement driven by climate change. Climate change will manifest in diverse ways and have distinct impacts on various regions and populations. In this context, human mobility can be an empowered adaptation strategy or an unwelcome imperative for survival with a high human cost.[1]

This book is a sequel to *Forcible Displacement Throughout the Ages: Towards an International Convention for the Prevention and Punishment of the Crime of Forcible Displacement* (2012). Displacement can be categorized into several forms: The first is displacement as a result of armed conflict. This is the displacement of humans due to war or localized violence, such as enslavement and relocation of a group of people. The second is development-induced displacement, whereby populations are forcibly moved from their homes in the name of economic progress. Both of these strains of displacement were dealt with in *Forcible Displacement Throughout the Ages*. At the end of that book, the authors broached the topic of environmental displacement, the third genus of displacement. The prediction was advanced that "[t]he political, geographical, economic, and social changes that we will undergo as a species due to the changes in our environment will be *the issue* of our next generation and beyond" and that "[i]t may be that the displacements of our past will appear as

---

1   *See* Olivia Serdeczny, *What Does It Mean to "Address Displacement" Under the UNFCCC? An Analysis of the Negotiations Process and the Role of Research* 15–18 (German Dev. Inst., Discussion Paper 12/2017, 2017), *available at* http://climateanalytics.org/files/dp_12.2017.pdf (discussing these juxtaposed aspects of human mobility in the context of climate change).

© KONINKLIJKE BRILL NV, LEIDEN, 2022 | DOI:10.1163/9789004298880_002

nothing more than a rather tame dress rehearsal for those that lie ahead, as the competition for resources and space intensifies".[2]

But a full treatment of the issue of environmental displacement was left for another day; hence, the present book. In respect of environmental displacement, the archeological and mitochondrial record reveals that humans and their genetic predecessors have altered their movements in response to environmental changes throughout history: recent scientific models indicate that environmental changes were a key driver of human migration out of Africa, which eventually led to the population of the rest of the Earth with humans.[3]

There are examples from the ancient world of humans having to leave their homes due to environmental changes, both sudden and gradual. Some of these episodes are mythological, some historical, and some in between. Ovid (*Metamorphoses*) and Apollodorus (*The Library*) depict a mythical flood caused by a wrathful Zeus in the story of Deucalion (son of Prometheus) and Pyrrha (daughter of Epimetheus and Pandora)—the sole survivors who then repopulate the human species. Ovid also tells of the flight of Baucis and Philemon who escaped Zeus's destruction of their town by flood. The story of Noah from the Old Testament of the Bible is yet another account of a catastrophic flood. Muslim, Jewish, and Christian literature tells the story of the flight of Lot (Abraham's nephew) from the destruction of Sodom and Gomorrah by divine fire and brimstone. Ancient literature recounts many volcanic eruptions that resulted in local populations having to leave their homes. In 122 BCE, Mount Etna severely damaged the city of Catania (an event depicted by Virgil in *The Aeneid*). In 79 CE, Mount Vesuvius erupted and destroyed the cities of Pompeii and Herculaneum. Several ancient historians and authors tell of the fall of Helike in the northern Peloponnesos (Achaea). Poseidon, angered by the people of Helike, deluged the city and submerged it during the course of a single night in the winter of 373 BCE. (A more historical account attributes the disaster to an earthquake and subsequent landslides and/or tsunami.) Helike was subsequently silted over and disappeared. After intense archaeological efforts to discover the sunken city in the nineteenth and twentieth centuries CE, Helike was finally rediscovered in 2001. Some scholars credit the demise of Helike as the inspiration for Plato's account of the fall of Atlantis. In the Middle

---

2   GRANT DAWSON & SONIA FARBER, FORCIBLE DISPLACEMENT THROUGHOUT THE
    AGES: TOWARDS AN INTERNATIONAL CONVENTION FOR THE PREVENTION AND
    PUNISHMENT OF THE CRIME OF FORCIBLE DISPLACEMENT 187 (2012).

3   *See generally* Peter B. Demenocal & Chris Stringer, *Human Migration: Climate and the
    Peopling of the World*, 538 NATURE 49 (2016); Axel Timmermann & Tobias Friedrich, *Late
    Pleistocene Climate Drivers of Early Human Migration*, 538 NATURE 92 (2016).

Ages, Paestum was abandoned due to alterations in water drainage that led to the area becoming marshy and malarial. The silting of the harbor of Ephesus throughout its history caused its inhabitants to leave and live elsewhere. Similarly, as told by Pausanius, the residents of Priene and Myus abandoned their cities in the second century CE due to silting of the Maeander River and moved to Miletus. Herodotus (*Historia*) and Aristotle (*Meteorologica*) describe how the Ancient Egyptians had to relocate settlements in response to sedimentation changes in the Nile River. More recently, the Chacoan people (ancestral Puebloans) were forced to leave their settlement in the Chaco Canyon due to a fifty-year draught that started in 1130 CE.

As eloquently put by Amin Maalouf in his book, *Origins*, "[t]rees must accept their fate; they need their roots. Men do not. [...] What matters to us are roads." Our early journeys as a species were a spontaneous adaptation strategy in response to alterations in the environment, a quest for better food and other resources. There were no overt moral implications to these wanderings and the natural processes that inspired and necessitated them. Scientific inquiry has since advanced human understanding of the natural (and human-influenced) processes that lead to significant climate change. As early as 1896, Swedish scientist Svante Arrhenius published a predictive model that increasing carbon dioxide in the atmosphere would result in a general rise in temperature. As scientific knowledge of this impact has grown, the role of humans in altering the environment since the Industrial Revolution has raised issues of law and morality, particularly where anthropogenic influences cause environmental changes on a global basis over a relatively short time horizon, resulting in the movement of (potentially) millions of persons and having severe impacts upon the biodiversity of the planet.

As law and morality have come into focus, the concept of environmental displacement, or forced movement, often has been distinguished from migration, relocation, and other forms of movement that may be conceived as voluntary in nature. Notwithstanding the questionable conceptual feasibility and practical utility of this dichotomy, these distinctions between various types of movement mean that, in current discourse, environmental displacement is only one facet of the broader issue of human mobility in connection with climate change.

Up until the latter half of the twentieth century CE, the international community has attempted to use a complex network of international treaties to regulate issues of morality, including those relating to displacement, by enshrining moral values and "rights" into legal codes. The accelerating difficulties presented by climate change and its interaction with human mobility have, however, outpaced this rights-based approach. Current efforts to mitigate global warming will not prevent massive human movements. Existing legal frameworks are in many cases insufficient to provide protection or assistance to those who must move or those who wish to move pre-emptively. This situation has driven the development of an adaptive approach to human mobility in the context of climate change—an approach characterized by the creation of cooperative strategies between disciplines at local, national, regional, and international levels to prevent involuntary mobility and to facilitate movement when necessary. This book will analyze the conceptualization of human mobility—or "climate change mobility" as referred to herein—in the context of climate change, including an elucidation of the historical context and the nature of climate change drivers and human movement connected with climate change. The shift in focus away from a rights-based approach to an adaptive approach will then be discussed through an examination of the underpinnings of each approach and an assessment of the capacity of each of these mechanisms to address climate change mobility. This assessment will include a closer look at the Great Green Wall project, viewed through the lens of complexity theory, as an embodiment of the adaptive approach. The book concludes with a consideration of the way forward, given the current state of these approaches and the existing political landscape.

The current political climate suggests that there will be no new legal instruments or protocols to expand existing protections under rights-based frameworks emerging in the near future. The existing frameworks provide only a patchwork of protection for some climate change mobility scenarios. The rights-based approach alone will therefore not be sufficient to prevent, enable, or protect humans on the move from climate change. At the same time, recent jurisprudence, particularly in connection with human rights law, suggests that judicial and quasi-judicial action can play a role in addressing climate change mobility. More research is needed to analyze emerging findings and create transformational adaptation strategies, such as supporting affected populations to remain where they currently live (i.e., *in situ* adaptation measures); strengthening the resilience of communities that must move or are already displaced, as well as the communities that host them; and planning for consent-based relocation as a last resort adaptation option. Under the adaptive approach, climate change mobility is increasingly addressed within existing and emerging legal and policy instruments, as well as intergovernmental and civil society initiatives and institutions. Increased coordination, consultation, data sharing, and funding distribution will be crucial to building a complementary approach across institutions and policy fields. Other strategies to be considered therefore include tasking a new or existing body with ensuring this coordination. One possibility would be the continued expansion of the mandate of the Task Force on Displacement under the UNFCCC to fulfill this role.

As significant population shifts occur and the habitable territory of entire States disappears under the expanding oceans, the rebarbative scope of the human movement we may face in the future and the resulting scale of human suffering may call for an approach that is beyond the classical, post-enlightenment codification-based approach to legal theory. Law is a tool for regulating human behavior, but the law has its limits. Climate change mobility will test those limits and may call for approaches that have not yet been devised.

In a book dealing with international law, the role of States will play a critical part. This is even more so in respect of the topic of environmental displacement and other forms of human mobility. There has been a paradigm shift away from States in relation to climate change mitigation, due to the lack of tangible progress by national governments to reduce greenhouse gas emissions and a concomitant shift towards cities and private industry assuming the mantel of prime movers in the realm of climate change mitigation.[4] Nevertheless, it is undeniable that States still firmly control their borders and, to a lesser extent, movement of people within international boundaries. Moreover, international law is created by States, and States wield vast economic and regulatory power, which can be used for implementing and enforcing those laws. For these reasons, we are not yet at some type of utopian (or dystopian) post-Westphalian epoch, in which States have become an anachronistic relic of a past age.

As expressed by David Luban, "[w]hile States will remain the preeminent actors on the world stage for the foreseeable future, the image of more or less self-contained territorial sovereigns is no longer accurate."[5] Luban articulates the international legal precept of responsibility to humanity (R2H) as an "outward-facing conception of state sovereignty [...] that [...] incorporates a duty to take the interests of outsiders—'humanity'—into account in national decision-making, and as a legal characteristic of national sovereignty."[6] This evolutive reformulation of the traditional and normative concept of state sovereignty is not to be underestimated, as it acknowledges the continuing importance of States, while at the same time seeks to harness the power of the State to address collective threats, such as global climate change and its effects upon human mobility. States still matter; and, it is for this reason that

---

4   *See generally* MICHAEL BLOOMBERG & CARL POPE, CLIMATE OF HOPE: HOW CITIES, BUSINESSES, AND CITIZENS CAN SAVE THE PLANET (2017).

5   David Luban, *Responsibility to Humanity and Threats to Peace: An Essay on Sovereignty*, 38(2) BERKELEY J . INT'L L. 185, 210 (2021).

6   *Id.* at 232.

the reluctance of States to enter into new legal obligations for the protection of those displaced due to environmental change is relevant. Such normative lethargy on behalf of States has applied pressure to the adaptive approach and fueled the fashioning of transformational adaptation strategies. Put simply, legal scholars, civil society, policy-makers within their own governments, and practitioners in the field have been forced to forego a newfangled international agreement in this area and instead made to work within the parameters of soft-law instruments and voluntary, non-binding policy initiatives. And this is not necessarily a politico-legal phenomenon from which to shrink. In the area of preserving communities that are at risk from slow onset climate change, it is both the result and the means that matter. A plethora of laws on the books that remain unenforced is of little assistance to anyone and can even be part of the problem—as regulatory confusion sets in and policy-makers focus their efforts on promulgating edentate laws, rather than their enforcement.

In 2014, Barack Obama expressed the view that "there's one issue that will define the contours of this century more dramatically than any other, and that is the urgent and growing threat of a changing climate."[7] Obama correctly frames the issue as one of identity—a concern that is often central in the human psyche. He says climate change will define "this century"; however, it may be even more veridical to speak of climate change—and, more critically, our response to climate change—as what will define, not our century, but rather ourselves—as individuals, communities, States, and a species. Past generations set humanity on our present suicide-course with the delicate environment, but our generation is the first to have both the knowledge of the consequences of our actions on the planetary ecosystem and the knowledge of what we must do to mitigate and possibly reverse it.[8] We need to quickly decide what to do with this knowledge—and then do it.

7  Barack Obama, Remarks by the U.S. President at United Nations Climate Change Summit (23 Sept. 2014), https://obamawhitehouse.archives.gov/the-press-office/2014/09/23/remarks-president-un-climate-change-summit.

8  PETER LAWRENCE, JUSTICE FOR FUTURE GENERATIONS: CLIMATE CHANGE AND INTERNATIONAL LAW 1 (2014) ("The preponderance of scientific evidence indicates that we need a total decarbonisation of the global economy by 2050—the elimination of GHG [global greenhouse gas] emissions from human activities—to have a reasonable chance of avoiding dangerous anthropogenic climate change").

# PART 1

## *Conceptualizing Climate Change Mobility*

∵

# CHAPTER 1

# Human Mobility in an Evolving Context

> We are at an epochal, transitional moment in the history of life on
> Earth. There is no other time as risky, but no other time as promis-
> ing for the future of life on our planet.
> — CARL SAGAN

⋰

Animals, including humans and their genetic predecessors, have altered their
movements in response to environmental changes throughout history.[1] These
movements were a natural adaptation strategy in response to alterations in the
environment.[2] There were no moral implications to those natural processes
or to the human movement they drove. The role of humans in altering the
environment over the past few centuries, however, has raised issues of law and
morality, particularly where anthropogenic influences cause environmental
changes on a global basis over a relatively short time, resulting in the movement of (potentially) millions of persons and having severe impacts on the

---

1   *See* BENOÎT MAYER, THE CONCEPT OF CLIMATE MIGRATION: ADVOCACY AND ITS
    PROSPECTS 14–15 (2016) [hereinafter 'MAYER, CLIMATE MIGRATION']; Kathryn A. Hoppe
    & Paul L. Koch, *Reconstructing the Migration Patterns of Late Pleistocene Mammals from
    Northern Florida, USA*, 68 QUATERNARY RES. 347, 347–349 (2007); Jean P. Dorst, *Origin and
    Evolution of Migration*, ENCYC. BRITANNICA, https://www.britannica.com/science/migrat
    ion-animal/Origin-and-evolution-of-migration (last visited 5 May 2021); INTERNATIONAL
    ORGANIZATION FOR MIGRATION, MIGRATION, ENVIRONMENT AND CLIMATE CHANGE:
    ASSESSING THE EVIDENCE 13 (Frank Laczko & Christine Aghazarm eds., 2010), *available
    at* http://publications.iom.int/bookstore/free/migration_and_environment.pdf; Robert
    McLeman & Barry Smit, *Migration as an Adaptation to Climate Change*, 76(1–2) CLIMATIC
    CHANGE 31, 32–33 (May 2006); Pinar Bilgin, *Resisting Post-Truth Politics, a Primer: Or, How
    Not to Think about Human Mobility and the Global Environment*, 8(1) GLOBAL POL'Y 55, 56
    (2017).
2   *See* JANE MCADAM, CLIMATE CHANGE, FORCED MIGRATION, AND INTERNATIONAL LAW
    3 (2012) ("Movement away from disasters and their effects has always been a rational, adap-
    tive response. Similarly, movement away from the impacts of longer-term processes, such as
    drought, is a well-documented survival strategy.").

© KONINKLIJKE BRILL NV, LEIDEN, 2022 | DOI:10.1163/9789004298880_003

biodiversity of the planet.[3] Human mobility in other contexts has been intimately tied to issues of law and morality in recent history. For example, in the
twentieth century, massive human displacements occurred before, during,
and after World War I and World War II. These were primarily government-
driven displacements designed to alter the demographic composition of the
population. Examples include the persecution and flight of the Jews from Nazi
Germany in the 1930s, the removal of the Tartars from the Crimean Peninsula
by the former Union of Soviet Socialist Republics (USSR) on 18 May 1944, and
the displacement of Germans throughout Europe following the close of the
war.[4] These (and many other) displacements were the direct impetus for the
development of the 1951 Convention Relating to the Status of Refugees and its
1967 Protocol.[5] Thus, up until the latter half of the twentieth century, the legal
apparatus surrounding human mobility was largely focused on protecting persons displaced due to persecution and armed conflict. Existing legal and policy
frameworks were not created with a view to addressing human mobility in the
context of climate change impacts. A new era in human mobility is therefore
developing which requires an evolved approach.[6]

---

3   *See* François Gemenne, *One Good Reason to Speak of 'Climate Refugees'*, 49 FORCED
    MIGRATION REV. 70, 71 (2015) [hereinafter 'Gemenne, *Climate Refugees*'] (opining, in the
    context of arguing that the term "refugee" should apply to human mobility in connection
    with climate change, that such movement is "the result of a persecution that we are inflicting
    on the most vulnerable").

4   *See generally* GRANT DAWSON & SONIA FARBER, FORCIBLE DISPLACEMENT THROUGHOUT
    THE AGES: TOWARDS AN INTERNATIONAL CONVENTION FOR THE PREVENTION
    AND PUNISHMENT OF THE CRIME OF FORCIBLE DISPLACEMENT (2012); JEAN-MARIE
    HENCKAERTS, MASS EXPULSION IN MODERN INTERNATIONAL LAW AND PRACTICE
    (1995); EUGENE MICHEL KULISCHER, THE DISPLACEMENT OF POPULATIONS IN EUROPE
    (1943); Alfred-Maurice de Zayas, *International Law and Mass Population Transfers*, 16 HARV.
    INT'L L.J. 207 (1975).

5   *See* Convention Relating to the Status of Refugees art. 1, 28 July 1951, 189 U.N.T.S. 137; Protocol
    Relating to the Status of Refugees art. 1, 31 Jan. 1967, 606 U.N.T.S. 267; Sadako Ogata, *Foreword*
    to THE REFUGEE CONVENTION, 1951: THE TRAVAUX PREPARATOIRES ANALYSED WITH A
    COMMENTARY BY DR PAUL WEIS 4, 4 (undated; published in print posthumously in 1995),
    *available at* http://www.unhcr.org/protection/travaux/4ca34be29/refugee-convention-1951-
    travaux-preparatoires-analysed-commentary-dr-paul.html; UNHCR, Introductory Note to
    the 1951 Refugee Convention 2 (Dec. 2010), http://www.unhcr.org/3b66c2aa10.

6   *See* Gemenne, *Climate Refugees*, *supra* note 3, at 70 ("Some geologists advocate the use of
    the term 'Anthropocene' to signal a new geological era, the Age of Humans, where we have
    become the major force of transformation of the Earth. [...] Even if humans have indeed
    replaced natural drivers of changes as the principal agents of changes on this planet, most
    humans are actually the victims of these changes, and not their agents.").

The magnitude of climate change mobility will quickly surpass the conflict-related displacement from the last century. There is no standardized methodology for predicting how many persons will move in connection with climate change impacts.[7] Norman Myers, a British environmentalist, began devising estimates of what he referred to as "environmental refugees" in 1995.[8] Although often associated with climate change, Myers' estimates relate to broader environmental impacts, whether related to climate change or otherwise.[9] Distinguishing broader environmental impacts from climate change is one (but far from the only) stumbling block which has hindered a cohesive conceptualization of human mobility in the context of climate change.[10] With this caveat in mind, Myers predicted in a 2005 publication that there could be up to 200 million "environmental refugees" by 2050, which would mean one in every 45 people.[11] This estimate, often associated with what has been called a "maximalist" or "alarmist" view,[12] has been widely cited but also heavily criticized as

---

7    See MCADAM, *supra* note 2, at 24–30; Oli Brown, *The Numbers Game*, 31 FORCED MIGRATION REV. 8, 8 (2008). On methodologies, see also DOMINIC KNIVETON ET AL., CLIMATE CHANGE AND MIGRATION: IMPROVING METHODOLOGIES TO ESTIMATE FLOWS 37–53 (IOM Migration Research Series No. 33, 2008), *available at* https://publicati ons.iom.int/system/files/pdf/mrs-33.pdf.

8    NORMAN MYERS WITH JENNIFER KENT, ENVIRONMENTAL EXODUS: AN EMERGENT CRISIS IN THE GLOBAL ARENA 8 (1995), *available at* http://climate.org/archive/PDF/Environmen tal%20Exodus.pdf (estimating that 162 million persons are at risk displacement from sea-level rise and 50 million at risk from drought and "other climate dislocations").

9    See Frank Biermann & Ingrid Boas, *Preparing for a Warmer World: Towards a Global Governance System to Protect Climate Refugees*, 10 GLOBAL ENVTL. POL. 60, 62 (2010); *see also* Kirsten Hastrup & Karen Fog Olwig, *Introduction: Climate Change and Human Mobility* to CLIMATE CHANGE AND HUMAN MOBILITY: CHALLENGES TO THE SOCIAL SCIENCES 1, 1 (Kirsten Hastrup & Karen Fog Olwig eds., 2012) (noting Myers' acknowledgement, in a publication from 2002, that his numbers would include a wide range of movement, including those who move out of necessity as well as "voluntary opportunists").

10   This distinction is discussed further in Chapter 2.

11   OSCE Economic Forum, Prague, 23–27 May 2005, *Environmental Refugees: An Emergent Security Issue*, at 1, OSCE Doc. EF.NGO/4/05 (22 May 2005) (*prepared by* Norman Myers), *available at* http://www.osce.org/eea/14851?download=true; *see also* OLI BROWN, MIGRATION AND CLIMATE CHANGE 11–12 (IOM Migration Research Series No. 31, 2008), *available at* https://publications.iom.int/fr/system/files/pdf/mrs-31_en.pdf?language=en; Mostafa Mahmud Naser, *Climate Change, Environmental Degradation, and Migration: A Complex Nexus*, 36 WM. & MARY ENVTL. L. & POL'Y REV. 713, 750 (2012).

12   For a history and analysis of "maximalist" versus "minimalist" views, see MCADAM, *supra* note 2, at 24–30; MAYER, CLIMATE MIGRATION, *supra* note 1, at 9–12; Astri Suhrke, *Environmental Degradation and Population Flows*, 47(2) J. INT'L AFF. 473, 474–79 (1994); James Morrissey, *Rethinking the 'Debate on Environmental Refugees': From 'Maximalists and Minimalists' to 'Proponents and Critics'*, 19 J. POL. ECOLOGY 36, 37–41 (2012); François Gemenne, Environmental Changes and Migration Flows: Normative Frameworks and

lacking empirical evidence.[13] More recent estimates and figures are, however, even more alarming.

A 2018 report published by the World Bank, entitled *Groundswell: Preparing for Internal Climate Migration*, estimated that by 2050 up to 143 million persons could migrate internally from just three regions (Sub-Saharan Africa, South Asia, Latin America) due to slow onset climate change impacts, which the report defined as "[c]hanges in climate parameters—such as temperature, precipitation, and associated impacts, such as water availability and crop production declines—that occur over long periods of time".[14] This estimate therefore does not include other regions, any cross-border movement, or movement in response to rapid onset events which may be influenced by climate change (such as cyclones or floods).

The Internal Displacement Monitoring Centre (IMDC) gathers data on internal movements due to conflicts and natural disasters. Its study shows that, in 2019 alone, 24.9 million persons were displaced internally due to natural disasters; this amount was three times the number of persons displaced internally due to conflict that year.[15] The vast majority of those natural disasters were weather-related (hydro-meteorological disasters), including extreme temperatures, floods, droughts, landslides, wildfires, cyclones, hurricanes, and typhoons.[16] Climate change impacts increase the frequency and intensity of these hydro-meteorological disasters.[17] These figures are global, reflecting worldwide internal movement. However, like the World Bank's *Groundswell* report, this data does not reflect cross-border movement relating to climate change impacts. Also, whereas *Groundswell* predicts movement relating to

---

Policy Responses Volume I, 117–32 (3 Apr. 2009) (Doctoral Thesis, Institut d'Etudes Politiques de Paris & University of Liège), *available at* https://orbi.uliege.be/handle/2268/137601 [hereinafter 'Gemenne Thesis']; *see also* Benoît Mayer, *"Environmental Migration" as Advocacy: Is It Going to Work?*, 29(2) REFUGE 27, 30–32 (2014) (identifying four schools of thought behind the debate, or "normative enterprises" as he terms them).

13    *See* MCADAM, *supra* note 2, at 26–27; KNIVETON ET AL., *supra* note 7, at 32–33; Gemenne Thesis, *supra* note 12, at 122–23. *See also* Hastrup & Olwig, *supra* note 9, at 1 (noting that "[n]umbers quickly take on a life of their own").

14    KANTA KUMARI RIGAUD ET AL., GROUNDSWELL: PREPARING FOR INTERNAL CLIMATE MIGRATION x, xiv (2018), *available at* https://openknowledge.worldbank.org/handle/10986/29461.

15    INTERNAL DISPLACEMENT MONITORING CENTRE, 2020 GLOBAL REPORT ON INTERNAL DISPLACEMENT, pt. 1, at 9, *available at* https://www.internal-displacement.org/global-report/grid2020/.

16    Of the total disaster displacements, 23.9 million were weather related; only 947,000 were geophysical disasters, such as volcanic eruptions and earthquakes. *Id.* at 10.

17    *Id.* at 81.

slow-onset climate change impacts, the IDMC data relates to the effects of rapid onset hazard events, such as landslides, floods, or hurricanes. A trajectory in which climate change-related displacements continue at a comparable (or increased) rate to the figures compiled by the IDMC would make Myers' early predictions appear conservative by comparison.

In addition to the raw impact of slow and rapid onset weather-related events which are amplified by climate change, alterations to the earth's climate will transform the physical aspects of certain habitable lands, rendering them unfit to sustain human life. These environmental (and climate change) impacts tend to exacerbate other existing economic, social, and political vulnerabilities. Such vulnerabilities, in combination with environmental impacts, drive human mobility and can lead to devastating conflict.[18] As David Luban observes:

> In its broadest terms, climate change will make some parts of the Earth, especially the poorest, unable to sustain their human populations. Coastal plains will flood; semi-arid regions will become deserts. If catastrophic storms proliferate, ever-larger numbers of people will be internally displaced. Other forms of environmental degradation and pollution threaten water supplies. For example, one research team claims that two-thirds of the world's people currently face severe water shortages. Already, the Chinese government reports that four-fifths of the well water in China is unfit to drink or bathe in.
>
> The threat to peace arising from these developments is obvious: as resources and living space become more scarce, environmental and climate refugees will flee from unlivable regions into countries that do not want them, and, in some cases, cannot support them. This will serve as an invitation to violence, confinement, or even genocide. Those who cannot leave may plunge their countries into civil conflicts, as some believe was the case in Darfur during the drought of the early 2000s.[19]

A report entitled *Shoring Up Stability: Addressing Climate & Fragility Risks in the Lake Chad Region* explains this cause and effect dynamism in the Lake Chad

---

18    *See, e.g.,* MCADAM, *supra* note 2, at 20–24; Walter Kälin & Nina Schrepfer, *Protecting People Crossing Borders in the Context of Climate Change: Normative Gaps and Possible Approaches* 4–6 (UNHCR, Legal & Protection Policy Research Series, PPLA/2012/01, Feb. 2012), *available at* https://www.unhcr.org/4f33f1729.pdf; Naser, *supra* note 11, at 751–54.

19    David Luban, *Responsibility to Humanity and Threats to Peace: An Essay on Sovereignty,* 38(2) BERKELEY J . INT'L L. 185, 204–05 (2021) (citations omitted).

region, an area which comprises areas of Cameroon, Chad, Niger, and Nigeria. *Shoring Up Stability* describes a "climate conflict trap"—a "vicious circle" whereby "climate change contributes to the drivers of conflict and conflict affects peoples' adaptation capacities".[20] The report describes that the intersection of climate change and conflict in the Lake Chad region presents four risks in particular:

- ongoing conflict deteriorates adaptive capacity, making it more difficult to meet the challenges presented by climate variability;
- climate change aggravates competition over natural resources caused by displacement and other conflict-related challenges;
- climate change factors combined with existing social instability compounds the risk of recruitment by armed opposition groups; and
- governmental military responses to ongoing unrest and violence can damage the resilience of communities and further restrict access to livelihoods and to essential resources, making it more difficult for those communities to adapt to climate change.[21]

Given that climate change impacts tend to combine with or exacerbate other drivers of human mobility, it can be difficult to untangle them in order to identify whether climate change was a decisive factor in driving human mobility—at least from a theoretical perspective. Some scholars consider the multi-causal nature of human mobility relating to climate change to be one of the most complex conceptual hurdles to quantifying, and indeed addressing, climate change mobility.[22] A number of migration scholars, generally associated with what has been called a "minimalist" or "skeptical" view,[23] have called attention to the lack of empirical data to support the view that environmental factors have a discernable and independent influence on human mobility. Some have questioned whether environmental (including, by extension, climate change) factors can or should be established as independent or primary drivers of human mobility at all.[24]

---

20    JANANI VIVEKANANDA ET AL., SHORING UP STABILITY: ADDRESSING CLIMATE AND FRAGILITY RISKS IN THE LAKE CHAD REGION 12–13, 45–68 (2019), *available at* https://shoring-up-stability.org/.

21    *Id.* at 13.

22    *See, e.g.,* MCADAM, *supra* note 2, at 20–30; Gemenne Thesis, *supra* note 12, at 164–65.

23    *See supra* note 12.

24    *See, e.g.,* MAYER, CLIMATE MIGRATION, *supra* note 1, at 6–21, 31–38; Richard Black, *Environmental Refugees: Myth or Reality?* 1, 13–14 (UNHCR, New Issues in Refugee Research Working Paper No. 34, Mar. 2001), *available at* https://www.unhcr.org/research/working/3ae6a0d0o/environmental-refugees-myth-reality-richard-black.html; Steve Lonergan, *The Role of Environmental Degradation in Population Displacement,* 4 ENVTL CHANGE & SECURITY REP. 5, 6 (1998); MCADAM, *supra* note 2, at 5.

Shifting the focus from theory to practice, however, others advocate against undue attention to conceptual debates over causation, lest the issue paralyze action or distract from the provision of aid to those who need it.[25] Scott Leckie, founder of the non-profit organization Displacement Solutions, has acknowledged that the issue of causation may be relevant in some rare legal contexts, but overall considers the focus on causation to be deleterious, referring to the so-called "climate displacement causation conundrum" as a "rapidly decomposing red herring":

> In debating circles the unfortunate over-emphasis on causation issues is a fortunately rapidly decomposing red herring comprising arguments in support of a position which may sound reasonable during theoretical discussions by those safely ensconced in ivy-covered buildings, but which simply bears little or no resemblance to real-life circumstances affecting ever-larger numbers of people. Clearly what is infinitely more important than any preoccupation with causation is determining who is under threat from the effects of climate change, where they reside, and the degree of urgency associated with finding rights-based solutions to their predicaments.[26]

Notwithstanding polarized debates and cautionary views on the extent to which one can accurately define or quantify the nexus between climate change and human mobility, there is widespread recognition that climate

---

25   *See* Scott Leckie, *Using Human Rights to Resolve the Climate Displacement Problem: The Promise of the Peninsula Principles*, *in* REPAIRING DOMESTIC CLIMATE DISPLACEMENT: THE PENINSULA PRINCIPLES 1, 5–7 (Scott Leckie & Chris Huggins eds., 2016) ("While the causation issue may be of relevance in the comparatively rare instances of individual asylum seekers arguing that climate change was the cause of their alleged persecution, for the vulnerable coastal and inland communities of the countries just mentioned, the causation issue is in practice much ado about very little."); Bruce Burson, *The Preamble*, *in* REPAIRING DOMESTIC CLIMATE DISPLACEMENT: THE PENINSULA PRINCIPLES 36, 47 (Scott Leckie & Chris Huggins eds., 2016) ("While definitions matter in that they define boundaries of applicability of legal regimes—including the legal regime of the Peninsula Principles—it is nevertheless important not to get too distracted by debates on terminology. Although complex in nature, there is an increasingly recognised and understood relationship between environmental stressors and human mobility generally, and the provision of comprehensive protection to affected individuals and communities via a coherent legal regime which responds to the complexities involved is more important than the label used.").

26   Leckie, *supra* note 25, at 7.

change does, directly or indirectly, impact human mobility.[27] Even where the analytical value of linking human mobility and climate change has been questioned, there is little denying that the concept has mobilized scholarly debate, public interest, and political action. Benoît Mayer, skeptical of the analytical accuracy or value of defining a category of human mobility in connection with climate change, considers "climate migration" to be more of a "broad nebula of political discourses and arguments" than any particular phenomenon of movement.[28] He concludes, however, that the concept of "climate migration" nevertheless has value for its political currency, as the concept has "built a significant momentum in recent years, hence, possibly, creating opportunities for reforms in global governance."[29]

Justice-based approaches suggest that the conceptual linchpin uniting the varied human mobility scenarios arising with climate change transcends political currency.[30] Addressing climate change mobility as a composite phenomenon is anchored in concepts of fairness and morality.[31] Human interaction with the environment is driving climate change; a justice perspective observes that not all humans have contributed to climate change equally and not all humans will carry equivalent burdens arising out of climate change impacts. Some humans have therefore driven climate change that will require others to move and generally experience loss as a result.[32] Climate change mobility scenarios are therefore also fused into a singular concept by the notion that it is an injustice which drives humans to move, which in turn breeds further injustice.

27   *See* MCADAM, *supra* note 2, at 30; Morrissey, *supra* note 12, at 40, 45; Gemenne, *Climate Refugees*, *supra* note 3, at 70.

28   MAYER, CLIMATE MIGRATION, *supra* note 1, at 38.

29   *Id.*

30   For a legal perspective on climate change mobility from corrective and distributive justice standpoint, see generally FANNY THORNTON, CLIMATE CHANGE AND PEOPLE ON THE MOVE: INTERNATIONAL LAW AND JUSTICE (2018).

31   *See id.* at 8 (observing, in a comparison between law and justice, that justice "refers to 'fairness', 'moral rightness', or, as has been stated, a system in which each entity receives what it is due, 'including all rights both natural and legal' (quoting *Justice*, LEGAL DICTIONARY, https://dictionary.law.com/Default.aspx?selected=1086 (last visited 2 June 2021)) and at 44 (observing that justice concerns underlie a number of protection, or as referred to herein, rights-based approaches, but that underlying a true justice-based approach is the establishment of a relationship between a "doer and sufferer, or haves and have-nots").

32   Fanny Thornton identifies two additional prevalent justice-based claims in connection with climate change mobility: First, some humans have driven climate change that will require others to move, but those required to move are trapped and cannot. Second, certain places are disproportionately and disadvantageously impacted by climate change mobility, either because they are places that people must move from or because they are places to where people move. THORNTON, *supra* note 30, at 7.

# CHAPTER 2

# Climate Change Mobility as an Evolving Concept

> The difference between talents and character is adroitness to keep
> the old and trodden round, and power and courage to make a new
> road to new and better goals.
>
> – RALPH WALDO EMERSON

∴

Climate change will manifest in diverse ways and have distinct impacts on
regions and populations. Human mobility in the context of climate change will
vary in nature, depending upon the environmental impact driving the movement as well as the adaptive capacity of the persons and the infrastructure
of the country affected by climate change.[1] The amorphous nature of climate
change and the human mobility it drives have resisted conceptual consensus and the assignment of strict academic or legal definitions. As discussions
about climate change mobility have evolved, terminology has proliferated, but
without a consistent view as to which terms should be used or how those terms
should be defined.[2]

The propagation of terms is not solely the byproduct of conflicting viewpoints or attempts to apply incompatible existing frameworks. As Professor
Jane McAdam observed, climate change mobility will take on many forms and
cannot properly be addressed by a "one-size-fits-all" definition or approach.[3]
The mutability of the terminology used is therefore, in part, a reflection of the
varied forms that human mobility can take in the context of climate change.
It also stems from a broad range of conceptual viewpoints as various actors

---

1 *See* JANE MCADAM, CLIMATE CHANGE, FORCED MIGRATION, AND INTERNATIONAL LAW
4–5 (2012) [hereinafter 'MCADAM, FORCED MIGRATION'].
2 *See, e.g.,* Koko Warner, *Assessing Institutional and Governance Needs Related to Environmental
Change and Human Migration* 1 (German Marshall Fund, Study Team on Climate-Induced
Migration, June 2010), *available at* https://archive.unu.edu/africa/activities/files/Warner_K
_2010_Assessing_Institutional_and_Governance_Needs_Related_to_Environmental_Cha
nge.pdf [hereinafter 'Warner, *Assessing Institutional and Governance Needs*'].
3 MCADAM, FORCED MIGRATION, *supra* note 1, at 5.

and institutions have sought to address the issue through the lens of existing or prospective legal and policy frameworks and create definitions for varying purposes.[4]

Most definitions attempt, to varying degrees, to define two aspects of human mobility in the context of climate change.[5] The first is the nature of the climate change impacts that drive human mobility. Climate change impacts have often been distinguished from broader environmental changes, but without consensus as to the defining factors. The second is the nature of the human mobility that is driven by climate change impacts. Some have sought to address this as a singular phenomenon—a simplified approach that does not attempt to distinguish between the many potential human mobility scenarios[6]—or by attempting to demarcate subcategories thereof.

## A        Climate Change Drivers of Human Mobility

Discussions about climate change as a driver of human mobility find their roots in broader environmentalist discourse about human movement in connection with environmental impacts.[7] As is widely recognized in the literature,

---

4   *See* Jane McAdam, *Environmental Migration*, *in* GLOBAL MIGRATION GOVERNANCE 153, 157–58 (Alexander Betts ed., 2011) [hereinafter 'McAdam, *Environmental Migration*']; Walter Kälin & Nina Schrepfer, *Protecting People Crossing Borders in the Context of Climate Change: Normative Gaps and Possible Approaches* 30 (UNHCR, Legal & Protection Policy Research Series, PPLA/212/01, Feb. 2012), *available at* https://www.unhcr.org/4f33f1729.pdf ("The terminological debate amongst humanitarian, migration management and development actors and the difficulties to achieve consensus is to a considerable extent related to mandate issues and responsibilities of the respective institutions, who are trying to defend their own position."); Warner, *Assessing Institutional and Governance Needs*, *supra* note 2, at 1–2 (noting that "[d]efinitions of the 'problem' (i.e., as a migration, humanitarian, development, security, or environmental issue) allow an assignment of authority to address environmentally induced migration." According to Warner, problems of definition stem from this issue along with the problem of establishing that human mobility is caused by climate change.). *See also* Bonnie Docherty & Tyler Giannini, *Confronting a Rising Tide: A Proposal for a Convention on Climate Change Refugees*, 33 HARV. ENVTL. L. REV. 349, 372 (2009) (emphasizing that their proposed definition of climate change refugees is intended for use in a new binding legal instrument and not for general policy).

5   *See* Docherty & Giannini, *supra* note 4, at 364; Mostafa Mahmud Naser, *Climate Change, Environmental Degradation, and Migration: A Complex Nexus*, 36 WM. & MARY ENVTL. L. & POL'Y REV. 713, 732 (2012).

6   *See* MCADAM, FORCED MIGRATION, *supra* note 1, at 5.

7   *See* McAdam, *Environmental Migration*, *supra* note 4, at 157; Angela Williams, *Turning the Tide: Recognizing Climate Change Refugees in International Law*, 30 L. & POL'Y 502, 506 (2008).

"environmental refugee" is one of the earliest terms applied to persons moving in connection with climate change, but with no agreed definition. Lester Brown, founder of the Earth Policy and Worldwatch Institutes, coined this term in the 1970s.[8] Essam El-Hinnawi, author of a much-cited report for the United Nations Environment Programme (UNEP), entitled *Environmental Refugees*, and Norman Myers subsequently popularized the term in the 1980s and 1990s.[9] Both El-Hinnawi and Myers gave the term their own definitions, adopting broad language that sought to encompass both climate change and other environmental factors as drivers of human mobility.

El-Hinnawi defined "environmental refugees" as including "those people who have been forced to leave their traditional habitat, temporarily or permanently, because of a marked environmental disruption (natural and/or triggered by people) that jeopardized their existence and/or seriously affected the quality of their life".[10] Myers gave another broad definition to the same term, explicitly including climate change as a potential driver of mobility:

> Environmental refugees are persons who can no longer gain a secure livelihood in their traditional homelands because of environmental factors of unusual scope, notably *drought, desertification, deforestation, soil erosion, water shortages and climate change, also natural disasters such as cyclones, storm surges and floods.* In face of these environmental threats, people feel they have no alternative but to seek sustenance elsewhere,

---

8   *See, e.g.*, Fabrice Renaud et al., *Control, Adapt or Flee: How to Face Environmental Migration?* 11 (UNU-EHS, InterSecTions No. 5/2007, May 2007), *available at* http://citese erx.ist.psu.edu/viewdoc/download?doi=10.1.1.505.4042&rep=rep1&type=pdf [hereinafter 'Renaud et al., *Control, Adapt or Flee*']; James Morrissey, *Rethinking the 'Debate on Environmental Refugees': From 'Maximalists and Minimalists' to 'Proponents and Critics'*, 19 J. POL. ECOLOGY 36, 41 (2012) (crediting Lester Brown with coining the term but noting that the term "has conceptual roots reaching as far back as the 1930s").

9   *See* Koko Warner et al., *Climate change, Environmental Degradation and Migration*, 55 NAT. HAZARDS 689, 693 (2010); Morrissey, *supra* note 8, at 36, 37, 41, 42. Some authors also credit Jodi Jacobson as defining and popularizing this term with a publication for the Worldwatch Institute. *See, e.g.*, Gaim Kibreab, *Environmental Causes and Impacts of Refugee Movements: A Critique of the Current Debate*, 21(1) DISASTERS 20, 21 (1997); Richard Black, *Environmental Refugees: Myth or Reality?* 1–2 (UNHCR, New Issues in Refugee Research Working Paper No. 34, Mar. 2001), *available at https://www.unhcr.org/ research/working/3ae6a0doo/environmental-refugees-myth-reality-richard-black.html.*

10  ESSAM EL-HINNAWI, ENVIRONMENTAL REFUGEES (1985), *available at* https://digital library.un.org/record/121267?ln=en (also defining "environmental disruption" as "any physical, chemical and/or biological changes in the ecosystem (or the resource base) that render it, temporarily or permanently, unsuitable to support human life.").

whether within their own countries or beyond and whether on a semi-permanent or permanent basis.[11]

These definitions indicate that El-Hinnawi and Myers were, in their view, addressing broader "environmental" drivers of human mobility, which encompassed both natural and anthropogenic changes, and not climate change drivers alone.

The term "environmental refugees", though heavily criticized by those referred to as "minimalist" proponents,[12] gained influence at the end of the twentieth century CE. Some have continued to address "environmental" drivers broadly. For example, Professor Michel Prieur proposed a *Draft Convention on the International Status of Environmentally-Displaced Persons*, which would

---

11    NORMAN MYERS WITH JENNIFER KENT, ENVIRONMENTAL EXODUS: AN EMERGENT CRISIS IN THE GLOBAL ARENA 18–19 (1995), *available at* http://climate.org/archive/PDF/Environmental%20Exodus.pdf (emphasis added) (The quoted definition was a "concise" version of a longer "working definition" proposed in this paper at page 18: "Environmental refugees are persons who can no longer gain a secure livelihood in their traditional homelands because of what are primarily environmental factors of unusual scope. These factors include drought, desertification, deforestation, soil erosion and other forms of land degradation; resource deficits such as water shortages; decline of urban habitats through massive over-loading of city systems; emergent problems such as climate change, especially global warming; and natural disasters such as cyclones, storm surges and floods, also earthquakes, with impacts aggravated by human mismanagement. There can be additional factors that exacerbate environmental problems and that often derive in part from environmental problems: population growth, widespread poverty, famine and pandemic disease. Still further factors include deficient development policies and government systems that 'marginalize' people in senses economic, political, social and legal. In certain circumstances, a number of factors can serve as 'immediate triggers' of migration, e.g. major industrial accidents and construction of outsize dams. Of these manifold factors, several can operate in combination, often with compounded impacts. In face of environmental problems, people concerned feel they have no alternative but to seek sustenance elsewhere, either within their countries or in other countries, and whether on a semi-permanent or permanent basis.").

12    For a history and analysis of the "maximalist" vs. "minimalist" views, see MCADAM, FORCED MIGRATION, *supra* note 1, at 24–30; BENOÎT MAYER, THE CONCEPT OF CLIMATE MIGRATION: ADVOCACY AND ITS PROSPECTS 9–12 (2016) [hereinafter 'MAYER, CLIMATE MIGRATION']; Astri Suhrke, *Environmental Degradation and Population Flows*, 47(2) J. INT'L AFF. 473, 474–79 (1994); Morrissey, *supra* note 8, at 37–41; François Gemenne, Environmental Changes and Migration Flows: Normative Frameworks and Policy Responses Volume I, at 117–32 (3 Apr. 2009) (Doctoral Thesis, Institut d'Etudes Politiques de Paris & University of Liège), *available at* https://orbi.uliege.be/handle/2268/137601 [hereinafter 'Gemenne Thesis']. *See also* Benoît Mayer, *"Environmental Migration" as Advocacy: Is It Going to Work?*, 29(2) REFUGE 27, 30–32 (2014) (identifying four schools of thought behind the debate, or "normative enterprises" as he terms them).

establish rights for persons forcibly displaced by a "sudden" or "gradual environmental disaster", defined broadly as any "rapidly occurring degradation"
or "slow-progressive or planned degradation" of the environment that is "of
natural and/or human origin".[13] Others have pushed the focus of the debate
towards the subcategory of "climate change" drivers rather than the broader
"environmental" factors presented by El-Hinnawi and Myers.[14] There is, however, disagreement as to how climate change drivers should be distinguished
from broader environmental impacts. Two prominent proposals for the creation of new instruments to address climate change mobility provide some
insight into the difficulties of making this distinction in practice.

In an oft-cited proposal for a protocol on recognition, protection, and resettlement of "climate refugees" to the United Nations Framework Convention
on Climate Change (UNFCCC), Frank Biermann and Ingrid Boas noted that,
although the term "climate refugee" was already present in the literature, the
term remained, at that time, undefined and/or conceptually undistinguished
from the broader category of "environmental refugees".[15] Biermann and Boas
considered it important to address climate change as a specific driver of human
mobility both analytically, to increase knowledge about the growing impact
of climate change on human mobility, and politically, to develop appropriate
responses and governance regimes.[16]

Biermann and Boas therefore attempted to define a narrower category of
"climate refugees" as "people who have to leave their habitats, immediately or
in the near future, because of sudden or gradual alterations in their natural
environment related to at least one of three impacts of climate change: sea-
level rise, extreme weather events, and drought and water scarcity".[17] The latter

---

13    Michel Prieur et al., Draft Convention on the International Status of Environmentally-
      Displaced Persons, ch. 1, art. 2 (third version, May 2013), https://cidce.org/wp-content/
      uploads/2016/08/Draft-Convention-on-the-International-Status-on-environmentally-
      displaced-persons-third-version.pdf.

14    *See, e.g.*, Frank Biermann & Ingrid Boas, *Preparing for a Warmer World: Towards a Global
      Governance System to Protect Climate Refugees* 3 (Global Governance Project, Global
      Governance Working Paper No. 33, 2007), *available at* https://sarpn.org/documents/
      d0002952/Climate_refugees_global_governance_Nov2007.pdf [hereinafter 'Biermann &
      Boas 2007']; Docherty & Giannini, *supra* note 4, at 367.

15    Biermann & Boas 2007, *supra* note 14, at 3. This proposal was republished in updated form
      in 2010: Frank Biermann & Ingrid Boas, *Preparing for a Warmer World: Towards a Global
      Governance System to Protect Climate Refugees*, 10 GLOBAL ENVTL. POL. 60 (2010) [here-
      inafter 'Biermann & Boas 2010']. Where the two versions of the proposal are substantively
      identical, citations hereinafter are made to the more recent publication of their proposal.

16    Biermann & Boas 2010, *supra* note 15, at 63.

17    *Id.* at 67.

half of this definition restricts the category to persons moving in relation to three exclusive climate change impacts (sea level rise, extreme weather events, and drought/water scarcity).[18] Biermann and Boas arrived at this list by excluding what they considered to be (i) climate change impacts with little or no connection to forced movement, (ii) measures taken to mitigate or adapt to global warming, (iii) environmental impacts that are unconnected to climate change or "unrelated to human activities", and (iv) drivers of human mobility that are the indirect result of climate change.[19] Biermann and Boas thus attempted to define a sub-category of climate change drivers by process of elimination to arrive at environmental changes that were, in their view, "direct, largely undisputed climate change impacts".[20]

Though Biermann and Boas intended to limit the scope of "climate refugees" to exclude indirect impacts of climate change, their definition indicates that the human movement must only be "related to" the three specified impacts of climate change. This language could be interpreted broadly, creating a standard whereby one of the specified climate change impacts would only have to be a contributing, not sole or arguably even primary, factor in triggering the movement. As such, their definition possibly still would apply in instances where, for example, one of the three specified climate change impacts, such as water scarcity, gave rise to armed conflict (i.e., an indirect impact) which then triggered human movement.[21]

In a contrasting approach, Bonnie Docherty and Tyler Giannini proposed a new international convention for the protection of persons they defined as

---

18    Although they narrowed the definition according to the kinds of environmental drivers they viewed as climate change specific, Biermann and Boas retained an extremely broad category of movement in their definition of "climate change refugees", declining to restrict the definition according to criteria already recognized under existing international legal frameworks that apply differing protection regimes to, inter alia, voluntary versus involuntary moment, as well as internal versus cross-border movement. *See* discussion *infra* in Chapter 2(B).

19    Biermann & Boas 2010, *supra* note 15, at 63–64.

20    *Id.* at 64. *See also* Docherty & Giannini, *supra* note 4, at 368.

21    Some, such as Black, a prominent minimalist, have expressed doubt that such an indirect causal link between conflict, environmental impacts, and movement could be established. *Black, supra* note 9, at 10 ("The point is that in conflict, as much as in migration, it is difficult or impossible to isolate particular causes, outside the broader context within which these processes develop; indeed, conflict and migration themselves are part of a dialectical relationship with this broader 'context', such that a simple causal link from environmental degradation to conflict to migration is hardly likely to be found.").

"climate change refugees".[22] They sought to limit the scope of the convention to climate change (rather than broader environmental) impacts from an account-ability standpoint because, in their view, the international community (and in particular those States contributing most to climate change) should be respon-sible for mitigating the impact on persons who have to move because of climate change.[23] Instead of defining specific climate events which would be covered by the proposed convention, Docherty and Giannini sought to establish more flexible criteria, which would allow for advancements in scientific knowledge, to determine whether an environmental impact should be attributed to cli-mate change.[24] They therefore proposed that a new international convention should provide protection to persons whose movement met six specific crite-ria: (i) forced movement that entailed (ii) temporary or permanent relocation (iii) across national borders, [in connection with][25] (iv) sudden or gradual onset environmental disruption (v) that is "consistent with climate change"[26] and

---

22    Docherty & Giannini, *supra* note 4.

23    *Id.* at 367.

24    *Id.* at 370–71; *see also* David Hodgkinson et al., *'The Hour When the Ship Comes In': A Convention for Persons Displaced by Climate Change*, 36(1) MONASH U. L. REV. 69, 84–85 (2010) (agreeing that any new instrument must be "sufficiently flexible to reflect develop-ments in scientific understanding over time").

25    The words "in connection with" are used here for demonstrative purposes only. Docherty and Giannini did not propose language that would indicate the way in which the first three criteria (relating to the nature of the movement) must be linked to the last three criteria (relating to the nature of the environmental impact).

26    Docherty and Giannini noted that the United Nations' Intergovernmental Panel on Climate Change (IPCC) has identified such environmental impacts, which include "warmer temperatures, more frequent droughts, more intense storms, and rising sea lev-els". By contrast to Biermann and Boas who enumerated an exclusive list of events which should be considered as related to climate change, Docherty and Giannini sought to allow for the advancement of scientific knowledge about the impact of climate change on the environment by including the above-cited language. Docherty & Giannini, *supra* note 4, at 370 (referring to INTERGOVERNMENTAL PANEL ON CLIMATE CHANGE, FOURTH ASSESSMENT REPORT: CLIMATE CHANGE 2007: SYNTHESIS REPORT 30, 53 (2007) [hereinafter 'IPCC FOURTH ASSESSMENT REPORT']). The IPCC is an international body established in 1988 by the United Nations Environment Programme (UNEP) and the World Meteorological Organization (WMO) and endorsed by the UN General Assembly. Its man-date is to provide a policy-neutral assessment on the current state of scientific knowl-edge on climate change. *History*, INTERGOVERNMENTAL PANEL ON CLIMATE CHANGE, https://www.ipcc.ch/about/history/#:~:text=The%20Intergovernmental%20Panel%20 on%20Climate%20Change%20(IPCC)%20was%20established%20by,UN%20Gene ral%20Assembly%20in%201988. (last visited 18 May 2021).

(vi) that can be established to be attributable to a human contribution by a "more likely than not"[27] standard.[28]

The first three criteria in Docherty and Giannini's proposal define the movement for which protection would be provided, i.e., forced relocation across international borders.[29] The last three criteria in Docherty and Giannini's proposal define which drivers of movement would be covered by their convention, i.e., environmental impacts that are consistent with, and "more likely than not" attributable to, climate change. Docherty and Giannini's proposal does not, however, include language indicating the nature of the connection required between the first three criteria (which define the movement) and the last three criteria (which define the climate change driver).[30] The words "in connection with" placed in brackets in the above quoted definition were not included by Docherty and Giannini (nor was any other language); they were inserted by the present authors here to show that the first three criteria must be connected in some way with the last three. Docherty and Giannini's proposal is therefore ambiguous as to the relationship required between the climate change driver and the movement. It is in doubt whether their convention would require that the movement be "caused by" or "(directly or indirectly) related to" the climate change driver. In light of the multi-causal nature of human mobility in the context of climate change, the language establishing the relationship between the movement and the climate change driver could greatly expand or limit the scope of any potential new convention. To employ a similar example to that

27    Docherty and Giannini also derived the "more likely than not" standard from the IPCC's Fourth Assessment Report; it equates to a likelihood of greater than fifty percent. By adopting this standard the authors sought to acknowledge scientific uncertainty but not allow such uncertainty to bar action, consistent with the precautionary principle articulated in the UNFCCC. Docherty & Giannini, *supra* note 4, at 371 (referring to IPCC FOURTH ASSESSMENT REPORT, *supra* note 26, at 27, 39–41). Hodgkinson et al. considered that a much higher standard of "very likely" (i.e., ninety percent) would be more appropriate for a new convention, to narrow the scope of potentially eligible persons and better allocate resources. They considered that a new convention using such a standard would address primarily slow onset hazard events. Hodgkinson et al., *supra* note 24, at 85–86.
28    Docherty & Giannini, *supra* note 4, at 372.
29    Although adopting a broader and more flexible approach to identifying climate change drivers, Docherty and Giannini proposed more restrictive criteria, modelled after existing legal frameworks, as to the persons who would be eligible for protection under a new international convention. *See* discussion *infra* in Chapter 2(B).
30    Docherty and Giannini did not propose language indicating the extent to which the movement itself must be related to the climate change driver. See *supra* note 25. As discussed, Biermann and Boas used the words "related to", a potentially broad standard suggesting that climate change would have to be a contributing, although not sole or even arguably primary, factor in the movement.

used in relation to the proposal by Biermann and Boas, scenarios may arise in which climate change impacts reduce access to natural resources, such as water. The scarcity of such essential resources may give rise to armed conflict (an indirect impact of climate change). Persons may flee abroad, to escape the conflict and/or to gain better access to basic resources. Absent language establishing the extent to which the climate change driver must be the direct or primary cause of the movement (or otherwise), it is unclear whether any of the persons who have fled in such a scenario should be protected under Docherty and Giannini's proposed convention.[31]

Although these and other commentators have sought to address a narrower category of "climate change", as opposed to "environmental", drivers, the above examples demonstrate the wide range of potential approaches in making this would-be distinction in practice. The distinction between "environmental" and "climate change" impacts is sometimes understood as natural versus anthropogenic causes,[32] but this is not a true dichotomy given that "environmental" is often understood as encompassing both natural and anthropogenic changes.[33] Further, although climate change is by definition anthropogenic in nature,[34] other anthropogenic environmental impacts may be unrelated in a direct manner to climate change, such as repercussions from the construction of massive dams or major industrial accidents.[35]

---

31    Docherty and Giannini also considered that only "forced" movement "due to threats to a refugee's survival" should qualify for protection under their proposed convention. Docherty & Giannini, *supra* note 4, at 369. They did not expand on how a distinction would be made between voluntary and forced movement in certain situations. *See* discussion *infra* in Chapter 2(B). Taking for example the scenario presented above, Docherty and Giannini did not indicate whether movement to gain better access to scarce resources should be considered as "forced".

32    McAdam, *Environmental Migration*, *supra* note 4, at 157.

33    El-Hinnawi and Myers defined "environmental" as encompassing both natural and anthropogenic causes (quoted *supra* and in note 11). *See also* Diane Bates, *Environmental Refugees? Classifying Human Migrations Caused by Environmental Change*, 23(5) POPULATION & ENV'T 465, 469–71 (2002).

34    United Nations Framework Convention on Climate Change art. 1(2), 9 May 1992, 1771 U.N.T.S. 107 (" 'Climate change' means a change of climate which is attributed directly or indirectly to human activity that alters the composition of the global atmosphere and which is in addition to natural climate variability observed over comparable time periods.").

35    Myers used these examples in his long working definition of "environmental refugees". *See supra* note 11. *See also* Bates, *supra* note 33, at 469–71; Pablo Bose & Elizabeth Lunstrum, *Introduction: Environmentally Induced Displacement and Forced Migration*, 29(2) REFUGE 5, 5 (2014).

As a matter of science, it is increasingly possible to determine whether a particular environmental change stems from natural or anthropogenic causes. It is already well established that human activity, beginning from the Industrial Revolution, has caused the increase of greenhouse gases in the Earth's atmosphere. As the Intergovernmental Panel on Climate Change (IPCC) has observed:

> The atmospheric concentrations of the greenhouse gases carbon dioxide ($CO_2$), methane ($CH_4$), and nitrous oxide ($N_2O$) have all increased since 1750 due to human activity. In 2011 the concentrations of these greenhouse gases were 391 ppm, 1803 ppb, and 324 ppb, and exceeded the preindustrial levels by about 40%, 150%, and 20%, respectively.[36]

Scientists have established that the change in weather patterns now being experienced is most likely caused by the increase in the amount of various greenhouse gases in the atmosphere since the Industrial Revolution and the resulting increase in mean temperature.[37] It has been more difficult for scientists to parse out whether specific environmental changes in a community, country, or region would have occurred if humans had not increased the amount of greenhouse gases in the atmosphere. Recent advances in attribution science, however, have made it increasingly possible to determine the connection between climate change and extreme weather events.[38]

---

36   INTERGOVERNMENTAL PANEL ON CLIMATE CHANGE, CLIMATE CHANGE 2013: THE PHYSICAL SCIENCE BASIS: SUMMARY FOR POLICYMAKERS, CONTRIBUTION OF WORKING GROUP I TO THE FIFTH ASSESSMENT REPORT OF THE IPCC 11 (2013) [hereinafter 'IPCC FIFTH ASSESSMENT PHYSICAL SCIENCE'] (citation omitted); *see also* INTERGOVERNMENTAL PANEL ON CLIMATE CHANGE, CLIMATE CHANGE 2007: THE PHYSICAL SCIENCE BASIS: SUMMARY FOR POLICYMAKERS, CONTRIBUTION OF WORKING GROUP I TO THE FOURTH ASSESSMENT REPORT OF THE IPCC 2 (2007) [hereinafter 'IPCC FOURTH ASSESSMENT PHYSICAL SCIENCE'].

37   IPCC FIFTH ASSESSMENT PHYSICAL SCIENCE, *supra* note 36, at 5, 11, 15, 17; *see also* IPCC FOURTH ASSESSMENT PHYSICAL SCIENCE, *supra* note 36, at 2–3, 15, 17.

38   For example, World Weather Attribution analyzes "the possible influence of climate change on extreme weather events, such as storms, extreme rainfall, heatwaves, cold spells, and droughts." *About*, WORLD WEATHER ATTRIBUTION, https://www.worldweatherattribution.org/about/ (last visited 18 May 2021). *See also* Angela Chen, *Climate Change Attribution*, MIT TECHNOLOGY REVIEW (26 Feb. 2020), https://www.technologyreview.com/10-breakthrough-technologies/2020/#climate-change-attribution ("Earlier this decade, scientists were reluctant to link any specific event to climate change. But many more extreme-weather attribution studies have been done in the last few years, and rapidly improving tools and techniques have made them more reliable and convincing. [...] These and other improvements have allowed scientists to state with increasing statistical certainty that yes, global warming is often fueling more dangerous weather events.").

Although some, like Biermann and Boas or Docherty and Giannini, have considered the distinction between natural and anthropogenic environmental impacts to be an important one when formulating legal definitions, the utility of establishing such a distinction would be of limited value from a humanitarian perspective given that the impact of any given environmental hazard will be the same whether it is "naturally" occurring or climate change driven. Docherty and Giannini emphasized that their proposal is "designed for a binding instrument rather than for a general policy"; in limiting the scope of their proposed convention they therefore sought, amongst other aims, to balance humanitarian needs with existing legal precedents and standards.[39] There may also be political implications to distinguishing climate change from other environmental impacts: a focus on climate change may be significant from an advocacy perspective but may produce a politically chilling—or mobilizing—effect.[40]

Walter Kälin, former Representative of the Secretary-General on the Human Rights of Internally Displaced Persons, has taken a pragmatic approach, proposing a typology for triggers of displacement scenarios without attempting to distinguish between their natural and anthropogenic roots, instead focusing on the character of the environmental change, as well as how such changes would impact human mobility in light of existing protection and assistance frameworks.[41] An informal group on Migration/Displacement and Climate

---

39    Docherty & Giannini, *supra* note 4, at 372.

40    For example, McAdam observed that the mandate of the Nansen Initiative (discussed *infra* in Chapter 5) is to address human mobility in the context of "disasters" and not "climate change" impacts specifically, although earlier drafts of the mandate had referred to "disasters 'particularly in the context of climate change' ". This choice to focus broadly on disasters rather than climate change specifically was fundamental to obtaining the support of some States, but does not prevent the Nansen Initiative from addressing disasters with anthropogenic roots. McAdam suggested, however, that from a climate justice perspective this approach may be considered to "miss[] an important opportunity to highlight the impact of climate change on human mobility and, in particular, to leverage climate change funding and assistance". Jane McAdam, *Creating New Norms on Climate Change, Natural Disasters and Displacement: International Developments 2010–2013*, 29(2) REFUGE 11, 18–19 (2014).

41    Walter Kälin, Remarks During Panel on Disaster Risk Reduction and Preparedness: Addressing the Humanitarian Consequences of Natural Disasters, Including the Impact of Climate Change (16 July 2008), https://www.brookings.edu/on-the-record/the-climate-change-displacement-nexus/. This typology formed the basis for subsequent submissions and publications by the author. *See* Representative of the UN Secretary-General on the Human Rights of Internally Displaced Persons (Walter Kälin), Working Paper Submitted to the IASC Working Group, *Working paper: Displacement and Climate Change: Towards Defining Categories of Affected Persons*, at 2–6 (1 Sept. 2008), *available at* https://interagencystandingcommittee.org/other/documents-public/rsg-climate-change-and-displacement [hereinafter 'Kälin, *Towards Defining Categories*']; Walter Kälin, *Conceptualising Climate-Induced*

Change mandated by the Inter-Agency Standing Committee (IASC)[42] adopted
in large part Kälin's proposed typology:[43]

- "Hydro-meteorological extreme hazard events" (i.e. rapid/sudden
  onset hazard events);
- "Environmental degradation and/or slow onset extreme hazard
  events";
- "Significant permanent losses in State territory as a result of sea level
  rise etc."; and
- "Armed conflict/violence over shrinking natural resources".[44]

---

Displacement, in CLIMATE CHANGE AND DISPLACEMENT: MULTIDISCIPLINARY
PERSPECTIVES 81, 84–86 (Jane McAdam ed., 2010) [hereinafter 'Kälin, Conceptualising'];
Kälin & Schrepfer, supra note 4, at 13–16. See also McAdam, Environmental Migration, supra
note 4, at 159–60; Jane McAdam, Climate Change Displacement and International Law:
Complementary Protection Standards 10–11 (UNHCR, Legal & Protection Policy Research
Series, PPLA/2011/03, May 2011), available at https://www.unhcr.org/4dffi6e99.pdf.

42   The IASC, established in June 1992 in response to the UN General Assembly Resolution
     46/182, provides a forum for coordination between humanitarian actors from both UN
     and non- UN bodies. The IASC Working Group develops policies to implement IASC deci-
     sions and oversees the work of thematically-driven subsidiary bodies within the IASC.
     In an effort to facilitate dialogue on climate change mobility, the IASC Working Group
     mandated an informal group on Migration/Displacement and Climate Change (IASC
     Informal Group), inter alia, to identify climate change related causes of human mobil-
     ity and their potential impacts, as well as applicable legal frameworks. Informal Group
     on Migration/Displacement and Climate Change of the IASC, Climate Change, Migration
     and Displacement: Who will be affected?, at 1, n.1 (Working paper, 31 Oct. 2008), available
     at https://www.unhcr.org/protection/environment/4a1e4fb42/climate-change-migrat
     ion-displacement-affected-working-paper-submitted.html [hereinafter 'IASC Informal
     Group, Who Will Be Affected'].
43   Kälin's proposed typology included five categories of climate change drivers; the IASC
     Informal Group adopted four of these. Kälin's fifth (unadopted) category of climate
     change drivers is evacuation and displacement following designation by governments of
     high-risk areas as too dangerous for habitation due to climate change impacts. Id. at 2–3;
     Kälin & Schrepfer, supra note 4, at 15–16; Kälin, Towards Defining Categories, supra note
     41, at 4; see also Kälin, Conceptualising, supra note 41, at 85–86; McAdam, Environmental
     Migration, supra note 4, at 159–60. Kolmannskog and Trebbi recognized a category similar
     to Kälin's fifth in a slightly different conceptualization of four categories of climate change
     drivers. Vikram Kolmannskog & Lisetta Trebbi, Climate Change, Natural Disasters and
     Displacement: A Multi-Track Approach to Filling the Protection Gaps, 92 INT'L REV. RED
     CROSS 713, 717–20 (2010); see also Vikram Kolmannskog, The Point of No Return: Exploring
     Law on Cross-Border Displacement in the Context of Climate Change, 34 REFUGEE WATCH
     28, 29–30 (2009).
44   IASC Informal Group, Who Will Be Affected, supra note 42, at 2–3. For variations on this
     typology, see supra note 43.

There is some overlap between these categories.[45] The fourth category, armed conflict over resources which have become scarce due to climate change, is generally considered an indirect impact of climate change. Climate change impacts which reduce access to natural resources (such as water), food production, or land (and thus may give rise to armed conflict) would arguably already fall under one of the first three categories.[46] This category is significant, however, because human mobility in the context of armed conflict, generally considered involuntary in nature, may give rise to existing protection mechanisms under international law.[47] Similarly, the third category—significant permanent losses in State territory as a result of sea level rise—could be considered as an issue falling within the scope of the second category, i.e., environmental degradation and/or slow onset extreme hazard events. However, rising sea levels present unique challenges and legal issues for small island States. The overlap between categories is therefore due to the unique legal and operational issues raised by armed conflict and sea level rise which set them apart from the other categories. In this respect, this typology was intended as an analytical tool used to identify human mobility scenarios and is not an exhaustive or theoretically flawless list.[48] The climate change drivers identified in this typology therefore provide a useful point of reference and will be used throughout this book.

## B        The Nature of Human Mobility in the Context of Climate Change

Since the issue of climate change mobility has come to the fore over the last few decades, scholars and practitioners have attempted to conceptualize human

---

45    *See* Kälin, *Towards Defining Categories*, *supra* note 41, at 2, n.3.

46    Kälin cited water and food production as examples of resources which could become scarce and consequently give rise to armed conflict. As examples of environmental degradation and slow onset disasters, he included reduced access to water, as well as desertification, recurring flooding, and seawater intrusion on coastal areas, all of which could impact food production. Kälin & Schrepfer, *supra* note 4, at 13–16; Kälin, *Towards Defining Categories*, *supra* note 41, at 2–3; Kälin, *Conceptualising*, *supra* note 41, at 84–86.

47    *See* Kälin, *Towards Defining Categories*, *supra* note 41, at 5–6; Kälin, *Conceptualising*, *supra* note 41, at 92.

48    *See* Kälin, *Towards Defining Categories*, *supra* note 41, at 2. For a view on the unfeasibility of creating a comprehensive list of scenarios, *see generally* MAYER, CLIMATE MIGRATION, *supra* note 12, at 16–38 ("The physical effects of climate change produce series of social effects which, like the concentric circles that an impact produces on a water surface, extend ad infinitum and at absurdum in time and space. It is hardly an exaggeration to state that the impacts of climate change can have virtually any consequence on any form of migration [...]" (quotation at 24)).

mobility and the people who move in the context of climate change through various criteria, including whether the movement is voluntary or involuntary, within or across national borders, or permanent or non-permanent.[49] Certain of these criteria coincide with existing legal frameworks for human mobility and are arguably vital to providing protection thereunder.[50] Some, however, have considered that certain of these criteria are unnecessary, impractical, or unhelpful for addressing climate change mobility.

Whether climate change mobility should be considered voluntary or involuntary is the most heavily debated criterion and underlies much of the terminological debate.[51] Some reject that a distinction can or should be made between voluntary and involuntary movement in the context of climate change. For example, Biermann and Boas consider that any distinction between voluntary and involuntary movement would correspond to the adaptive capacity of the persons moving and the strength of available resources.[52] They also consider that making a legal distinction based on the purportedly voluntary or involuntary nature of the movement would be detrimental because it would, in their view, falsely diminish the scope of the actual problem and create arbitrarily differing protection regimes.[53]

Others, such as Docherty and Giannini, consider that there is an important distinction to be made between voluntary and involuntary movement, in large part because it coincides with distinctions required under existing legal frameworks.[54] To recall, their proposed convention would provide protection for climate change mobility that constitutes forced relocation (temporary or permanent) across national borders.[55] These criteria show that, although they adopted a broader and more flexible approach to identifying climate change

---

49    *See* Graeme Hugo, *Environmental Concerns and International Migration*, 30(1) INT'L MIGRATION REV. 105, 106 (1996); MOSTAFA M. NASER, THE EMERGING GLOBAL CONSENSUS ON CLIMATE CHANGE AND HUMAN MOBILITY 2 (2021) (giving also a visual illustration of these as "key climate-related mobility variables").

50    *See* Kälin & Schrepfer, *supra* note 4, at 28–29.

51    *See* Hugo, *supra* note 49, at 106; Hodgkinson et al., *supra* note 24, at 88–89; Gemenne Thesis, *supra* note 12, at 168–70. *See also* François Gemenne, *One Good Reason to Speak of 'Climate Refugees'*, 49 FORCED MIGRATION REV. 70, 70 (2015) [hereinafter 'Gemenne, *Climate Refugees*'].

52    Biermann & Boas 2010, *supra* note 15, at 65. *See also* Hodgkinson et al., *supra* note 24, at 88–89 (rejecting the inclusion of a subjective assessment of voluntary/involuntary movement in their proposed convention).

53    Biermann & Boas 2010, *supra* note 15, at 65.

54    Docherty & Giannini, *supra* note 4, at 368–69. *See also* Kälin & Schrepfer, *supra* note 4, at 43, 62.

55    Docherty & Giannini, *supra* note 4, at 372.

drivers (as discussed earlier), Docherty and Giannini, modelling after existing legal frameworks, proposed more restrictive criteria than Bierman and Boas, as to the persons eligible for protection under a new international convention.

Making a distinction between voluntary and forced movement in practice, however, is difficult. It is widely acknowledged that there is no bright-line distinction between voluntary and involuntary movement in the context of climate change. Rather, entirely voluntary and involuntary movement each lie at opposite ends of a spectrum, with movements characterized by varying degrees of control or compulsion falling somewhere in between these two extremes.[56] In addition, true voluntariness in this context does not equate to complete freedom of choice but rather to the ability to decide between reasonable choices.[57]

Fabrice Renaud and his colleagues consider that the relative (in)voluntary nature of movement can be determined by examining factors, such as the nature of the climate change driver as slow or rapid onset, the relative contribution of socio-political compulsion or economic motivation, and adaptive capacity.[58] By contrast, Walter Kälin and Nina Schrepfer consider this kind of *ex ante* approach to be impractical because determining the relative causality between such factors would be "exceedingly difficult or even impossible".[59] Instead, Kälin and Schrepfer propose a three-pronged *ex post* examination for determining whether persons who have moved in connection with climate change can or should be forced to return to their homes—what they call a "returnability test":

    a.   Is it *permissible* under international law to send the person back, particularly in light of the principle of *non-refoulement*?

---

56    Margareta Wahlström, *Chairperson's Summary*, *in* The Nansen Conference, Oslo, Norway, 6–7 June 2011, *Climate Change and Displacement in the 21st Century*, at 18, 18, ¶ 6 (*text by* Christian Gahre), *available at* https://www.unhcr.org/4ea969729.pdf [hereinafter 'Wahlström Nansen Summary']; Bates, *supra* note 33, at 467–68; Hugo, *supra* note 49, at 107; Jane McAdam & Elizabeth Ferris, *Planned Relocations in the Context of Climate Change: Unpacking the Legal and Conceptual Issues*, 4 CAMBRIDGE J. INT'L & COMP. L. 137, 143 (2015).

57    Kälin & Schrepfer, *supra* note 4, at 62–63.

58    *See generally* Fabrice G. Renaud et al., *A Decision Framework for Environmentally Induced Migration*, 49 INT'L MIGRATION e5 (2011) [hereinafter 'Renaud et al., *Decision Framework*'].

59    Kälin and Schrepfer also critiqued the model proposed by Renaud and his colleagues as not taking into account categories of persons who leave their home voluntarily but are later unable to return due to the occurrence of a rapid onset disaster and a subsequent lack of recovery therefrom. Kälin & Schrepfer, *supra* note 4, at 63, 66–67.

    b.   Is it *feasible* (i.e., factually possible) to return the person in light of existing conditions in the country of origin following climate change impacts (e.g., is the path of return physically or administratively blocked)?

    c.   Is it *reasonable*, in light of humanitarian considerations, to return a person (e.g., is the government willing and able to provide protection and would living conditions be consistent with international standards)?[60]

If the answer to any of these three questions is "no", then they consider that the person should be permitted to stay, without any need to determine whether he or she moved voluntarily at the outset.[61] Neither the approach of Renaud nor that of Kälin and Schrepfer has yet been adopted as a common framework.

Another significant criterion, which has been the subject of debate, is whether the movement is within national borders or transnational. Unlike voluntariness, identifying the national or international nature of the movement poses little difficulty in most cases.[62] The debate in this respect centers on whether the distinction is relevant and justifiable in the context of climate change mobility. The law and governance of internal movement is rooted in issues of sovereignty, which make the establishment of overarching international laws a highly sensitive issue.[63] The distinction between internal and international movement is therefore already made in existing legal frameworks, which may already provide varying degrees of protection to climate change mobility. For example, the United Nations High Commissioner for Refugees (UNHCR) considers that in many cases people displaced by environmental disasters and climate change will be internally displaced and are already protected under international humanitarian and human rights law, as reflected in the 1998 Guiding Principles on Internal Displacement.[64]

Some commentators disagree, however, that existing frameworks should guide the conceptualization of climate change mobility. For example, in attempting to define "climate refugees", Biermann and Boas rejected the

---

60    *Id.* at 65–66.

61    *Id.*

62    Gemenne Thesis, *supra* note 12, at 166.

63    *See, e.g.*, Docherty & Giannini, *supra* note 4, at 369.

64    Guiding Principles on Internal Displacement, UN Doc. E/CN.4/1998/53/Add.2 (11 Feb. 1998); UNHCR, UNHCR, ENVIRONMENT & CLIMATE CHANGE 8 (Volker Türk et al. eds., updated version, 2015), *available at* https://www.unhcr.org/540854f49.pdf. There is, however, disagreement as to whether the Guiding Principles provide full protection in all climate change mobility scenarios. *See* discussion *infra* in Chapter 4(D).

criterion of internal versus transnational movement, considering that it had little relevance to understanding human mobility in the context of climate change.[65] Biermann and Boas also considered that making such a distinction in protection mechanisms could ultimately disadvantage larger developing nations, which are expected to experience the greatest numbers of persons moving internally in connection with climate change.[66]

Distinctions have also been drawn between temporary and permanent movement, although there is little guidance as to how to classify movement as one or the other without the benefit of hindsight.[67] Temporary movement is often associated with rapid onset hazards, but people may temporarily leave their homes in response to slow onset hazards or environmental degradation.[68] Those who move in emergency response to rapid onset hazards may never return to their homes, making what was at first a temporary move ultimately a permanent one.[69] There is no meaningful measure of time to mark the transition from temporary to permanent; any imposed cut-off point would be arbitrary.[70]

Moreover, the value of dichotomizing temporary and permanent movement is questionable. Identifying movement as "temporary" could be relevant to projected population movement scenarios. In the context of protection frameworks, some countries have either practice or domestic law providing temporary protection in the wake of rapid onset hazards, but temporary protection does not necessarily correlate with temporary movement.[71] Jane McAdam and Elizabeth Ferris have pointed out that, from an operational standpoint, temporary evacuation and permanent planned relocation implicate "different decision-making structures", which means involvement of actors from different sectors applying adapted policies and powers.[72] The involvement of "different decision-making structures", however, is more closely related to the nature of the movement as emergency or planned rather than its temporary or permanent nature. Following a rapid onset environmental hazard, those who move temporarily and those who ultimately never return to their homes will

---

65   Biermann & Boas 2010, *supra* note 15, at 66. By contrast, Hodgkinson and his colleagues acknowledge this as an important conceptual distinction but consider that a new instrument must address both. Hodgkinson et al., *supra* note 24, at 83.

66   Biermann & Boas 2007, *supra* note 14, at 6.

67   *See* MYERS WITH KENT, *supra* note 11, at 18–19.

68   *See* Renaud et al., *Decision Framework*, *supra* note 58, at e9, e14; Kälin & Schrepfer, *supra* note 4, at 60.

69   *See* Renaud et al., *Decision Framework*, *supra* note 58, at e16, fig.1.

70   Gemenne considered that temporary versus permanent movement must also be perceived as a continuum. Gemenne Thesis, *supra* note 12, at 172.

71   *See, e.g.*, Wahlström Nansen Summary, *supra* note 56, at 19, ¶ 22.

72   McAdam & Ferris, *supra* note 56, at 161.

require the same assistance. Docherty and Giannini rejected the need to make such a distinction for the purposes of a new convention, noting that no such distinction was made under the Refugee Convention and observing that the need for humanitarian assistance does not depend upon the temporary or permanent nature of the movement.[73]

Debates over terminology reflect disagreements on criteria, especially perceptions as to whether climate change mobility is voluntary or involuntary. The word "refugee" has been widely used in connection with climate change, including in the seminal term discussed above: "environmental refugee".[74] The term "refugee" is a defined legal term under the Refugee Convention.[75] With some exceptions, there is broad agreement that persons who move because of climate change do not generally fall within the existing legal definition of "refugee", which only applies to persons subject to persecution.[76] The use of the word "refugee" in connection with climate change mobility has therefore been heavily criticized as a "legal misnomer" which risks undermining existing protection mechanisms.[77] Others consider the word "refugee" is nonetheless

---

73    Docherty & Giannini, *supra* note 4, at 369. Biermann and Boas and Hodgkinson et al. also considered the distinction unnecessary. Biermann & Boas 2010, *supra* note 15, at 65–66; Hodgkinson et al., *supra* note 24, at 84.

74    *See* discussion on the term "environmental refugee" *supra* in Chapter 2(A).

75    Convention Relating to the Status of Refugees art. 1(A)(2), 28 July 1951, 189 U.N.T.S. 137 [hereinafter 'Refugee Convention'], as amended by Protocol Relating to the Status of Refugees art. 1(2), 31 Jan. 1967, 606 U.N.T.S. 267 [hereinafter 'Refugee Protocol'], discussed *infra* in Chapter 4(A).

76    Under the Refugee Convention, the term "refugee" applies to "any person who: [...] owing to well-founded fear of being persecuted for reasons of race, religion, nationality, membership of a particular social group or political opinion, is outside the country of his nationality and is unable or, owing to such fear, is unwilling to avail himself of the protection of that country; or who, not having a nationality and being outside the country of his former habitual residence as a result of such events, is unable or, owing to such fear, is unwilling to return to it." Refugee Convention, *supra* note 75, art. 1(A)(2), as amended by Refugee Protocol, *supra* note 75, art. 1(2). For an analysis, see Jane McAdam et al., *International Law and Sea-Level Rise: Forced Migration and Human Rights* 31–32 (Fridtjof Nansen Inst., FNI Report 1/2016, Jan. 2016), *available at* https://www.fni.no/getfile.php/131 711-1469868996/Filer/Publikasjoner/FNI-R0116.pdf. The potential exceptions to this analysis are discussed in Chapter 4 in connection with the asylum framework.

77    *See, e.g.*, Kälin & Schrepfer, *supra* note 4, at 28; UNHCR, *Climate Change, Natural Disasters and Human Displacement: A UNHCR Perspective* 8–9 (Policy Paper, 2009), *available at* https://www.unhcr.org/protection/environment/4901e81a4/unhcr-policy-paper-climate-change-natural-disasters-human-displacement.html; Stephen Castles, *Environmental Change and Forced Migration: Making Sense of the Debate* 8 (UNHCR, New Issues in Refugee Research Working Paper No. 70, Oct. 2002), *available at* https://www.unhcr.org/research/working/3de344fd9/environmental-change-forced-migration-making-sense-debate-step hen-castles.html; Wahlström Nansen Summary, *supra* note 56, at 19, ¶ 21; OLI BROWN,

most appropriate, either as a non-legal term best suited to convey the urgency of the issue and the dire circumstances of persons moving in the context of climate change, or as a legal term in need of revision or expansion.[78] Avidan Kent and Simon Behrman opine that the "current definition of the refugee in international law has indeed become 'entrenched' in outdated preconceptions," observing that "legal categories of any sort must always be open to question, and to revision."[79] As discussed, new terms incorporating the word "refugee" have been proposed as the cornerstone of new legal instruments that would convey a new form of refugee status (and concomitant legal rights and protections) on certain categories of persons who move in connection with climate change.[80]

Some scholars have considered "migrant" a more suitable term for persons moving in connection with climate change. For example, following the view that the term "environmental refugee" had "no legal grounding in international refugee law", the International Organization for Migration (IOM) in 2007 proposed instead the term "environmental migrant" to define a broad category of persons, similar to the definitions El-Hinnawi and Myers had proposed for "environmental refugee", without explicit reference to climate change as a driver:

> Environmental migrants are persons or groups of persons who, for compelling reasons of sudden or progressive changes in the environment that adversely affect their lives or living conditions, are obliged to leave their

---

MIGRATION AND CLIMATE CHANGE 13–14 (IOM Migration Research Series No. 31, 2008), *available at* https://publications.iom.int/fr/system/files/pdf/mrs-31_en.pdf?language=en; INTERNATIONAL ORGANIZATION FOR MIGRATION, MIGRATION, ENVIRONMENT AND CLIMATE CHANGE: ASSESSING THE EVIDENCE 18 (Frank Laczko & Christine Aghazarm eds., 2010), *available at* http://publications.iom.int/bookstore/free/migration_and_envi ronment.pdf; AVIDAN KENT & SIMON BEHRMAN, FACILITATING THE RESETTLEMENT AND RIGHTS OF CLIMATE REFUGEES: AN ARGUMENT FOR DEVELOPING EXISTING PRINCIPLES AND PRACTICES 53–55 (2018).

78   *See, e.g.,* MYERS WITH KENT, *supra* note 11, at 19–20; European Parliamentary Assembly, Report of the Committee on Migration, Refugees and Population, *Environmentally Induced Migration and Displacement: A 21st Century Challenge,* ¶ 50, Doc. 11785 (2008) (*rapporteur* Tina Acketoft), *available at* https://assembly.coe.int/nw/xml/XRef/Xref-XML2HTML-en.asp?fileid=12098&lang=en [hereinafter 'EU 2008 Report']; Renaud et al., *Decision Framework, supra* note 58, at e12–13, e24, n.2; Biermann & Boas 2010, *supra* note 15, at 66–67; Gemenne, *Climate Refugees, supra* note 51, at 71.

79   KENT & BEHRMAN, *supra* note 77, at 43, 46–53 (quotations at 43).

80   *See generally* Docherty & Giannini, *supra* note 4; Biermann & Boas 2010, *supra* note 15.

habitual homes, or choose to do so, either temporarily or permanently, and who move either within their country or abroad.[81]

The IOM's broad definition of "environmental migrant" explicitly encompasses voluntary and involuntary (as well as temporary and permanent, internal and international) movement; nevertheless, from a legal perspective, the stand-alone term "migrant" is often understood as conveying voluntary movement.[82] Thus, in a 2008 report, Oli Brown observed that the term "climate migrant" could imply "the 'pull' of the destination more than the 'push' of the source country and carries negative connotations which reduce the implied responsibility of the international community for their welfare".[83] Brown therefore used another term, "forced climate migrant", in his report to convey the involuntary nature of the movement he addressed therein.[84]

Others have also used other descriptive variations of the term "migrant" to convey varying levels of voluntariness. For example, Fabrice Renaud and his colleagues proposed that human mobility could be divided into three categories of "environmental migrants" which would correspond with various factors, including voluntariness as a predominant criterion: (i) "environmental emergency migrants", (ii) "environmentally forced migrants", and

---

81    International Organization for Migration Council, 94th Sess., Geneva, Switzerland, 27–30 Nov. 2007, *Discussion Note: Migration and the Environment*, at 1–2, Doc. No. MC/INF/288 (1 Nov. 2007) (emphasis in original omitted). *See also* BROWN, *supra* note 77, at 15.

82    *See* Kälin & Schrepfer, *supra* note 4, at 28–29 (noting that the term "obfuscates the distinction between forced and voluntary movements that is important from a legal protection perspective. While it is true that social scientists often use migration as a generic term encompassing both voluntary and forced movements, international law does not use the term 'migrant' in the context of forced movements but refers to 'displaced persons' and 'refugees'. At the same time, the legal term 'migrant worker' denotes one, albeit particularly important sub-category of voluntary movement, suggesting that the hitherto not defined term 'migrant' should be used for persons migrating voluntarily" (citations omitted)). *See also* GRANT DAWSON & SONIA FARBER, FORCIBLE DISPLACEMENT THROUGHOUT THE AGES: TOWARDS AN INTERNATIONAL CONVENTION FOR THE PREVENTION AND PUNISHMENT OF THE CRIME OF FORCIBLE DISPLACEMENT 43 (2012) ("The term 'migration' can be used in a non-criminal context as part of the natural movement of populations, and so can obscure the discussion [about the involuntary nature of forcible displacement] at times.").

83    BROWN, *supra* note 77, at 14. *See also* McAdam, *Environmental Migration*, *supra* note 4, at 157 (observing that "[t]ensions between 'refugee' and 'migrant' labels strike at the heart of the debate—do (or should) states have international protection obligations towards the displaced, or should they retain the discretion to pick and choose new migrants?"); EU 2008 Report, *supra* note 78, ¶ 50.

84    BROWN, *supra* note 77, at 15.

(iii) "environmentally motivated migrants".[85] In an earlier publication presenting a similar concept, Renaud originally used the term "environmental refugee" for the first category but, given its incompatibility with the legal definition of refugees under the 1951 Convention, replaced the term with "environmental emergency migrants".[86]

Others have used variations of the term "displaced" in formulating terms, such as "environmentally displaced persons" and "climate change displaced persons".[87] The term "displaced" or "displacement" conveys involuntary movement.[88] David Hodgkinson and his colleagues refer to "CCPDs" (meaning "climate change displaced persons"), distinguishing this category of persons from voluntary forms of migration and expressing a desire to distance their proposal from asylum regimes.[89]

Within the last two decades, human mobility has been increasingly recognized as a form of adaptation to climate change.[90] With this shift, the terms "relocation" and "resettlement" have appeared with increasing frequency in the literature.[91] "Relocation" often refers to permanent movement that

---

85   Renaud et al., *Decision Framework, supra* note 58, at e14–15.

86   *Id.* at e14, e24, n.2 (2011); *see also* Renaud et al., *Control, Adapt or Flee, supra* note 8, at 29–30.

87   *See* Prieur et al., *supra* note 13, *passim* (using the term "environmentally-displaced persons"); Jane McAdam & Ben Saul, *An Insecure Climate for Human Security? Climate-Induced Displacement and International Law, in* HUMAN SECURITY AND NON-CITIZENS: LAW, POLICY AND INTERNATIONAL AFFAIRS 357, *passim* (Alice Edwards & Carla Ferstman eds., 2009) (using the term "climate-induced displacement"); Margit Ammer, *Climate change and Human Rights: The Status of Climate Refugees in Europe* 26–27 (Ludwig Boltzmann Inst. of Hum. Rts., Research Project on Climate Change for the Swiss Initiative to Commemorate the 60th Anniversary of the Universal Declaration of Human Rights, June 2009) (using the terms "international climate displacees" and "internal climate displacees"); Hodgkinson et al., *supra* note 24, at 87–90 (using the term "climate change displaced persons" or the short form "CCDPs").

88   For a discussion of the meaning of the term "displacement" and its variations, see DAWSON & FARBER, *supra* note 82, at 43–46.

89   Hodgkinson et al., *supra* note 24, at 87–90.

90   *See* Gemenne, *Climate Refugees, supra* note 51, at 70. On the nexus between migration and adaptation, see François Gemenne & Julia Blocher, *How Can Migration Serve Adaptation to Climate Change? Challenges to Fleshing Out a Policy Ideal* 183(4) GEOGRAPHICAL J. 336, 340–41 (2017).

91   *See* DANIEL PETZ, PLANNED RELOCATIONS IN THE CONTEXT OF NATURAL DISASTERS AND CLIMATE CHANGE: A REVIEW OF THE LITERATURE 5 (2015), *available at* https://www.brookings.edu/wp-content/uploads/2016/06/brookings-planned-relocations-annotated-bibliography-june-2015.pdf (noting a "clear rise of interest in the topic of planned relocations (both reactive and preemptive) in recent years" and observing that the bulk of the literature reviewed on this topic was published between 2010 and 2015).

implicates government involvement in the planning, oversight, or execution of the move.[92] With respect to the permanent nature of relocation, a temporary relocation may be more appropriately termed an "evacuation".[93] Although a distinction has been made between forced and voluntary relocation, some would argue that, in the context of climate change, any distinction between voluntary and involuntary planned relocation is in any case "artificial": "In all types of Planned Relocation, distinctions between 'forced' versus 'voluntary' movement are somewhat artificial. Arguably, all those who participate in planned relocation are being compelled to move by forces beyond their control—disasters and environmental change, including the effects of climate change".[94] "Resettlement" is sometimes used synonymously with "relocation"[95] or as referring to "forced relocation".[96] A more recent view, however, considers

---

92    *See* UNHCR, Expert Consultation in Sanremo, Italy, 12–14 Mar. 2014, *Report: Planned Relocation, Disasters and Climate Change: Consolidating Good Practices and Preparing for the Future*, ¶ 31 (2014) (*prepared by* Sanjula Weerasinghe with Susan Martin et al.), *available at* https://www.unhcr.org/54082cc69.pdf [hereinafter 'Sanremo Report'] (according to the report, "most participants agreed that 'planned relocation' is ordinarily instigated, supervised, and carried out by the State or under its responsibility, or carried out by communities in their own interests, in coordination with the State, or suggested or petitioned for by communities and put into practice by the State"). *See also* Elizabeth Ferris, *Planned Relocation, Disasters and Climate Change: Consolidating Good Practices and Preparing for the Future* 8 (Background Document for Expert Consultation in Sanremo, Italy on 12–14 Mar. 2014), *available at* https://www.brookings.edu/wp-content/uploads/2016/06/Planned-Relocations-Backgrond-paper-March-2014.pdf (defining relocation as "physical movement of people instigated, supervised and carried out by State authorities (whether national or local)", although not presenting this as a universally applicable definition).

93    *See* Sanremo Report, *supra* note 92, at 10; McAdam & Ferris, *supra* note 56, at 140.

94    Brookings Inst. et al., Guidance on Protecting People from Disasters and Environmental Change Through Planned Relocation, at 7 (7 Oct. 2015), https://www.brookings.edu/wp-content/uploads/2016/06/GUIDANCE_PLANNED-RELOCATION_14-OCT-2015.pdf.

95    *See* Sanremo Report, *supra* note 92, ¶ 29; *see also* Alex de Sherbinin et al., *Preparing for Population Displacement and Resettlement Associated with Large Climate Change Adaptation and Mitigation Projects* 1 (Background Paper for Workshop in Bellagio, Italy, 2–6 Nov. 2010) (defining "resettlement" as "population movement planned directly by the government or private developers, where an area is chosen in order to resettle the population"). Sherbinen et al.'s definition is broader in the sense that it includes movement planned by private actors, not only by government actors alone.

96    *See* JEAN-MARIE HENCKAERTS, MASS EXPULSION IN MODERN INTERNATIONAL LAW AND PRACTICE 2 (1995) (defining forced relocation as "forcible resettlement pursuant to governmental policies"). By contrast, forcible displacement is generally associated with armed conflict, ethnic tensions, or serious human rights violations. *See* DAWSON & FARBER, *supra* note 82, at 43 (citing HENCKAERTS) (defining internal displacement

resettlement as a distinct part of the relocation process. In this context, resettlement refers to establishing the means for relocated persons to reestablish their communities and livelihoods.[97]

This shift towards adaptation manifested in the Cancun Adaptation Framework, adopted by the Conference of the Parties to the UNFCCC in 2010 as part of the Cancun Agreements.[98] Paragraph 14(f) of the Cancun Adaptation Framework invites the Parties "to enhance action on adaptation", including "[m]easures to enhance understanding, coordination and cooperation with regard to climate change induced displacement, migration and planned relocation, where appropriate, at the national, regional and international levels".[99] This was the first time that the UNFCCC Conference of the Parties agreed on a text regarding migration, displacement, and planned relocation.[100]

Although the Cancun Adaptation Framework refers to "displacement, migration and planned relocation", it does not provide any definition of these terms. These terms have since been generally grouped under the umbrella

as "uprooting caused by civil war, internal strife, ethnic tensions and other situations where serious human rights violations occur" and forced relocation as "forcible resettlement pursuant to governmental policies, such as the implementation of development projects"). *See also* Sanremo Report, *supra* note 92, at 10, n.8, ¶ 29; Ferris, *supra* note 92, at 8; Elizabeth Ferris, *When Protecting People from Natural Disasters and Environmental Change Means Relocating Them*, BROOKINGS INST. (12 June 2015), https://www.brookings.edu/blog/planetpolicy/2015/06/12/when-protecting-people-from-natural-disasters-and-environmental-change-means-relocating-them/.

97    Sanremo Report, *supra* note 92, at 10 ("resettlement" as "a component of planned relocation, means: the process of enabling persons to establish themselves permanently in a new location, with access to habitable housing, resources and services, measures to restore/recover assets, livelihoods, land, and living standards, and to enjoy rights in a non-discriminatory manner"). McAdam and Ferris acknowledge resettlement as relating to relocation in this manner, but consider that relocation can in some cases occur without resettlement. McAdam & Ferris, *supra* note 56, at 141.

98    *See generally* UNFCCC, Cancun, Mex., 29 Nov.–10 Dec. 2010, *Report of the Conference of the Parties on its Sixteenth Session*, pt. 2, at 3, ¶ 2(b), UN Doc. FCCC/CP/2010/7/Add.1 (15 Mar. 2011), [hereinafter 'UNFCCC, Cancun Report'], discussed *infra* in Chapter 5(A). On the evolution of party views on adaptation and human mobility through UNFCCC discussions between 2007 and 2010, see Koko Warner, *Human Migration and Displacement in the Context of Adaptation to Climate Change: the Cancun Adaptation Framework and Potential for Future Action*, 30(6) ENV'T & PLAN. C: GOV'T & POL'Y 1061, 1063–70 (2012) [hereinafter 'Warner, *Cancun Adaptation Framework*'].

99    UNFCCC, Cancun Report, *supra* note 98, ¶ 14(f).

100   *See* Warner, *Cancun Adaptation Framework*, *supra* note 98, at 1061.

term "human mobility".[101] Although there is no official uniform definition,[102] they have generally been interpreted as follows:

- displacement: primarily forced movement;[103]
- migration: primarily voluntary movement;[104] and
- planned relocation: an organized process of moving persons to a new location, usually within the same country.[105]

There seems to be, however, some disagreement as to whether the term "planned relocation" only refers to planned collective movement made with the consent of and in consultation with those moving, or whether it may also refer to movement planned and executed by, for example, the government without the consent of those moving.[106] In this respect, consent may be considered

---

101   *See* Advisory Group on Climate Change and Human Mobility, *Human Mobility in the Context of Climate Change*, at 3 (Recommendations for UNFCCC COP 20, Lima, Peru, Dec. 2014), *available at* https://www.iom.int/sites/default/files/migrated_files/pbn/docs/Human-Mobility-in-the-context-of-Climate-Change.pdf [hereinafter 'Advisory Group COP20 Recommendations']; UNHCR, *Policy Brief: Displacement at COP 22*, at 2 (Policy Brief for UNFCCC COP 22, Marrakech, Morocco, Nov. 2016), *available at* http://disasterdisplacement.org/wp-content/uploads/2016/11/UNHCR-COP22-Policy-Brief-1.pdf;   1 NANSEN INITIATIVE, AGENDA FOR THE PROTECTION OF CROSS-BORDER DISPLACED PERSONS IN THE CONTEXT OF DISASTERS AND CLIMATE CHANGE 17, ¶ 22 (2015) [hereinafter 'NANSEN PROTECTION AGENDA'].
102   *See, e.g.*, Elizabeth Ferris, Climate change, Migration and the Incredibly Complicated Task of Influencing Policy, Keynote Address at the Brookings Institute Conference on Human Migration and the Environment: Futures, Politics, Invention (1 July 2015), http://cmsny.org/wp-content/uploads/FERRIS-1-JULY-2015.pdf ("In the absence of a clear paradigm—which sets out the questions to be asked and posits relationships between them—many of us have latched on to the language of article 14(f) of the 2010 Cancun Adaptation Framework [...]. But there are differences in understanding what these terms—climate change induced displacement, migration and planned relocation—mean. And there are differences in approaches to influencing policy.").
103   *See* Advisory Group COP20 Recommendations, *supra* note 101, at 3; NANSEN PROTECTION AGENDA, *supra* note 101, at 17, ¶ 22.
104   *See* Advisory Group COP20 Recommendations, *supra* note 101, at 3; NANSEN PROTECTION AGENDA, *supra* note 101, at 17, ¶ 20 (defining "migration" as "human movements that are preponderantly voluntary insofar as people, while not necessarily having the ability to decide in complete freedom, still possess the ability to choose between different realistic options" (emphasis in original omitted)).
105   *See* Advisory Group COP20 Recommendations, *supra* note 101, at 3; NANSEN PROTECTION AGENDA, *supra* note 101, at 17, ¶ 21.
106   *See* Advisory Group COP20 Recommendations, *supra* note 101, at 3 (defining "planned relocation" as "[a]n organized relocation, ordinarily instigated, supervised and carried out by the state with the consent or upon the request of the community"); NANSEN

distinct from the concept of voluntariness discussed earlier. A community may be compelled to move by severe climate change impacts (i.e., involuntary movement), but also consent to a plan to relocate collectively in cooperation with government and other actors. Consent is a significant factor in understanding the nature of planned relocation; whether a community agrees to, and participates in formulating, a plan to relocate will most likely have a real impact on the process of moving and on the well-being of the persons moving. At the same time, whether those moving perceive their movement to be "voluntary" may also impact their experience of the move and its outcome.

Moreover, the increasing recognition of human mobility as a form of adaptation should not be understood as an endorsement of mobility (in any of its forms) as a beneficial or even acceptable outcome of climate change. Moving—whether considered voluntarily or otherwise—can mean leaving behind one's home, family, land, community, or country and can lead to loss of territory, cultural identity, or indigenous knowledge for individuals and entire communities.[107] In addition, as Scott Leckie points out, many who move face difficult living conditions that are often worse than the ones they fled:

> Despite the rising voices of those proclaiming the virtues of migration, we can rest assured that in the absence of well-thought-out government plans and policies to address the growing problem of climate displacement, most of those affected will be migrating not to better homes on better lands in better locations, but rather to drab and often dangerous neighbourhoods which are in all likelihood far worse than the areas whence they came.[108]

Even voluntary climate change mobility can have detrimental impacts on individuals and communities (including receiving communities). Any such

---

PROTECTION AGENDA, *supra* note 101, ¶ 21 (defining "planned relocation" as a "planned process in which persons or groups of persons move or are assisted to move away from their homes or places of temporary residence, are settled in a new location, and provided with the conditions for rebuilding their lives" (emphasis in original omitted)) (quoting from Brookings Inst. et al., *Guidance on Planned Relocation within National Borders: To Protect People from Impacts of Disasters and Environmental Change, Including Climate Change* (Draft, 5 June 2015)); *see also* Ferris, *supra* note 92, at 8–9; Sanremo Report, *supra* note 92, ¶ 10.

107　*See* Petra Tschakert et al., *Climate Change and Loss, as if People Mattered: Values, Places and Experiences*, 8(5) WIRES CLIMATE CHANGE e476, e482–83 (2017).

108　Scott Leckie, *Using Human Rights to Resolve the Climate Displacement Problem: The Promise of the Peninsula Principles, in* REPAIRING DOMESTIC CLIMATE DISPLACEMENT: THE PENINSULA PRINCIPLES 1, 11 (Scott Leckie & Chris Huggins eds., 2016).

movement is a complex process that requires significant time and resources.[109] For these and other reasons, mobility as an adaption strategy is generally considered an option of last resort.[110]

Some have questioned whether framing human mobility as an issue of adaptation at all is ultimately unhelpful or even damaging.[111] For example, migration expert François Gemenne views the shifting focus towards adaptation as a political tool for diminishing the need to take responsibility for anthropogenic climate changes that are disproportionately impacting persons in less industrialized nations.[112] Gemenne describes the focus on adaptation as the result of a process of de-victimizing persons moving in connection with climate change, who were once commonly referred to as "climate refugees".[113] Gemenne opines that the inclusion of human mobility in the Cancun Adaptation Framework marked "a paradigm shift: that migration in the context of climate change was no longer a disaster to avoid at all costs but a strategy that ought to be encouraged and facilitated."[114] Gemenne expresses regret at having supported the recognition of migration as a positive adaptive strategy, advocating for a return

---

109    Robin Bronen, *Climate Displacement: Preparation and Planning, in* REPAIRING DOMESTIC CLIMATE DISPLACEMENT: THE PENINSULA PRINCIPLES, *id.*, at 89, 90 ("Relocation is complicated, can be severely harmful to people, is a long-term development process and can be expensive to plan and implement. In order to identify and mitigate adverse social impacts and impoverishment risks, planning must begin as soon as it is established that relocation must occur. New multi-level and multi-disciplinary relationships between national, regional, tribal and local government actors must be created in order for them to work in concert together and with climate-affected populations. For these reasons, relocation should only occur as a last resort, if there are no other adaptation strategies to protect people from the climate-induced environmental changes in the places where they reside.").

110    *Id.*

111    *See* Christine Gibb & James Ford, *Should the United Nations Framework Convention on Climate Change Recognize Climate Migrants?*, 7 ENVTL. RES. LETT. 1, 3–4 (2012); KNOMAD, Symposium on Environmental Change and Migration: State of the Evidence, Washington, D.C., U.S.A., 28–29 May 2014, *Thematic Working Group on Environmental Change and Migration*, at 12 (*by* Wesley Wheeler), *available at* https://www.knomad.org/sites/defa ult/files/2017-03/KNOMAD_Symposium_Report_Final_TWG11%20%28final%20vers ion%29.pdf; Gemenne, *Climate Refugees, supra* note 51, at 70–71; MD SHAMSUDDOHA, CLIMATE-INDUCED DISPLACEMENT AND MIGRATION: POLICY GAPS AND POLICY ALTERNATIVE: A LIKELY LEGAL INSTRUMENT FOR A RIGHTS-BASED POLITICAL SOLUTION 9 (2015), *available at* https://unfccc.int/files/adaptation/groups_committ ees/loss_and_damage_executive_committee/application/pdf/briefing_paper_climate_ induced_displacement_and_migration.pdf.

112    Gemenne, *Climate Refugees, supra* note 51, at 71.

113    *Id.*

114    *Id.* at 70.

to the term "climate refugees", "because it recognises that these migrations are first and foremost the result of a persecution that we are inflicting on the most vulnerable."[115] Gemenne thus warns of the dangers of perceiving human mobility in the context of climate change simplistically as a beneficial option to those negatively impacted by climate change.

Addressing human mobility as part of adaptation measures thus entails an attempt, where possible, to build resilience and avert undesirable mobility and to confront the inevitability of some mobility, albeit unwelcome.[116] In the context of climate change, adaptation (including human mobility) may thus equate to balancing between two undesirable outcomes in order to assist communities that must move from their homes due to the effects of climate change.

---

115    *Id.* at 71.

116    The notion of adaptation in the context of mitigation efforts, particularly within the UNF-CCC, is discussed in further detail in Chapter 5.

# PART 2

## *Exploring a Rights-Based Approach to Climate Change Mobility*

∴

# CHAPTER 3

# The Development of a Rights-Based Approach and the Integration of an Adaptive Approach

> One must have gone against the stream to know what it means to
> go with the stream.
> — FRIDTJOF NANSEN

∴

The second half of the twentieth century CE—and especially the post-World War II era—was characterized by a proliferation of libertarian initiatives to codify human rights in a variety of legal instruments. Examples include the Universal Declaration of Human Rights (UDHR),[1] the International Covenant on Civil and Political Rights (ICCPR),[2] the International Covenant on Economic, Social and Cultural Rights (ICESCR),[3] the 1951 Convention Relating to the Status of Refugees and its 1967 Protocol,[4] and the European Convention on Human Rights (ECHR).[5] While the Cold War raged and the super powers waged their power struggles through proxies and poured their resources into assembling unimaginably destructive conventional, nuclear, chemical, biological, and radiological weapons arsenals, the international community was, at the same time, focused on adopting dozens of treaties to enshrine moral values into legal mandates, including the protection of the individual from unwarranted governmental intrusion. For these reasons, when legal scholars first began to discern that environmental changes would influence human movement, it was only natural that they would frame the issue in terms of

---

1 Universal Declaration of Human Rights, G.A. Res. 217 (III) A, UN Doc. A/RES/217(III) (10 Dec. 1948).
2 International Covenant on Civil and Political Rights, 19 Dec. 1966, 999 U.N.T.S. 171.
3 International Covenant on Economic, Social and Cultural Rights, 16 Dec. 1966, 993 U.N.T.S. 3.
4 Convention Relating to the Status of Refugees art. 1, 28 July 1951, 189 U.N.T.S. 137; Protocol Relating to the Status of Refugees art. 1, 31 Jan. 1967, 606 U.N.T.S. 267.
5 Council of Europe, European Convention for the Protection of Human Rights and Fundamental Freedoms, 4 Nov. 1950, 213 U.N.T.S. 221.

legal protections for those displaced due to environmental impacts, i.e., what is referred to in this book as a "rights-based approach".

However, it rather quickly became apparent that States were not about to extend classical post-World War II refugee protections to persons who had fled their homes due to land degradation and desertification. Hence, alternatives to the codification of legal rights for a brand new, and rather amorphous, group of people were needed. At the same time, it became increasingly clear that continuing attempts to mitigate global warming itself would not be sufficient to prevent human mobility in connection with climate change impacts.[6] These factors were the impetus for an adaptive approach to human mobility in the context of climate change. The development of an adaptive approach over the past two decades has been slow and subtle. It is a complex process whereby international organizations, States, non-governmental organizations (NGOs), scientists, scholars, and affected communities interact in a variety of settings in order to define the problem at hand and devise foresightful solutions to the emerging crises connected with human mobility and climate change.

Therefore, as used in this book:

–   A "rights-based approach" is characterized by a post hoc, top-down approach in which States have the duty to provide varying forms of protection to persons that have already moved internally or internationally. The scope of protection is determined by international legal frameworks that establish positive obligations for States, most often vis-à-vis individuals who fulfill certain pre-defined criteria.[7]

---

6       The Fourth Assessment Report of the Intergovernmental Panel on Climate Change (IPCC) promoted this realization and marked a shift in UNFCCC discussions towards adaptation. *See* Koko Warner, *Human Migration and Displacement in the Context of Adaptation to Climate Change: the Cancun Adaptation Framework and Potential for Future Action*, 30(6) ENV'T & PLAN. C: GOV'T & POL'Y 1061, 1062 (2012) ("A second strand of discussion was introduced around the time of the Intergovernmental Panel on Climate Change's (IPCC's) 'Fourth assessment report' in 2007 and the release of the Stern (2006) Review: scientists and policy makers began to concur that some impacts of climate change may already be manifest and that adaptation was therefore a necessary complement to mitigation in order to cushion the blow to society from some of the expected impacts of climate change"). *See also* Stephen Castles, *Afterword: What Now? Climate-Induced Displacement after Copenhagen, in* CLIMATE CHANGE AND DISPLACEMENT: MULTIDISCIPLINARY PERSPECTIVES, 239, 239–40 (Jane McAdam ed., 2010).

7       Jolanda van der Vliet also used the term "rights-based approach" in a manner similar to the one used herein. Her analysis compares, however, a rights-based approach with a "security approach" (based on "the interdependence between human vulnerability and national security") and a "responsibility approach" (based on the obligation of polluting States to those nations most affected by climate change). Jolanda van der Vliet, *A Legal*

This term, as used in this book, should not be confused with references in the literature to a "(human) rights-based approach", which refers to taking human rights into account, or using human rights as a starting point, in making policy decisions or in formulating new instruments.[8] Human rights law is one component of the rights-based approach explored in this book. More broadly speaking, however, human rights considerations must always be taken into account in any policy or legal approach.

— An "adaptive approach" is characterized by pre-emptive or transformational strategies which aim to prevent involuntary movement or to facilitate movement where it can be considered voluntary or inevitable.[9] Under the adaptive approach, human mobility is recognized as a potential adaptation strategy (without, however, advocating that human mobility is a positive, or even acceptable outcome of climate change). An adaptive approach is generally driven by local or regional input, but potentially implemented on a national or international level. There are also opportunities, as explored in this book, for international frameworks to impact local, regional, and national policies and strategies.[10]

---

*Mapping Exercise, in* 'CLIMATE REFUGEES': BEYOND THE LEGAL IMPASSE? 16, 17–19 (Simon Behrman & Avidan Kent eds., 2018).

8    *See, e.g.,* Human Rights Council Res. 14/6, Mandate of the Special Rapporteur on the Human Rights of Internally Displaced Persons, 14th Sess., 23 June 2010, UN Doc. A/HRC/14/37, at 19 (23 Oct. 2012).

9    Castles describes "adaptation" (to global warming in a broader sense, and not only in connection with human mobility) as meaning "designing and implementing measures to help communities affected by climate change to modify the ways they work and live to be able to cope with new environmental conditions". Castles, *supra* note 6, at 240.

10   Mostafa Naser also recognizes some of the policy approaches within the frameworks underpinning the adaptive approach as foundational for "emerging global consensus towards recognition and protection of climate change and human mobility". He presents these approaches under six policy areas, discussing in particular various institutional approaches: climate change, disaster risk reduction and management, human rights, refugees, migration, and sustainable development. *See generally* MOSTAFA M. NASER, THE EMERGING GLOBAL CONSENSUS ON CLIMATE CHANGE AND HUMAN MOBILITY (2021) (quotation at 39). Avidan Kent and Simon Behrman also discuss the role of various institutions (describing not only a legal but "institutional gap" for addressing climate change mobility). AVIDAN KENT & SIMON BEHRMAN, FACILITATING THE RESETTLEMENT AND RIGHTS OF CLIMATE REFUGEES: AN ARGUMENT FOR DEVELOPING EXISTING PRINCIPLES AND PRACTICES 122–160 (2018). The adaptive approach as discussed in this book describes the intersection of legal and policy frameworks with both institutional and governmental action.

These two approaches are identified in this book not as a true dichotomy, but as analytical constructs which illustrate trends in the way in which advocates, commentators, and institutions address human mobility in the context of climate change. In reality, there is no bright line between a rights-based and an adaptive approach. For example, setting in place new legal mechanisms to provide protection to persons who move in the context of climate change may be necessary for some carefully defined categories of persons. Such an approach would be considered consistent with a rights-based approach when it seeks to establish legal protection which would apply *after* persons have moved, i.e., post hoc protection, rather than seeking to adapt to climate change and minimize the need for persons to move, or otherwise plan relocations where necessary. It is also possible to use legal frameworks to inform adaptive strategies, but this would be considered an adaptive approach to the extent that the legal mechanism sets in motion pre-emptive plans such as relocation. This would be the case particularly where such programs were not legally binding and took the form of governmental strategies that were voluntarily adopted by States and/or communities on a case-by-case basis.

As these examples illustrate, a rights-based and an adaptive approach are not (and should not be) mutually exclusive. An adaptive approach is not (and must never be) devoid of human rights considerations, some of which underpin the rights-based approach. To the contrary, human rights considerations must also form the basis for any future pre-emptive or protective actions.[11] Moreover, neither a rights-based nor an adaptive approach would alone be sufficient to address the broad range of issues connected with human mobility and climate change. Focusing solely on a rights-based approach would ignore

---

11    *See* Human Rights Council Res. 10/4, Human Rights and Climate Change, 10th Sess., 25 Mar. 2009, UN Doc. A/HRC/10/29, at 12 (9 Nov. 2009) ("Affirming that human rights obligations and commitments have the potential to inform and strengthen international and national policymaking in the area of climate change, promoting policy coherence, legitimacy and sustainable outcomes"); Report of the UN High Commissioner for Human Rights on the Relationship Between Human Rights and the Environment, ¶ 54, UN Doc A/HRC/19/34, Human Rights Council, 19th Sess. (16 Dec. 2011); Robin Bronen, *Climate-Induced Community Relocations: Creating an Adaptive Governance Framework Based in Human Rights Doctrine*, 35 N.Y.U. REV. L. & SOC. CHANGE 357 (2011); Bruce Burson, *Protecting the Rights of People Displaced by Climate Change: Global Issues and Regional Perspectives, in* CLIMATE CHANGE AND MIGRATION: SOUTH PACIFIC PERSPECTIVES 159, 169–71 (Bruce Burson ed., 2010); Margareta Wahlström, *Chairperson's Summary, in* The Nansen Conference, Oslo, Norway, 6–7 June 2011, *Climate Change and Displacement in the 21st Century*, at 18, 19, ¶¶ 12–13 (*text by* Christian Gahre), *available at* https://www.unhcr.org/4ea969729.pdf; JANE MCADAM, CLIMATE CHANGE, FORCED MIGRATION, AND INTERNATIONAL LAW 254–66 (2012).

opportunities to mitigate the impact of climate change on human mobility and exacerbate the problem it seeks to address.[12] At the same time, adaptive strategies cannot always prevent human movement or provide adequate protection to those who must move.[13] Adaptive measures must therefore be supplemented by corresponding protective measures. Addressing climate change mobility will therefore require a successful integration of an adaptive approach to a rights-based approach.

---

12  *See* Bonnie Docherty & Tyler Giannini, *Confronting a Rising Tide: A Proposal for a Convention on Climate Change Refugees*, 33 HARV. ENVTL. L. REV. 349, 360 (2009).

13  Walter Kälin & Nina Schrepfer, *Protecting People Crossing Borders in the Context of Climate Change: Normative Gaps and Possible Approaches* 17 (UNHCR, Legal & Protection Policy Research Series, PPLA/2012/01, Feb. 2012), *available at* https://www.unhcr.org/4f33f1729. pdf ("addressing the cause of climate change and adapting to its effects can have a preventive effect on displacement and migration. At the same time, measures to mitigate and *ex ante* adapt to climate change and its effects are often insufficient to prevent population movements making it necessary to also addressing its humanitarian consequences"); Walter Kälin, *Conceptualising Climate-Induced Displacement*, *in* CLIMATE CHANGE AND DISPLACEMENT: MULTIDISCIPLINARY PERSPECTIVES, *supra* note 6, at 81, 83; Frank Biermann & Ingrid Boas, *Preparing for a Warmer World: Towards a Global Governance System to Protect Climate Refugee*s, 10 GLOBAL ENVTL. POL. 60, 61 (2010).

# The Underpinnings of a Rights-Based Approach

A nation's greatness is measured by how it treats its weakest members.

— MOHANDAS KARAMCHAND GANDHI

∴

The rights-based approach to human mobility relies in large part on the application of existing legal instruments that often provide post hoc protection to pre-defined categories of persons. Human mobility is the focus of a complex network of legal frameworks which exist on the international, regional, and national levels. These legal frameworks, many of which were created at a time when the impacts of climate change were not widely known or in full focus, are ill-equipped to address the unique and varied aspects of human mobility in the context of climate change.

This chapter will explore the extent to which some of the most prominent instruments under existing international frameworks for human mobility could provide protection to persons moving in the context of climate change, including the asylum framework, protection for stateless persons, protection for migrant workers, protection for internally displaced persons, and human rights protections. These international frameworks establish minimum standards which should drive national frameworks.

Exploring the boundaries of some of the international legal frameworks which underpin the rights-based approach is a common point of departure for many advocates and scholars when addressing the challenge of climate change mobility. Although mapping and analysis of various legal instruments can be found throughout the literature on climate change mobility, this chapter compiles a comprehensive view of relevant frameworks and discusses them as components of a broader rights-based approach. As will be seen, climate change mobility does not fall squarely within existing international frameworks. As it currently exists, the rights-based approach to climate change mobility is more of a patchwork that has been compiled from instruments originally designed for other purposes. For this reason, existing rights-based frameworks are often described as leaving a critical protection "gap" for climate change mobility.

© KONINKLIJKE BRILL NV, LEIDEN, 2022 | DOI:10.1163/9789004298880_006

Despite these gaps, these rights-based frameworks may provide protection in specific cases. The human rights framework, in particular, has taken on increasing relevance in climate change litigation *fora*, including with respect to climate change mobility in particular.

## A    The Asylum Framework

### 1)    *The 1951 Convention Relating to the Status of Refugees*
The original text of the 1951 Convention Relating to the Status of Refugees was adopted on 28 July 1951 and entered into force on 22 April 1954 (Refugee Convention).[1] The Refugee Convention establishes minimum standards of treatment and prohibits expulsion of refugees. The principle of *non-refoulement* is the cornerstone of the Refugee Convention, a non-derogable obligation which prohibits States Parties from sending refugees (back) to territories where they might face persecution.[2]

The Refugee Convention was initially devised as an instrument for protection of refugees in Europe following World War II.[3] The original text of the Refugee Convention limited the rights afforded by the Convention to persons who were displaced on account of events that occurred in Europe before 1 January 1951.[4]

---

1    Convention Relating to the Status of Refugees, 28 July 1951, 189 U.N.T.S. 137 [hereinafter 'Refugee Convention'].

2    Protocol Relating to the Status of Refugees art. 33(1), 31 Jan. 1967, 606 U.N.T.S. 267 [hereinafter 'Refugee Protocol']; UNHCR, *Note on the Principle of Non-Refoulement*, ¶ 1, UN Doc EC/SCP/2 (23 Aug. 1977) [hereinafter 'UNHCR Note on Non-Refoulement']. For an analysis of the *non-refoulement* obligation and its non-derogable character, see Sir Elihu Lauterpacht & Daniel Bethlehem, *The Scope and Content of the Principle of* Non-Refoulement: *Opinion*, *in* REFUGEE PROTECTION IN INTERNATIONAL LAW: UNHCR'S GLOBAL CONSULTATIONS ON INTERNATIONAL PROTECTION 87 (Erika Feller et al. eds., 2003). For a detailed explanation of *non-refoulement* and its application in practice, see Jenny Poon, *Drawing upon International Refugee Law*, *in* 'CLIMATE REFUGEES': BEYOND THE LEGAL IMPASSE? 157, 159–162 (Simon Behrman & Avidan Kent eds., 2018).

3    *See* Sadako Ogata, *Foreword* to THE REFUGEE CONVENTION, 1951: THE TRAVAUX PREPARATOIRES ANALYSED WITH A COMMENTARY BY DR PAUL WEIS 4 (undated; published in print posthumously in 1995), *available at* http://www.unhcr.org/protection/travaux/4ca34be29/refugee-convention-1951-travaux-preparatoires-analysed-commentary-dr-paul.html; UNHCR, Introductory Note to the 1951 Refugee Convention, at 2 (Dec. 2010), http://www.unhcr.org/3b66c2aa10 ("The 1951 Convention, as a post-Second World War instrument, was originally limited in scope to persons fleeing events occurring before 1 January 1951 and within Europe. The 1967 Protocol removed these limitations and thus gave the Convention universal coverage.").

4    Refugee Convention, *supra* note 1, arts. 1(A)(2), 1(B)(1).

The 1967 Protocol Relating to the Status of Refugees (Refugee Protocol) broadened the scope of the Refugee Convention by removing its geographical and temporal delimitations.[5] Notwithstanding its expanded scope since 1967, the Refugee Convention was written in a vastly different context than that which exists today, before the massive impact of global climate change on human mobility came to the fore. It is therefore unsurprising that the legal definition of a refugee under that instrument generally does not cover the protection of people displaced by environmental (or climate change) events.

The Refugee Convention (as amended by the Refugee Protocol) defines a refugee as an individual who:

> owing to well-founded fear of being persecuted for reasons of race, religion, nationality, membership of a particular social group or political opinion, is outside the country of his nationality and is unable or, owing to such fear, is unwilling to avail himself of the protection of that country; or who, not having a nationality and being outside the country of his former habitual residence as a result of such events, is unable or, owing to such fear, is unwilling to return to it.[6]

Under this definition, the scope of protection under the Refugee Convention is limited to persons who (i) have crossed an international border (ii) because of fear of persecution for one of five enumerated reasons (race, religion, nationality, membership of a particular social group or political opinion) and who are (iii) unable or unwilling to return to their home State because of such persecution.[7] The Refugee Convention therefore does not apply to persons who move within national borders, whatever the reason for the movement. With respect to international movement, it is widely agreed that environmental or climate change impacts alone do not qualify as persecution, as defined by the Refugee Convention.[8] The Refugee Convention therefore does not, generally

---

5     Refugee Protocol, *supra* note 2, art. 1.

6     Refugee Convention, *supra* note 1, art. 1(A)(2), as amended by the Refugee Protocol, *supra* note 2, art. 1. Hereinafter references to the Refugee Convention alone refer to the Refugee Convention as amended by the Refugee Protocol, unless stated otherwise.

7     *See* Walter Kälin & Nina Schrepfer, *Protecting People Crossing Borders in the Context of Climate Change: Normative Gaps and Possible Approaches* 31 (UNHCR, Legal & Protection Policy Research Series, PPLA/2012/01, Feb. 2012), *available at* https://www.unhcr.org/4f33f1729.pdf (identifying these three key elements of the definition of a refugee under the Refugee Convention).

8     A small body of case law from New Zealand and Australia, discussed *infra*, supports this view. For an analysis, see *id.* at 31–34; Jane McAdam, *Climate Change Displacement and International Law: Complementary Protection Standards* 12–14 (UNHCR, Legal & Protection

speaking, provide protection for climate change mobility. Notwithstanding, it is not excluded that the requirements of the Refugee Convention may be met in circumstances that relate to climate change or environmental impacts, i.e., where climate change impacts intersect with existing vulnerabilities and warrant protection under the Refugee Convention. As Bruce Burson has observed:

> The existence of complex relationships between environmental degradation, conflict, and migration means that it is an oversimplification to insist on immutable distinctions between environmentally displaced persons and those eligible for recognition as Convention refugees. Given the potential for issues of environmental degradation to collide with issues of poverty, inequality, discriminatory modes of governance, and human rights violations, the environmental issue may acquire attributes which potentially bring affected persons within the scope of the Convention.[9]

However, in any such cases, the occurrence of climate change impacts is, with respect to operation of the Refugee Convention, only a contributing factor and would not, without the intervention of other political and social factors, constitute persecution or give rise to protection under the Refugee Convention.[10]

---

Policy Research Series, PPLA/2011/03, May 2011), *available at* https://www.unhcr.org/4dffi6egg.pdf [hereinafter 'McAdam, *Complimentary Protection*']; Angela Williams, *Turning the Tide: Recognizing Climate Change Refugees in International Law*, 30 L. & POL'Y 502, 507–10 (2008). *But see* Jessica Cooper, Note, *Environmental Refugees: Meeting the Requirements of the Refugee Definition*, 6 N.Y.U. ENVTL L.J. 480, 502–26 (1998) (arguing that government action or inaction which furthers environmental degradation constitutes persecution within the meaning of the Refugee Convention; similar arguments have, however, been rejected by some national courts in asylum cases); Heather Alexander & Jonathan Simon, *"Unable to Return" in the 1951 Refugee Convention: Stateless Refugees and Climate Change*, 26(3) FLA. J. INT'L L. 531 (2014) (arguing, against generally accepted interpretation, that there is no persecution requirement under the Refugee Convention for stateless persons who are unable to return to their country of habitual residence).

9   Bruce Burson, *Environmentally Induced Displacement and the 1951 Refugee Convention: Pathways to Recognition*, *in* ENVIRONMENT, FORCED MIGRATION AND SOCIAL VULNERABILITY 3, 6–7 (Tamer Afifi & Jill Jäger eds., 2010). *See also, generally,* MATTHEW SCOTT, CLIMATE CHANGE, DISASTERS AND THE REFUGEE CONVENTION (2020) (challenging the "dominant view" that the Refugee Convention is "an inherently peripheral instrument for addressing the legal status of persons displaced across borders in the context of disasters and climate change" (quotation at 1)).

10  *See* Jane McAdam, *From the Nansen Initiative to the Platform on Disaster Displacement: Shaping International Approaches to Climate Change, Disasters and Displacement*, 39(4) UNIV. NEW S. WALES L. J. 1518, 1535–36 (2016).

Australian and New Zealand courts have considered applications by individuals seeking refugee status in which climate change impacts are either peripheral or central factors.[11] No refugee status has yet been granted by those courts on climate change related grounds. The Refugee Review Tribunal of Australia considered the nexus of climate change impacts and refugee status in a 2009 decision on a refugee application by a citizen of Kiribati, based on climate change impacts in his home State. The Tribunal framed the applicant's argument as follows:

> The applicant fears return to his country of nationality because there is substantial scientific evidence that rising sea levels will devastate that country. He fears rising sea levels will see the further diminution of fresh water for drinking, washing and survival of food production crops. He fears ultimately that the country could be completely submerged by sea water and not [sic] longer habitable.[12]

The Tribunal rejected the application on the basis that the applicant's fear did not qualify as fear of persecution because of the applicant's race, religion, nationality, social group, or political opinion.[13] In particular, the Tribunal rejected that the production of carbon emissions could be considered an act of persecution aimed at any particular group.[14] The Tribunal acknowledged the plight of those fleeing climate change impacts, but considered that the existing laws in Australia did not apply to such circumstances: "There appears no doubt that the circumstances the applicant, and others living in Kiribati, face are serious and deserving of significant Governmental consideration and attention. They are not matters against which, however, the Refugees [sic] Convention as it applies in Australia is able to provide protection."[15] The Tribunal's statement suggests that climate change impacts alone would not be sufficient to trigger protection obligations under the Refugee

---

11    A report for the United States Library of Congress provides a list of relevant Australian and New Zealand cases. Kelly Buchanan, *New Zealand: "Climate Change Refugee" Case Overview* 7–8 (Law Library of Cong., Global Research Ctr., July 2015), *available at* https://www.loc.gov/law/help/climate-change-refugee/new-zealand-climate-change-refugee-case.pdf.

12    *RTT Case Number 0907346* [2009] RRTA 1168 (Refugee Review Tribunal, 10 Dec. 2009) ¶ 47 (Austl.).

13    *Id.* ¶ 48.

14    *Id.* ¶¶ 51, 52.

15    *Id.* ¶ 54.

Convention as implemented into Australian national law, absent legislative intervention.[16]

In two later, well-known cases, the New Zealand courts also rejected applications for refugee status based on climate change impacts.[17] The courts were, however, less categorical concerning the relationship between potential refugee status and climate change impacts. In the first case, Mr. Ioane Teitiota, a native of the Pacific island of Kiribati, requested refugee status in New Zealand because of the impact of sea level rise on his native island, including "storm surges, extreme high spring tides, flooding of residential areas, raised floors of residences, depletion of fishing stocks, diminution of arable land, contamination of drinking water by salt water, sewage contamination of water tables, and deterioration of the population's health."[18] Similar to the Australian case, the New Zealand courts rejected Mr. Teitiota's application, finding there was no evidence that he would be subjected to persecution upon returning to Kiribati and that the hardships caused by environmental degradation there were in any case indiscriminate.[19] The New Zealand High Court rejected, amongst other arguments, that the international community could be considered as the "persecutor" for its role in emitting carbon dioxide into the atmosphere. This argument, according to the High Court, "completely reverses the traditional refugee paradigm", in which a refugee flees persecution in his or her own State, which either perpetrates that persecution or fails to protect the individual in

---

16    Other Australian refugee case law in which climate change impacts were raised include *Mohammed Motahir Ali v Minister of Immigration et al.* [1994] FCA 887 (Federal Court, 4 Feb. 1994) (Austl.); *RTT Case Number N99/30231* [2000] RRTA 17 (Refugee Review Tribunal, 10 Jan. 2000) (Austl.); *RTT Case Number N00/34089* [2000] RRTA 1052 (Refugee Review Tribunal, 17 Nov. 2000) (Austl.); *RTT Case Number 1004726* [2010] RRTA 845 (Refugee Review Tribunal, 30 Sep. 2010) (Austl.).

17    Earlier New Zealand case law in which climate change impacts were raised in connection with refugee applications include *Refugee Appeal No. 72185* [2000] NZRSAA 335 (Refugee Status Appeals Authority, 10 Aug. 2000) (N.Z.); *Refugee Appeal No. 72186* [2000] NZRSAA 336 (Refugee Status Appeals Authority, 10 Aug. 2000) (N.Z.); *Refugee Appeal No. 72189* [2000] NZRSAA 355 (Refugee Status Appeals Authority, 17 Aug. 2000) (N.Z.); *Refugee Appeal No. 72179* [2000] NZRSAA 385 (Refugee Status Appeals Authority, 31 Aug. 2000) (N.Z.); *Refugee Appeal No. 72313* [2000] NZRSAA 491 (Refugee Status Appeals Authority, 19 Oct. 2000) (N.Z.); *Refugee Appeal No. 72314* [2000] NZRSAA 492 (Refugee Status Appeals Authority, 19 Oct. 2000) (N.Z.); *Refugee Appeal No. 72315* [2000] NZRSAA 493 (Refugee Status Appeals Authority, 19 Oct. 2000) (N.Z.); *Refugee Appeal No. 72316* [2000] NZRSAA 494 (Refugee Status Appeals Authority, 19 Oct. 2000) (N.Z.).

18    *Ioane Teitiota v. Chief Executive of the Ministry of Business Innovation & Employment* [2013] NZHC 3125, ¶ 18 (High Court, 26 Nov. 2013) (N.Z.), [hereinafter 'Teitiota High Court Decision'].

19    *Id.* ¶¶ 29–30.

question.[20] In this case, if the international community could be considered the perpetrator (which the court did not accept), Mr. Teitiota would be seeking refuge in an allegedly persecuting State.[21] In addition, any such alleged persecution would remain indiscriminate. Notwithstanding, the New Zealand Courts left open the possibility that, in other cases, climate change impacts could "create a pathway into the Refugee Convention or protected person jurisdiction".[22] As the New Zealand High Court explained:

> there is a complex inter-relationship between natural disasters, environmental degradation and human vulnerability. Sometimes a tenable pathway to international protection under the Refugee Convention can result. Environmental issues sometimes lead to armed conflict. There may be ensuing violence towards or direct repression of an entire section of a population. Humanitarian relief can become politicised, particularly in situations where some group inside a disadvantaged country is the target of direct discrimination.[23]

Following the final decision issued in his case by the New Zealand Supreme Court, Mr. Teitiota went on to bring a human rights-based claim before the Human Rights Committee. That claim and its outcome are discussed in detail in Chapter 4(E).

Shortly after the New Zealand Court of Appeal denied leave to appeal in the *Teitiota* case, the Immigration and Protection Tribunal issued a decision in another case raising issues of refugee protection and climate change impacts. In this new case, the Alesana family from the Pacific island nation of Tuvalu applied for New Zealand resident visas on the basis of refugee status, protected person status under human rights law, and/or humanitarian protection.[24] Their application relied in part on difficulties caused by climate change impacts in Tuvalu. The New Zealand Immigration and Protection Tribunal found that the family was not entitled to refugee or protected person status,

---

20    *Id.* ¶ 55.

21    *Id.*

22    *Ioane Teitiota v. Chief Executive of the Ministry of Business Innovation & Employment* [2015] NZSC 107, ¶ 13 (Supreme Court, 20 July 2015) (N.Z.) (citations omitted) [hereinafter 'Teitiota Supreme Court Decision'].

23    Teitiota High Court Decision, *supra* note 18, ¶ 27 (citations omitted).

24    AC *(Tuvalu)* [2014] NZIPT 800517-520 (Immigration and Protection Tribunal, 4 June 2014) (N.Z.) [hereinafter 'NZ Tuvalu Refugee Decision']; AD *(Tuvalu)* [2014] NZIPT 501370-371 (Immigration and Protection Tribunal, 4 June 2014) (N.Z.) [hereinafter 'NZ Tuvalu Humanitarian Appeals Decision'].

but granted visas pursuant to humanitarian protection. The outcome of this case was hailed by some news outlets as establishing the world's first "climate refugees".[25] However, the decision to grant the visas was not based on recognition of refugee status. The applicants abandoned their refugee claims, accepting that there was no basis for recognizing them as refugees in light of the findings in the recent *Teitiota* decision.[26] Moreover, the granting of discretionary humanitarian protection was not based on climate change impacts, but rather on strong family ties that the applicants had in New Zealand:

> The deportation of the appellants to Tuvalu would amount to an unusually significant disruption to a dense network of family relationships spanning three generations in New Zealand. It would also impact upon the quality of life for the husband's mother, a New Zealand resident, who relies on him for her mobility-related needs.[27]

Climate change was therefore not a determinative factor in the outcome; the Tribunal expressly declined to reach a conclusion as to whether the climate change factors relied upon by the applicants could have satisfied the conditions for granting humanitarian protection pursuant to New Zealand law:

> As for the climate change issue relied on so heavily, while the Tribunal accepts that exposure to the impacts of natural disasters can, in general terms, be a humanitarian circumstance, nevertheless, the evidence in appeals such as this must establish not simply the existence of a matter of broad humanitarian concern, but that there are exceptional

---

25  *See, e.g.*, Rachel Nuwer, *The World's First Climate Change Refugees Were Granted Residency in New Zealand*, SMITHSONIAN MAGAZINE (7 Aug. 2014), https://www.smithsonian mag.com/smart-news/worlds-first-climate-change-refugees-were-just-granted-reside ncy-new-zealand-180952279/; Ted Alvarez, *The World's First Official Climate Refugees Land in New Zealand*, GRIST (8 Aug. 2014), https://grist.org/living/the-worlds-first-offic ial-climate-refugees-land-in-new-zealand/; Vanessa Ellingham, *World First: Climate Refugees to Stay in New Zealand*, FAIR PLANET, EDITOR'S PICKS (4 Aug. 2014), https:// www.fairplanet.org/editors-pick/world-first-climate-refugees-to-stay-in-new-zealand/ . For an analysis of the case that dismantles this misconception, see Jane McAdam, *No "Climate Refugees" in New Zealand*, BROOKINGS, PLANETPOLICY (13 Aug. 2014), https:// www.brookings.edu/blog/planetpolicy/2014/08/13/no-climate-refugees-in-new-zealand/ ; Vernon Rive, *"Climate Refugees" Revisited: A Closer Look at the Tuvalu Decision*, VERNON RIVE LAW ACADEMIC (14 Aug. 2014), http://www.vernonrive.com/home/climate-refug ees-revisited-a-closer-look-at-the-tuvalu-decision.

26  NZ Tuvalu Refugee Decision, *supra* note 24, ¶ 45.

27  NZ Tuvalu Humanitarian Appeals Decision, *supra* note 24, ¶ 31.

circumstances of a humanitarian nature such that it would be unjust or unduly harsh to deport *the particular appellant* from New Zealand.

It is not, however, necessary on the facts of this appeal to reach any conclusion on this issue in relation to any of the appellants as the Tribunal is satisfied that by reason of the other factors identified in this case, there are exceptional circumstances of a humanitarian [sic] in the sense contemplated by Glazebrook J in *Ye v Minister of Immigration*, and that it would be unjust or unduly harsh for the appellants to be deported from New Zealand.[28]

The New Zealand courts also did not consider whether climate change impacts could qualify as exceptional circumstances leading to humanitarian protection in the *Teitiota* case.[29]

Examples of national case law therefore indicate, as does an analysis of the text of the Refugee Convention, that application of the Convention in climate change mobility cases is not the norm. Some national courts have held that climate change factors alone do not qualify as persecution under the Refugee Convention and therefore cannot, absent other factors, give rise to protection. As explored in the following sections, regional refugee instruments paint a more nuanced picture. Regional refugee instruments, unlike the Refugee Convention, tend to contain additional grounds for granting asylum that do not require persecution.

## 2)    *Regional Instruments*
a             The OAU Convention Governing the Specific Aspects of Refugee
             Problems in Africa

The Convention Governing the Specific Aspects of Refugee Problems in Africa (OAU Convention) was adopted by the Organization of African Unity (OAU) Assembly of Heads of State and Government on 10 September 1969 and entered into force on 20 June 1974. The OAU Convention is a regional instrument addressing cross-border movement and, by design, complements the provisions of the Refugee Convention.[30]

---

28     *Id.* ¶¶ 32–33 (emphasis in original).
29     Teitiota High Court Decision, *supra* note 18, ¶ 43 ("Unfortunately for the applicant, because he has chosen to remain illegally in New Zealand, he is, under current law, precluded from applying for an immigration permit on humanitarian grounds.").
30     Organization of African Unity Convention Governing the Specific Aspects of Refugee Problems in Africa art. 8(2), 10 Sept. 1969, 1001 U.N.T.S. 45 [hereinafter 'OAU Convention'] ("The present Convention shall be the effective regional complement in Africa of the 1951 United Nations Convention on the Status of Refugees.").

Amongst other innovations, the OAU Convention contains an expanded definition of a refugee.[31] The OAU Convention incorporates *verbatim* the definition of a refugee included in the Refugee Convention and further adds:

> [T]he term "refugee" shall also apply to every person who, owing to external aggression, occupation, foreign domination or events seriously disturbing public order in either part or the whole of his country of origin or nationality, is compelled to leave his place of habitual residence in order to seek refuge in another place outside his country of origin or nationality.[32]

The inclusion of "events seriously disturbing public order" opens the door to a more flexible interpretation of the drivers that could fall within the scope of the OAU Convention.[33] Opinions vary as to whether this language includes natural disasters, and State practice on this issue is inconclusive.[34] Although examples can be found in which States have granted refugee status in disaster-related situations, these have been intertwined with ongoing violence and conflict. For

---

31    The expanded refugee definition is often described as the most celebrated feature of the OAU Convention. Its breadth has, however, been exaggerated at times. For an analysis of the expanded definition of "refugee" in the OAU Convention and common misconceptions thereof, see generally Marina Sharpe, *The 1969 African Refugee Convention: Innovations, Misconceptions, and Omissions*, 58(1) MCGILL L.J. 95 (2012). On the origins of the definition of "refugee" found in the OAU Convention, see George Okoth-Obbo, *Thirty Years On: A Legal Review of the 1969 OAU Refugee Convention Governing the Specific Aspects of Refugee Problems in Africa*, 20(1) REFUGEE SURV. Q. 79, 109–12 (2001). On the OAU Convention's other innovations, see Fatoumata Lejeune-Kaba, *Q&A: OAU Convention Remains a Key Plank of Refugee Protection After 40 Years*, UNHCR, NEWS (9 Sept. 2009), http://www.unhcr.org/news/latest/2009/9/4aa7b80c6/qa-oau-convention-remains-key-plank-refugee-protection-africa-40-years.html.

32    OAU Convention, *supra* note 30, art. 1(2).

33    *See* Jane McAdam et al., *International Law and Sea-Level Rise: Forced Migration and Human Rights* 33, ¶ 86 (Fridtjof Nansen Inst., FNI Report 1/2016, Jan. 2016), *available at* https://www.fni.no/getfile.php/131711-1469868996/Filer/Publikasjoner/FNI-R0116.pdf [hereinafter 'McAdam et al., *Sea-Level Rise*']; Alice Edwards, *Refugee Status Determination in Africa*, 14 AFR. J. INT'L & COMP. L. 204, 225–26 (2006) [hereinafter 'Edwards, *Refugee Status in Africa*'].

34    For a review of differing positions amongst scholars and States, see McAdam et al., *Sea-Level Rise*, *supra* note 33, at 33–34; Tamara Wood, *Protection and Disasters in the Horn of Africa: Norms and Practice for Addressing Cross-border Displacement in Disaster Contexts* 23–29 (Technical Paper prepared for the Nansen Initiative, Jan. 2013), *available at* http://www.nanseninitiative.org/wp-content/uploads/2015/03/190215_Technical_Paper_Tamara_Wood.pdf [hereinafter 'Wood, *Horn of Africa*']; Edwards, *Refugee Status in Africa*, *supra* note 33, at 226–27.

example, during the 2011 drought in the Horn of Africa, Kenya granted *prima facie* refugee status to Somalis fleeing the impact of the drought. This took place during a period in which Kenya generally granted *prima facie* refugee status to Somalis fleeing conflict and violence in South Central Somalia. Kenya recognized and accepted that, within this *prima facie* category, it had welcomed an influx of refugees driven primarily by drought rather than conflict.[35] It is unclear the extent to which the language of the OAU Convention played a role or whether such status would have been granted without the existing state of conflict.[36] By contrast, Egypt maintained a more stringent, individual refugee status determination during this period. A study based on interviews with UNHCR personnel and asylum seekers reported that fleeing drought alone was not sufficient to satisfy the Egyptian requirements (in applying the OAU Convention) and that a connection to persecution or conflict was required.[37]

Tamara Wood considers that examples such as these show the difficulty in drawing a strict distinction between "natural" and "human" drivers of mobility, as they are often insufficient to address the complexity of the situations on the ground:

[35] *See* VIKRAM KOLMANNSKOG & TAMER AFIFI, DISASTER-RELATED DISPLACEMENT FROM THE HORN OF AFRICA 43–44 (Report No. 15. Bonn: UNU-EHS, Mar. 2014), *available at* https://reliefweb.int/sites/reliefweb.int/files/resources/Report%20No%2015_NRC.pdf.

[36] *See id.* at 44 ("[I]t is worth noticing that the official statement from the Government of Kenya (2011) last year employed the refugee label for this group as well, and claimed that, 'Kenya has welcomed all refugees and assisted them'. One could argue that many of the Somalis were in fact traditional refugees because armed conflict and persecution played a role in their displacement. 'In 2011 most people came due to drought and the fighting. Since there are two reasons, we accept them. The fighting is the reason considered,' said one Department of Refugee Affairs interviewee."); Wood, *Horn of Africa, supra* note 34, at 25, note 145 ("Representatives from government, UNHCR and refugee-related NGOs working in Kenya reported that the grant of prima facie status to Somalis in Kenya is based on the 1969 Convention, although it is difficult to identify exactly when or by whom the decision to grant status in this way was made. During field research by the author in 2012, some interviewees reported that the decision was made unilaterally by the Kenyan Government, others reported it was made by UNHCR, pursuant to the 2010 Eligibility Guidelines for Somalia. Yet others described the arrangement as the result of an agreement between the two. Somalis fleeing during the 2011 drought were also awarded prima facie refugee status in Yemen, though Yemen is not a party to the 1969 African Refugee Convention.").

[37] Nansen Initiative Secretariat, *Natural Hazards, Climate Change, and Cross-Border Displacement in the Greater Horn of Africa: Protecting People on the Move* 16 (Background Paper for the Greater Horn of Africa Regional Consultation, Nairobi, Kenya, 21–23 May 2014), *available at* https://www.nanseninitiative.org/portfolio-item/greater-horn-of-africa-background-paper/; KOLMANNSKOG & AFIFI, *supra* note 35, at 51.

Regardless of the view one takes on these questions, neat conceptual distinctions between 'human' and 'natural' causes of displacement do not always reflect realities, as conditions in Somalia and South Sudan well demonstrate. For example, while the 2011 Horn of Africa drought forced hundreds of thousands of Somalis across international borders in search of safety, food and other assistance, the majority of similarly drought-affected Kenyans stayed put, aided by the relatively higher levels of security and assistance in the country. Likewise, the distinction between 'economic migrants' on the one hand and refugees or 'forced migrants' on the other is blurry at best. People's reasons for movement are complex and often multifarious, not least in the case of fragile states.[38]

As Wood also points out, whether a natural disaster or environmental conditions force people to move will depend in part on the fragility of the state and its capacity for resilience.

If natural disasters—absent a concurrent situation of conflict and violence—can be considered to fall within the scope of drivers giving rise to protection under the OAU Convention (a conclusion which is optimistically speculative), such an interpretation should include, by extension, rapid onset hazard impacts arising from climate change.[39] It is less certain whether such an interpretation would also include slow onset hazard events. The impacts of any such disasters would still have to be significant enough to disrupt "public order", a term that is undefined in the OAU Convention and open to a wide range of varying interpretations.[40] Some consider that the phrase "events seriously disturbing public order" encompasses only disturbances arising from "human activity", thereby excluding environmental impacts.[41] Little

---

38    Tamara Wood, *Fragile States and Protection under the 1969 African Refugee Convention*, 43 FORCED MIGRATION REV. 17, 19 (2013).

39    *See* UNHCR, Expert Roundtable, Bellagio, Italy, 22–25 Feb. 2011, *Summary of Deliberations on Climate Change and Displacement*, at 4, ¶ 9 (Apr. 2011), *available at* http://www.unhcr.org/4da2b5e19.pdf [hereinafter 'UNHCR, Bellagio Roundtable Summary']. Whether rapid onset hazard impacts and/or slow onset hazard events fall within the scope of natural disasters is an issue addressed in the context of the Guiding Principles, which explicitly includes "natural or human-made disasters" as drivers of internal displacement. *See* discussion of the Guiding Principles in Chapter 4(D).

40    *See* Wood, *Horn of Africa*, *supra* note 34, at 28. For an analysis of the potential meaning of "public order", see Edwards, *Refugee Status in Africa*, *supra* note 33, at 218–20.

41    *See, e.g.*, Sharpe, *supra* note 31, at 113, n.109; Edwards, *Refugee Status in Africa*, *supra* note 33, at 225–26; Micah Bond Rankin, *Extending the Limits or Narrowing the Scope? Deconstructing the OAU Refugee Definition Thirty Years On* 20 (UNHCR, New Issues in

consideration is found on record as to whether such an interpretation could include climate change impacts due to their anthropogenic roots.[42] Even absent such an interpretation, climate change impacts can indirectly trigger protection under the OAU Convention should they, for example, give rise to conflict over scarce resources or, as in the example of Somalia, aggravate an existing state of conflict.[43]

b        The Cartagena Declaration on Refugees
The Cartagena Declaration on Refugees (Cartagena Declaration) was adopted in November 1984 by the Colloquium on the International Protection of Refugees in Central America, Mexico and Panama.[44] The Cartagena Declaration is a non-binding set of principles compiled by legal scholars to provide a common refugee framework for the region.[45] Although the Cartagena Declaration is

Refugee Research Working Paper No. 113, Apr. 2005), *available at* https://www.unhcr.org/research/working/425f71a42/extending-limits-narrowing-scope-deconstructing-oau-refugee-definition.html.

42    Cantor raises this question in a footnote with respect to similar language found in the Cartagena Declaration (discussed *infra*). David James Cantor, *Law, Policy, and Practice Concerning the Humanitarian Protection of Aliens on a Temporary Basis in the Context of Disasters, States of the Regional Conference on Migration and Others in the Americas* 18, n.67 (Background Study for Regional Workshop in San José, USA, on Temporary Protection Status and/or Humanitarian Visas in Situations of Disasters, 10–11 Feb. 2015), *available at* https://disasterdisplacement.org/wp-content/uploads/2015/07/150715_FINAL_BACKGROUND_PAPER_LATIN_AMERICA_screen.pdf ("Whether a 'man-made' natural disaster would engage the definition thus remains an open question.") (cited in McAdam et al., *Sea-Level Rise, supra* note 33, at 34, ¶ 88). Edwards also observed in a footnote, in relation to "ecological changes such as drought and famine", that "[i]t is of course arguable that such disasters have an element of human construction". Edwards, *Refugee Status in Africa, supra* note 33, at 225, n.116.

43    McAdam et al., *Sea-Level Rise, supra* note 33, at 35, ¶ 89. This has reportedly been the case in Latin America with respect to incorporation of the Cartagena Declaration which has a similar refugee definition, including "other circumstances which have seriously disturbed public order" in the enumerated drivers of mobility. *See* sources cited *infra* note 51.

44    Cartagena Declaration on Refugees, Colloquium on the International Protection of Refugees in Central America, Mexico and Panama, 22 Nov. 1984 [hereinafter 'Cartagena Declaration'].

45    Michael Reed-Hurtado, *The Cartagena Declaration on Refugees and the Protection of People Fleeing Armed Conflict and Other Situations of Violence in Latin America* 4 (UNHCR, Legal & Protection Policy Research Series, June 2013), *available at* https://www.unhcr.org/protection/globalconsult/51c800fe9/32-cartagena-declaration-refugees-protection-people-fleeing-armed-conflict.html; UNHCR, African & Latin American Groups of the Working Group on Solutions and Protection, paper submitted to the Executive Committee (1991), *Persons Covered by the OAU Convention Governing the Specific Aspects of Refugee Problems in Africa and by the Cartagena Declaration on Refugees*, at 7, UN Doc. EC/1992/SCP/CRP.6 (6 Apr. 1992).

itself not binding, its expanded definition of refugees, one of its most noted features,[46] has been widely incorporated into national laws in the region, even if often ineffectively implemented in practice.[47] In an approach inspired by the expanded definition of refugees contained in the OAU Convention, the Cartagena Declaration recommends that the definition of a refugee should:

> in addition to containing the elements of the 1951 Convention and the 1967 Protocol, include[ ] among refugees persons who have fled their country because their lives, safety or freedom have been threatened by generalized violence, foreign aggression, internal conflicts, massive violation of human rights or other circumstances which have seriously disturbed public order.[48]

The Cartagena Declaration's concept of refugees thus includes "other circumstances which have seriously disturbed public order" as potential drivers of human mobility which would fall within its scope. This phrase, similar to the one contained in the OAU Convention, raises the same questions as to whether natural disasters fall within this framework. According to a 2015 study, the prevailing view in the region is that environmental impacts are not included within the scope of the Cartagena Declaration, which is limited to disruptions caused by "human activity".[49] Again, there has been limited discussion on whether such an interpretation would include climate change impacts given their anthropogenic roots.[50]

In practice, disasters have indirectly triggered asylum protection under the definition in the Cartagena Declaration. Following the 2010 earthquake in Haiti, Ecuador and Mexico granted asylum to Haitian applicants. Ecuador and Mexico considered that these applicants had fled "other circumstances which have seriously disturbed public order" not because of the earthquake itself,

---

46    On other notable accomplishments of the Cartagena Declaration, *see* Reed-Hurtado, *supra* note 45, at 10–11.

47    States which have incorporated the Cartagena Declaration definition of refugees, or a version thereof, into their national laws include Argentina, Belize, Bolivia, Brazil, Chile, Colombia, Ecuador, El Salvador, Guatemala, Honduras, Mexico, Nicaragua, Paraguay, Peru and Uruguay. Cantor, *supra* note 42, at 17. For details on the specific provisions included in some of these national laws as well as implementation, see Reed-Hurtado, *supra* note 45, at 16–32.

48    Cartagena Declaration, *supra* note 44, art. III(3).

49    Cantor, *supra* note 42, at 18 (cited by McAdam et al., *Sea-Level Rise*, *supra* note 33, at 34, ¶ 88).

50    *See supra* note 42 and accompanying text.

but because of the ensuing "insecurity, violence and disrupting of police and justice structures" that disturbed public order.[51] This example suggests that, as Wood observed in connection with the application of OAU Convention, whether a natural disaster or environmental conditions will trigger asylum protection under laws coinciding with the Cartagena Declaration will depend in part on the fragility of the State and its capacity for resilience.

c          The Arab Convention on Regulating the Status of Refugees in the
           Arab Countries

The Arab Convention on Regulating Status of Refugees in the Arab Countries (Arab Refugee Convention) was adopted by the League of Arab States in 1994. It was, however, not ratified and has not entered into force. In 2017, the League of Arab States worked with the UNHCR to update the 1994 Arab Refugee Convention, but no changes have yet been adopted.[52] The 1994 Arab Refugee Convention therefore does not have binding legal force, and there is little prospect of this instrument—in its existing form—having a significant impact on climate change mobility.[53] Its definition of refugees is nevertheless noteworthy for its express inclusion of movement relating to natural disasters, a definition that could potentially serve as inspiration for future legal instruments.

The first clause of the definition of "refugee" in Article 1 of the Arab Refugee Convention is substantively identical to the definition in the 1951 Refugee Convention:

> Any person who is outside the country of his nationality or outside his habitual place of residence in case of not having a nationality and owing to well-grounded fear of being persecuted on account of his race, religion, nationality, membership of a particular social group or political opinion, unable or unwilling to avail himself of the protection of or return to such country.[54]

---

51    Cantor, *supra* note 42, at 17–18 (cited in McAdam et al., *Sea-Level Rise, supra* note 33, at 34–35, ¶¶ 88–89).

52    League of Arab States, Contribution to the UN Sixteenth Coordination Meeting on International Migration in New York, USA, 15–16 Feb. 2018, at 4, UN Doc. UN/POP/MIG-16CM/2018/4 (9 Feb. 2018).

53    *See* Kälin & Schrepfer, *supra* note 7, at 34 (noting that the Arab Refugee Convention "has not gained much practical relevance").

54    The contents of this definition are substantively identical to the 1951 Refugee Convention, cited *supra*, although the phrasing has been somewhat changed.

The second clause of Article 1 expands on this definition to include, amongst other factors, forced cross-border movement due to natural disasters disrupting public order:

> Any person who unwillingly takes refuge in a country other than his country of origin or his habitual place of residence because of sustained aggression against, occupation and foreign domination of such country or *because of the occurrence of natural disasters or grave events resulting in major disruption of public order in the whole country or any part thereof*.[55]

The Arab Refugee Convention is therefore progressive in its explicit inclusion of natural disasters as a driver of movement that could give rise to refugee protection. However, the natural disaster would have to result in "major disruption of public order" to give rise to refugee protection thereunder. This requirement that the disaster result in a disruption of public order suggests that, in practice, the refugee definition in the Arab Refugee Convention might not extend more protection than the definitions under the OAU Convention or the Cartagena Declaration. To recall, examples have already arisen in connection with both the OAU Convention and the Cartagena Declaration where refugee status has been granted under circumstances in which natural disasters have intersected with disturbances in public order.

d        The Bangkok Principles on the Status and Treatment of Refugees
The Asian-African Legal Consultative Committee (AALCC),[56] in consultation with the UNHCR, developed and adopted the Bangkok Principles on the Status and Treatment of Refugees on 17 August 1966 (1966 Bangkok Principles).[57] The AALCC formulated these Principles in view of its "advisory character", acknowledging that "it would be up to the Government of each participating State to

---

55    Emphasis added.

56    The Asian-African Legal Consultative Organization (AALCO) was first known as the Asian Legal Consultative Committee (ALCC) when it was formed in 1956 by its seven original Member States. This name was revised in 1958 to the Asian-African Legal Consultative Committee (AALCC) to reflect the membership of African countries. This organisation is today known as the AALCO and, as of the time of writing, has 48 Member States. *About AALCO*, AALCO, http://www.aalco.int/about (last visited 22 May 2021).

57    AALCC, Bangkok, Thailand, 8–17 Aug. 1966, *Report of the Eight Session, IX Final Report of the Committee Adopted at the Eighth Session*, at 209, ¶ 6 [hereinafter 'AALCC, 8th Session Final Report']; AALCC, Bangkok, Thailand, 8–17 Aug. 1966, *Report of the Eight Session, Annexure, Principles Concerning Treatment of Refugees*, at 211 *et seq.* [hereinafter '1966 Bangkok Principles'].

decide as to how it would give effect to the Committee's recommendations whether by entering into multilateral or bilateral arrangements or by recognizing the principles [...] in their own municipal laws."[58]

The AALCC adopted two subsequent addenda to the original text, in 1970 and in 1987.[59] On the occasion of the 30th anniversary of the original text, the AALCC agreed to review and revise the 1966 Bangkok Principles on the Status and Treatment of Refugees, again in consultation with the UNHCR.[60] Following this revision process, the AALCC, at its 40th session on 24 June 2001, adopted a revised and consolidated form of the 1996 Bangkok Principles on the Status and Treatment of Refugees (2001 Bangkok Principles).[61] At the same session, the AALCC changed its name to the Asian-African Legal Consultative Organization (AALCO).[62]

The original text of the 1966 Bangkok Principles contained a definition of the term "refugee" that was similar (although not identical) to the definition found in the Refugee Convention:

> a person who, owing to persecution or well-founded fear of persecution for reasons of race, colour, religion, political belief or membership of a particular social group: (a) leaves the State of which he is a national, or the Country of his nationality, or, if he has no nationality, the State or Country of which he is a habitual resident; or, (b) being outside such State or Country, is unable or unwilling to return to it or to avail himself of its protection.[63]

---

58    AALCC, 8th Session Final Report, *supra* note 57, at 209, ¶ 6.

59    The first addendum elaborated the right of return. AALCO, Addendum to the Principles Concerning Treatment of Refugees, 27 Jan. 1970. The second addendum incorporated principles of burden sharing. AALCO, Addendum to the Status and Treatment of Refugees, 13 Jan. 1987.

60    AALCC, Manila, Philippines, 4–8 Mar. 1996, *Report of the Thirty Fifth Session*, at 210, ¶ 7. *See also* AALCC, Cairo, Egypt, 19–23 Feb. 2000, *Status and Treatment of Refugees*, presented at the Thirty Nineth Session, at 1, *available at* http://www.aalco.int/39thsession/strcairoIV.pdf [hereinafter '*Status and Treatment of Refugees*'].

61    AALCC, New Delhi, India, 20–24 June 2001, *Resolutions Adopted at the Fortieth Session, Resolutions on Substantive Matters*, RES/40/3 (24 June 2001); Final Text of the AALCO's 1966 Bangkok Principles on Status and Treatment of Refugees as Adopted on 24 June 2001 at the AALCO's 40th Session, New Delhi, 24 June 2001 [hereinafter '2001 Bangkok Principles']. For a detailed history of the development of and revisions to the Bangkok Principles, see *Status and Treatment of Refugees, supra* note 60.

62    AALCC, New Delhi, India, 20–24 June 2001, *Resolutions Adopted at the Fortieth Session, Resolutions on Organisational Matters*, RES/40/ORG 3 (24 June 2001).

63    1966 Bangkok Principles, *supra* note 57, art. I. The Refugee Convention (as amended by the Refugee Protocol) defines Refugees as individuals who "owing to well-founded fear of being persecuted for reasons of race, religion, nationality, membership of a particular

Unlike the Refugee Convention, this definition does not include persecution for reasons of "nationality", but does include persecution for reasons of "colour". Whereas the Refugee Convention refers to political "opinion", the original text of the 1966 Bangkok Principles refer to political "belief". Also unique to the original text of the 1966 Bangkok Principles, an "Explanation" to the definition of "refugee" states that the "dependents of a refugee shall be deemed to be refugees."[64] Another "Explanation" to the refugee definition clarifies that the term "'leaves' includes voluntary as well as involuntary leaving."[65]

Amongst other revisions, the 2001 Bangkok Principles expanded the scope of the definition of "refugees" from the original 1966 text to include persecution for reasons of nationality, ethnic origin, and gender, and further revised "political belief" to become "political opinion".[66] The 2001 Bangkok Principles also included in the definition of refugee an entirely new paragraph, which is identical to language found in the OAU Convention:

> The term "refugee" shall also apply to every person who, owing to external aggression, occupation, foreign domination or events seriously disturbing public order in either part or the whole of his country of origin or nationality, is compelled to leave his place of habitual residence in order to seek refuge in another place outside his country of origin or nationality.[67]

As noted above in connection with the OAU Convention, the inclusion of "events seriously disturbing public order" could open the door to a more flexible interpretation of the drivers that could fall within the scope of the 2001 Bangkok Principles, such as climate change impacts. However, unlike the OAU Convention, the 2001 Bangkok Principles are not binding.[68] The Bangkok

---

social group or political opinion, is outside the country of his nationality and is unable or, owing to such fear, is unwilling to avail himself of the protection of that country; or who, not having a nationality and being outside the country of his former habitual residence as a result of such events, is unable or, owing to such fear, is unwilling to return to it". Refugee Convention, *supra* note 1, art. 1(A)(2), as amended by the Refugee Protocol, *supra* note 2, art. 1.

64 1966 Bangkok Principles, *supra* note 57, art. I.

65 *Id.*

66 2001 Bangkok Principles, *supra* note 61, art. I(1). AALCO also revisited provisions relating to asylum and standards of treatment, durable solutions, and burden sharing. See *Status and Treatment of Refugees*, *supra* note 60, at 1.

67 2001 Bangkok Principles, *supra* note 61, art. I(2).

68 *Id.* at Notes, Comments and Reservations made by the Member States of AALCO, Introductory Remarks, ¶ 2; *see also* AALCC, 8th Session Final Report, *supra* note 57, at 209, ¶ 6.

Principles are also generally not incorporated into the national laws of AALCO Member States.[69]

To the extent that the 2001 Bangkok Principles have not fully taken into account State concerns, notwithstanding their non-binding character, AALCO's members have made notes, comments, and reservations that are included as "an integral part of the main document of the Revised Bangkok Principles".[70] These include observations and reservations as to the definition of refugees contained therein.[71] The extent and detail of these reservations suggest that AALCO's Member States anticipated that the 2001 Bangkok Principles would be significant in the future development of regional refugee law and policy, despite their non-binding nature.[72]

Some, such as Pia Oberoi, have argued that the Bangkok Principles have been influential in the South Asia region.[73] She notes the particular significance of these standards for the region, given that none of the South Asian States (as she refers to them)—Bangladesh, Bhutan, India, the Maldives, Myanmar,

---

69   *See* Ruma Mandal, *Protection Mechanisms Outside of the 1951 Convention ("Complementary Protection")* 20 (UNHCR, Legal & Protection Policy Research Series, PPLA/2005/02, June 2005), *available at* https://www.unhcr.org/protection/globalconsult/435df0aa2/9-protect ion-mechanisms-outside-1951-convention-complementary-protection.html.

70   2001 Bangkok Principles, *supra* note 61, at Notes, Comments and Reservations made by the Member States of AALCO, Introductory Remarks, ¶ 1.

71   *Id.* at Notes, Comments and Reservations made by the Member States of AALCO, art. 1.

72   *See* Merrill Smith, *The Bangkok Principles on the Status and Treatment of Refugees*, RIGHTS IN EXILE (3 Dec. 2011), https://rightsinexile.tumblr.com/post/13676403836/the-bang kok-principles-on-the-status-and-treatment ("The Principles proclaim themselves to be 'declaratory and non-binding in character [...]'. Nevertheless, a look at all the notes, comments and reservations that form an integral part of the document reveals States negotiating something they seemed to take more seriously than a mere declaration. We can't call it law until some legislative, judicial and/or executive authority in the region says it is but, as a political matter it would seem difficult for any Member State to distance themselves from the Principles if they failed to object or to declare a reservation when they had opportunity to do so (demonstrated by those who actually did so)."); B. Sen, *Protection of Refugees: Bangkok Principles and After,* 34(2) J. INDIAN L. INST. 187, 189 (1992) ("The Bangkok Principles were thus somewhat restrictive in scope in the matter of recognition of refugee rights, but their strength lies in the fact that they represent a position which governments could be expected to accept in their approach to the problem of refugees.").

73   In support of her statement that the Bangkok Principles have been influential in the region, Oberoi gives the example that the government of Pakistan referred to the definition of refugees from the 1966 Bangkok Principles in its 1981 "Official Handbook on Refugee Management in Pakistan". Pia Oberoi, *Regional Initiatives on Refugee Protection in South Asia,* 11(1) INT'L J. REFUGEE L., 193, 195, n.7 (1999). Barry Sen, former Secretary-General of the AALCC, considered that the Bangkok Principles "had a good deal of impact on the future growth of refugee law". Sen, *supra* note 72, at 187.

Nepal, Pakistan, or Sri Lanka—are members of the 1951 Refugee Convention.[74] Others consider that the Bangkok Principles, being neither binding nor monitored, have not had a significant impact in practice.[75] UNHCR has opined that the Bangkok Principles are "important but have not achieved the same prominence and legal value as instruments in other regions."[76]

e        The European Union Qualification Directive

On 29 April 2004, the Council of the European Union adopted Directive 2004/83/EC on minimum standards for the qualification and status of third country nationals or stateless persons as refugees or as persons who otherwise need international protection and the content of the protection granted (EU Qualification Directive).[77] As indicated in the full title of the document, the EU Qualification Directive addresses not only the protection of refugees, but also subsidiary protection, i.e., protection (including from *refoulement*) which extends beyond the scope of the asylum framework.[78] The EU Qualification

---

74    Oberoi, *supra* note 73, at 193, n.1. In connection with the process to update the Bangkok Principles prior to 2001, Oberoi opined: "Given that these [Bangkok] Principles are the only codified and comprehensive standards of protection in Asia, it is important to ensure that they are kept relevant to the refugee experience of Asian states. Oberoi, *supra* note 73, at 197.

75    SARA ELLEN DAVIES, LEGITIMISING REJECTION: INTERNATIONAL REFUGEE LAW IN SOUTHEAST ASIA 4 (2008); *see also* Joyce Chia & Justice Susan Kenny, *Children of Mae La: Reflections on Regional Refugee Cooperation*, 13 MELB. J. INT'L L. 1, 15 (2012) (citing Davies on the same conclusion); Savitri Taylor, *Refugee Protection in the Asia Pacific Region*, RIGHTS IN EXILE PROGRAMME (undated), http://www.refugeelegalaidinformation.org/refugee-protection-asia-pacific-region; Manish Kumar Yadav, *Rights of Refugees and Internally Displaced Persons with a Special Reference to South Asian Region*, 4(12) INT'L J. HUMAN. & SOC. SCI. INVENTION 36, 43 (2015).

76    FRANCES NICHOLSON & JUDITH KUMIN, A GUIDE TO INTERNATIONAL REFUGEE PROTECTION AND BUILDING STATE ASYLUM SYSTEMS 22 (Handbook for Parliamentarians N° 27, 2017), *available at* https://www.unhcr.org/3d4aba564.pdf.

77    Directive 2004/83, of the Council of the European Union of 29 April 2004 on the Minimum Standards for the Qualification and Status of Third Country Nationals or Stateless Persons as Refugees or as Persons Who Otherwise Need International Protection and the Content of the Protection Granted, 2004 O.J. (L 304) 12 [hereinafter 'Qualification Directive'].

78    Subsidiary protection is sometimes referred to as being synonymous with "complementary protection", a term commonly used to refer to protection from *refoulement* beyond obligations arising under the Refugee Convention. Complementary protection is not a term defined in any international instrument. It has been used to refer to both mandatory protection obligations arising under international human rights law as well as discretionary extensions of protection. Margit Ammer, *Climate Change and Human Rights: The Status of Climate Refugees in Europe* 56–57 (Ludwig Boltzmann Inst. of Hum. Rts., Research Project on Climate Change for the Swiss Initiative to Commemorate the 60th Anniversary of the

Directive draws its subsidiary protection obligations "from international obligations under human rights instruments and practices existing in Member States."[79] The EU Qualification Directive does not seek to establish new law but instead to harmonize State practices by establishing common minimum standards of recognition for refugee and subsidiary protection.[80] The EU Qualification Directive restates the definition of Refugees set forth in the Refugee Convention and, unlike the OAU Convention and the Cartagena Declaration, does not expand it.[81] The EU Qualification Directive does, however, include subsidiary protection measures by defining, in addition to refugees, persons "eligible for subsidiary protection":

---

Universal Declaration of Human Rights, June 2009); JANE MCADAM, CLIMATE CHANGE, FORCED MIGRATION, AND INTERNATIONAL LAW 53 (2012) [hereinafter 'MCADAM, FORCED MIGRATION']; Mandal, *supra* note 69, at 2–3. Although the term "humanitarian protection" can be understood as a form of complementary protection, subsidiary protection is sometimes distinguished from humanitarian protection, for example in the Finnish Alien's Act. *See* Act No. 323 of 2009 (To Amend Provisions of the Aliens Act No. 301 of 2004), §§ 88 & 88a (Fin.). The EU Qualification Directive also distinguishes persons who "are allowed to remain in the territories of the Member States for reasons not due to a need for international protection but on a discretionary basis on compassionate or humanitarian grounds" as falling outside of its scope. Qualification Directive, *supra* note 77, preamble, ¶ 9. There is some disagreement as to whether temporary protection can be considered a form of complementary protection. *Compare* Alice Edwards, *Temporary Protection, Derogation and the* 1951 Refugee Convention, 13(2) MELB. J. INT'L L. 1, 10–11 (2012) [hereinafter 'Edwards, *Temporary Protection*'] ("Temporary protection needs to be distinguished from 'complementary' or 'subsidiary' forms of protection, the legal basis for which is rooted in human rights obligations of *non-refoulement*. Unlike temporary protection, complementary or subsidiary forms of protection are not normally emergency or provisional in nature and are applied on an individual case basis, rather than to mass movements of persons.") *with* François Gemenne, Environmental Changes and Migration Flows: Normative Frameworks and Policy Responses Volume I, at 327 (3 Apr. 2009) (Doctoral Thesis, Institut d'Etudes Politiques de Paris & University of Liège), *available at* https://orbi.uliege.be/handle/2268/137601 (identifying subsidiary/humanitarian protection and temporary protection as two main subsets of complementary protection).

79     Qualification Directive, *supra* note 77, preamble, ¶ 25.

80     *Id.* ¶ 6; European Parliament Directorate-General for Internal Policies, Policy Department C: Citizens' Rights and Constitutional Affairs, *"Climate Refugees": Legal and Policy Responses to Environmentally Induced Migration*, at 51, Doc. No. PE 462.422 (Dec. 2011) (*by* Albert Kraler et al.) [hereinafter 'Kraler Policy Paper']; Ammer, *supra* note 78, at 61. *See also* Gemenne, *supra* note 78, at 330 ("The Qualification directive [...] represents the first international attempt to harmonise these schemes of subsidiary protection and to guarantee minimal standards"). As these are minimum standards, Member States can maintain and adopt laws which have higher standards or which offer protection under additional circumstances.

81     *See* Qualification Directive, *supra* note 77, art. 2(c).

a third country national or a stateless person who does not qualify as a refugee but in respect of whom substantial grounds have been shown for believing that the person concerned, if returned to his or her country of origin, or in the case of a stateless person, to his or her country of former habitual residence, would face a real risk of suffering serious harm as defined in Article 15, and to whom Article 17(1) and (2) do not apply, and is unable, or, owing to such risk, unwilling to avail himself or herself of the protection of that country.[82]

Article 15 defines "serious harm" as consisting of:

(a) death penalty or execution; or
(b) torture or inhuman or degrading treatment or punishment of an applicant in the country of origin; or
(c) serious and individual threat to a civilian's life or person by reason of indiscriminate violence in situations of international or internal armed conflict.

As Ruma Mandal observes, Articles 15(a) and (b) are clearly derived from human rights obligations found in relevant treaties.[83] By contrast, the language in Article 15(c) is not directly linked to the language found in specific human rights treaties and is most comparable to the expanded refugee definitions found in the OAU Convention and Cartagena Declaration.[84] Subsidiary protection under the EU Qualification Directive (and/or under human rights obligations) could conceivably arise in connection with climate change impacts under the language used in Article 15(b), should they give rise to conditions amounting to inhuman treatment.[85]

Unlike the Refugee Convention and some of its regional counterparts, the EU Qualification Directive is recent and its drafters were aware of climate change impacts and their emerging influence on human mobility. The somewhat obscure drafting history shows that explicit reference to environmental

---

82    *Id.* art. 2(e).
83    Mandal, *supra* note 69, at 18, ¶ 46.
84    *Id.* at 18–19, ¶¶ 47–48.
85    Kraler Policy Paper, *supra* note 80, at 52–53. Jane McAdam similarly explores the possibility that *non-refoulement* obligations in connection with human rights norms, including the rights to life and not to be subjected to cruel, inhuman or degrading treatment, could apply in connection with climate change impacts. For an analysis of such obligations in the context of human mobility and climate change, see MCADAM, FORCED MIGRATION, *supra* note 78, at 52–98.

impacts was contemplated but ultimately omitted from the EU Qualification Directive.[86] Even if the EU Qualification Directive could be interpreted to apply (which is doubtful), or is ultimately amended (as some have suggested[87]) to include explicitly, climate change impacts, its protection could only apply in circumstances where the country of origin could not itself provide protection. Article 8 explicitly circumscribes application of the EU Qualification Directive to instances where there is no option for internal displacement to another part of the country of origin.[88]

The European Union has also institutionalized on an international level a temporary protection mechanism with the adoption of European Council Directive 2001/55/EC on minimum standards for giving temporary protection in the event of a mass influx of displaced persons and on measures promoting a balance of efforts between Member States in receiving such persons and bearing the consequences thereof (EU Temporary Protection Directive) on 20 July 2001.[89] Temporary protection is generally a discretionary protection mechanism beyond the asylum framework, defined by the EU Temporary Protection Directive as "a procedure of exceptional character to provide, in the event of a mass influx or imminent mass influx of displaced persons from third countries who are unable to return to their country of origin, immediate and temporary protection to such persons, in particular if there is also a risk that the asylum system will be unable to process this influx without adverse effects for its efficient operation, in the interests of the persons concerned and other persons requesting protection".[90]

---

86    *See* Vikram Kolmannskog & Finn Myrstad, *Environmental Displacement in European Asylum Law*, 11 EUR. J. MIGRATION & L. 313, 319–25 (2009). McAdam considered that the inclusion of environmental disasters as a ground for subsidiary protection "does not seem to have been entertained seriously in deliberations". Although she recognized this as being explicitly precluded from the EU Qualification Directive, she considered that this "does not foreclose the possibility that treatment resulting from such situations could amount to inhuman or degrading treatment". MCADAM, FORCED MIGRATION, *supra* note 78, at 103–04. It has also been stated, similar to the arguments relating to the provisions of the OAU Convention and Cartagena Declaration (discussed *supra*), that the terms of the EU Qualification Directive should be understood as applying only to "man-made situations". Ammer, *supra* note 78, at 61–63.

87    Kolmannskog & Myrstad, *supra* note 86, at 325; Kraler Policy Paper, *supra* note 80, at 53.

88    *See* Kraler Policy Paper, *supra* note 80, at 51–52.

89    Directive 2001/55/EC, of the Council of the European Union of 20 July 2001 on Minimum Standards for Giving Temporary Protection in the Event of a Mass Influx of Displaced Persons and on Measures Promoting a Balance of Efforts Between Member States in Receiving such Persons and Bearing the Consequences Thereof, 2001 O.J. (L 212) 12 [hereinafter 'Temporary Protection Directive'].

90    *Id.* art 2(a). For a discussion on the meaning of temporary protection, see Edwards, *Temporary Protection*, *supra* note 78, at 5–9.

The EU Temporary Protection Directive can be activated to provide temporary protection in cases of mass influx of displaced persons, the latter being defined as:

> third-country nationals or stateless persons who have had to leave their country or region of origin, or have been evacuated, in particular in response to an appeal by international organisations, and are unable to return in safe and durable conditions because of the situation prevailing in that country, who may fall within the scope of Article 1A of the Geneva Convention or other international or national instruments giving international protection, in particular: (i) persons who have fled areas of armed conflict or endemic violence; (ii) persons at serious risk of, or who have been the victims of, systematic or generalised violations of their human rights.[91]

Although environmental (or climate change) impacts are not explicitly included, the use of the words "in particular" has been interpreted as indicating a non-exhaustive list of drivers which could be understood as including those displaced by environmental impacts.[92] At the same time, Member States rejected a proposal to include specific language on displacement by natural disasters,[93] demonstrating scarce political will to enter into any commitments in this respect. Political will plays a large role in implementation of the EU Temporary Protection Directive because, despite its concretization of temporary protection measures, it remains a discretionary mechanism. Protection under the EU TPD must be triggered by a proposal by the European Commission and subsequent decision of the Council.[94] Although this means that cases involving environmental (or climate change) impacts can be given case-by-case consideration, it also makes such decisions highly political and unpredictable, as is generally also the case with national discretionary temporary protection schemes.

∴

---

91    Temporary Protection Directive, *supra* note 89, art. 2(c).
92    *See* Kraler Policy Paper, *supra* note 80, at 54; Kolmannskog & Myrstad, *supra* note 86, at 316–17.
93    *See* Kolmannskog & Myrstad, *supra* note 86, at 316.
94    Temporary Protection Directive, *supra* note 89, art. 5.

Regional asylum instruments tend to contain more flexible criteria for asylum protection than the 1951 Refugee Convention. Climate change and natural disasters are often still not explicitly included as possible drivers of refugee movement within the definitions contained in these regional instruments. Instead, most of these instruments (excepting only the EU Qualification Directive) include events seriously disturbing public order as potential drivers of refugee movements. Textual interpretation and application of this language in practice have not given a categorical answer as to whether natural disasters may constitute events seriously disturbing public order. Instead, whether a natural disaster or environmental conditions will trigger asylum protection under these regional instruments will depend in part on States' capacity and willingness to accept those displaced by natural disasters and other climate change impacts.

## B      Protection for Stateless Persons

The 1954 Convention Relating to the Status of Stateless Persons (1954 Convention) was adopted on 28 September 1954 and entered into force on 6 June 1960.[95] The 1954 Convention was modeled after, and in many instances mirrors the provisions of, the Refugee Convention.[96] The 1954 Convention affords stateless persons many of the same rights and obligations provided to refugees.[97] In addition to establishing similar (but not in all cases identical) minimum standards of treatment, the 1954 Convention contains a provision safeguarding stateless persons from expulsion that is identical to that contained in the Refugee Convention.[98] The 1954 Convention does not, however,

---

95    Convention Relating to the Status of Stateless Persons, 28 Sept. 1954, 360 U.N.T.S. 117 [hereinafter 'Convention on Statelessness']. Another convention on statelessness, the Convention on the Reduction of Statelessness, was adopted on 30 Aug. 1961. Any potential relevance of this treaty to human mobility in the context of climate change is more tenuous. *See generally* Convention on the Reduction of Statelessness, 30 Aug. 1961, 989 U.N.T.S. 175.

96    For a history of the conclusion of the 1954 Convention and an analysis of its provisions in relation to those of the Refugee Convention, see generally Nehemiah Robinson, *Convention Relating to the Status of Stateless Persons, Its History and Interpretation* (Commentary for the 1955 World Jewish Congress, reprinted by the UNHCR Division of International Protection, 1997), *available at* https://www.unhcr.org/3d4ab67f4.pdf.

97    *Id.* at 1.

98    Convention on Statelessness, *supra* note 95, art. 31; Refugee Convention, *supra* note 1, art. 32; *id.* at 60–63.

contain any provisions on *non-refoulement*.[99] The drafters, considering the proscription of *refoulement* expressed in Article 33 of the Refugee Convention to be a generally accepted principle, deemed it unnecessary to include any such explicit provision in the 1954 Convention.[100]

The 1954 Convention is potentially relevant to climate change mobility in cases where sea level rise and increasing frequency of rapid onset hazards threaten to render uninhabitable, or to submerge, the majority or entirety of the territory of small island States.[101] The Maldives, Tuvalu, the Marshall Islands, Nauru, and Kiribati are amongst the States whose existence may be

99    On the principle of *non-refoulement*, see *supra* note 2 and accompanying text.

100   *See* Final Act of the United Nations Conference on the Status of Stateless Persons, No. 5158, at 122, 124, 28 Sept. 1954, 360 U.N.T.S. 118, [hereinafter 'Final Act on Statelessness']; *see also Objectives and Key Provisions of the 1954 Convention Relating to the Status of Stateless Persons*, UNHCR (1 Oct. 2001), http://www.unhcr.org/protection/statelessness/3bd7d3 394/objectives-key-provisions-1954-convention-relating-status-stateless-persons.html. *But see* UNHCR, Expert Meeting, 27–28 May 2010, Prato, Italy, *The Concept of Stateless Persons under International Law: Summary Conclusions*, at 2, ¶ 5, *available at* http://www.unhcr.org/protection/statelessness/4cb2fe326/expert-meeting-concept-stateless-pers ons-under-international-law-summary.html [hereinafter 'UNHCR, Prato Conclusions'] (suggesting that the Refugee Convention offers a higher standard of protection than the 1954 Convention due to, in part, the former's explicit provision on *non-refoulement*); UNHCR Note on Non-Refoulement, *supra* note 2, ¶ 18 ("While the principle of non-refoulement is universally recognized, the danger of refoulement could be more readily avoided if the State concerned has accepted a formal legal obligation defined in an international instrument").

101   For an analysis of the potential impacts of climate change on small island States, see Lilian Yamamoto & Miguel Esteban, *Atoll Island States and Climate Change: Sovereignty Implications* 1, 7–34 (UNU-IAS Working Paper No. 166, Oct. 2011), *available at* https://i.unu. edu/media/unu.edu/publication/20972/atoll-island-states-and-climate-change_unu-ias-working-paper-166.pdf; *see also* INTERGOVERNMENTAL PANEL ON CLIMATE CHANGE, FOURTH ASSESSMENT REPORT: CLIMATE CHANGE 2007: IMPACTS, ADAPTATION AND VULNERABILITY, CONTRIBUTION OF WORKING GROUP II TO THE FOURTH ASSESSMENT REPORT OF THE IPCC 736 (2007); Gregory E. Wannier & Michael B. Gerrard, *Disappearing States: Harnessing International Law to Preserve Cultures and Society, in* CLIMATE CHANGE: INTERNATIONAL LAW AND GLOBAL GOVERNANCE 615, 617–618 (Oliver C. Ruppel et al. eds., 2013) [hereinafter 'Wannier & Gerrard, *Disappearing States*']. Sea level rise also has potential implications for small island State maritime entitlements and territorial sea as well. *See generally* Clive Schofield & David Freestone, *Options to Protect Coastlines and Secure Maritime Jurisdictional Claims in the Face of Global Sea Level Rise, in* THREATENED ISLAND NATIONS LEGAL IMPLICATIONS OF RISING SEAS AND A CHANGING CLIMATE 141, 144–48 (Michael B. Gerrard & Gregory E. Wannier eds., 2013); Rosemary Rayfuse, *International Law and Disappearing States: Utilising Maritime Entitlements to Overcome the Statehood Dilemma* 1–4 (UNSW Law Research Paper No. 2010-52, Nov. 2010), *available at* https://papers.ssrn.com/sol3/papers.cfm?abstract_id=1704835.

endangered by sea level rise.[102] The question is whether the citizens of these small island States would, under such circumstances, be rendered stateless within the meaning of the 1954 Convention.

The 1954 Convention defines a "Stateless Person" as one "who is not considered as a national by any State under the operation of its law."[103] With this definition, the drafters of the 1954 Convention sought to restrict its application to persons who are *de jure* stateless, i.e., those who possess no nationality as a matter of law.[104] The 1954 Convention does not apply, by design, to persons who are *de facto* stateless, i.e., those who possess a nationality but where such nationality is ineffective.[105] Thus, in the latter case, a person may possess the nationality of a State in which, for example, the government is not functioning or is unable to provide protection to its nationals.

Legal scholars generally consider that, so long as small island nations continue to exist as States and have not revoked nationality by operation of their laws, their nationals would at most become *de facto* stateless, in which case the 1954 Convention would not apply.[106] One exception to this line of thought

---

102    Etienne Piquet, *Climatic Statelessness: Risk Assessment and Policy Options,* 45(4) POPULATION & DEV. REV. 865, 871 (2019). In his analysis identifying endangered States, Piquet excludes islands that are colonies, overseas territories, or generally a part of States that will retain unendangered territory. Based on this and on the highest territory above sea level, Piquet identifies these five island nations as the principal States whose existence may be endangered by sea level rise.

103    Convention on Statelessness, *supra* note 95, art. 1(1). For an interpretation of this provision and its history, see Robinson, *supra* note 96, at 5–14; UNHCR, Prato Conclusions, *supra* note 100, at 2–5, ¶¶ 1–27.

104    Robinson, *supra* note 96, at 7–11.

105    *See* UNHCR, Prato Conclusions, *supra* note 100, at 2, ¶ 3. The Final Act of the United Nations Conference relating to the 1954 Convention contains a recommendation that when "a person has renounced the protection of the State of which he is a national," contracting States should, when they consider the reasons for such renunciation to be valid, "consider sympathetically the possibility of according to that person the treatment which the Convention accords to stateless persons". This recommendation, however, is non-binding and does not appear in the final text of the 1954 Convention. Final Act on Statelessness, *supra* note 100, at 122. *See also* Robinson, *supra* note 96, at 7–11. On the meaning of *de facto* stateless persons, see UNHCR, Prato Conclusions, *supra* note 100, at 6–8.

106    *See* UNHCR, Submission to the Sixth Session of the Ad Hoc Working Group on Long-Term Cooperative Action (AWG-LCA 6) under the UN Framework Convention on Climate Change, 1–12 June 2009, Bonn, Germany, *Climate Change and Statelessness, An Overview* 2 (15 May 2009), *available at* http://www.unhcr.org/protection/environment/4a1e50082/climate-change-statelessness-overview.html (cited in MCADAM, FORCED MIGRATION, *supra* note 78, at 141, n.153) [hereinafter 'UNHCR, *Climate Change and Statelessness*']; Kälin & Schrepfer, *supra* note 7, at 38–39.

is the theory advanced by Heather Alexander and Jonathan Simon, who argue that submerged island States, even if they continue to exist as States, cannot confer nationality without having a territory to which they can readmit their nationals, thereby leaving their citizens *de jure* stateless within the meaning of the 1954 Convention.[107] For now, the circumstances under which small island nations might cease to be States, or by which they may no longer confer nationality, remain questions of fertile debate.[108] The disappearance of a State's habitable territory due to environmental impacts therefore engenders great uncertainty.

Moreover, there is no binding definition of a "State" or formal criteria for statehood under international law that would provide conclusive guidance.[109] Legal scholars tend to analyze this issue in light of the four indicia of statehood set forth in the Montevideo Convention on the Rights and Duties of States (Montevideo Convention)[110]: "The state as a person of international law should possess the following qualifications: (a) a permanent population; (b) a defined territory; (c) government; and (d) capacity to enter into relations with the other states"[111] (collectively, the Montevideo Indicia). The Montevideo

---

107    Heather Alexander & Jonathan Simon, *No Port, No Passport: Why Submerged States Can Have No Nationals*, 26(2) WASH. INT'L L. J. 307 (2017).

108    *See* UNHCR, Prato Conclusions, *supra* note 100, at 5, ¶ 27; MCADAM, FORCED MIGRATION, *supra* note 78, at 127–28, 139; Sumudu Atapattu, *Climate Change: Disappearing States, Migration, and Challenges for International Law*, 4(1) WASH. J. ENVTL. L. & POL'Y 1, 18–19 (2014); Maxine Burkett, *The Nation* Ex-Situ: *On Climate Change, Deterritorialized Nationhood and the Post-Climate Era*, 2 CLIMATE L. 345, 354 (2011) [hereinafter 'Burkett, Nation Ex-Situ'].

109    *See, e.g.*, Thomas D. Grant, *Defining Statehood: The Montevideo Convention and its Discontents*, 37 COLUM. J. TRANSNAT'L L. 403, 404–14 (1999); UNHCR, *Climate Change and Statelessness*, *supra* note 106, at 1; Susin Park, *Climate Change and the Risk of Statelessness: The Situation of Low-lying Island States* 4 (UNHCR, Legal & Protection Policy Research Series, PPLA/2011/04, May 2011), *available at* https://www.unhcr.org/protect ion/globalconsult/4df9cb0c9/20-climate-change-risk-statelessness-situation-low-lying-island-states.html.

110    *See, e.g.*, Heather Alexander & Jonathan Simon, *Sinking Into Statelessness*, 19 TILBURG L. REV. 20, 22 (2014) [hereinafter Alexander & Simon, *Sinking Into Statelessness*']; Park, *supra* note 109, at 4–5; MCADAM, FORCED MIGRATION, *supra* note 78, at 128; UNHCR, Prato Conclusions, *supra* note 100, at 5, ¶ 23.

111    Montevideo Convention on the Rights and Duties of States art. 1, 26 Dec. 1933, 165 U.N.T.S. 21. Park observes that these characteristics are interlinked in that, for example, the permanent population is meant to inhabit the State's territory and the government is meant to have control over the territory and population. Park, *supra* note 109, at 5–6. Some consider that the fourth criterion, "capacity to enter into relations with the other states", to be a consequence of, rather than a prerequisite for, statehood. *See, e.g.*, MCADAM, FORCED MIGRATION, *supra* note 78, at 133 ("The capacity to enter into relations with other States

Indicia alone are insufficient to determine the creation, much less the continuing existence, of States under international law, although they have provided a common point of departure for analysis.[112] Although climate change impacts could threaten to upset the existence of one or all of the Montevideo Indicia,[113] there is no consensus as to whether the presence or absence of any of these particular indicia for any specific period of time would be decisive.[114] Given the general presumption for the continuity of existing States under international law,[115] most, but not all, scholars tend to consider that the absence of one or more of these indicia, at least temporarily,[116] would not terminate a State's existence.[117] If a small island State were, by some means, to cease to exist as a political entity, this may extinguish the legal status of the

is a conflation of the requirements of government and independence. It is, accordingly, a consequence, rather than a criterion, of statehood") (citing James Crawford, THE CREATION OF STATES IN INTERNATIONAL LAW 61 (2nd ed., 2006)); Grant, *supra* note 109, at 434–35.

112    For an analysis of the Montevideo Convention, see Grant, *supra* note 109, at 414–18, 434–53. For a view on competing theories of State creation, see generally William Thomas Worster, *Law, Politics, and the Conception of the State in State Recognition Theory*, 27 B.U. J. INT'L L. 115 (2009).

113    For an analysis on each of the Montevideo indicia in relation to rising sea levels, see MCADAM, FORCED MIGRATION, *supra* note 78, at 129–35.

114    *Compare* Alexander & Simon, *Sinking Into Statelessness*, *supra* note 110, at 22–23 (considering habitable territory to be indispensable) *with* Grant, *supra* note 109, at 435 (opining that an existing State would not lose its statehood because it has lost its territory or effective control thereover), *and with* MCADAM, FORCED MIGRATION, *supra* note 78, at 137–38 (suggesting that State continuity in the absence of one or more indicia may depend in large part on the view of other States).

115    Atapattu, *supra* note 108, at 14; Park, *supra* note 109, at 6–7; Walter Kälin, *Conceptualising Climate-Induced Displacement*, *in* CLIMATE CHANGE AND DISPLACEMENT: MULTIDISCIPLINARY PERSPECTIVES, *supra* note 6, at 81, 101 [hereinafter 'Kälin, *Conceptualising*']. *But see* Alexander & Simon, *Sinking Into Statelessness*, *supra* note 110, at 23–24 (arguing that the presumption of continuance cannot preserve the existence of a State in the absence of territory).

116    *See* Park, *supra* note 109, at 7, 8, 14 (considering that the presumption for continuity of a State likely only operates for temporary loss of territory or exile of the population).

117    Grant, *supra* note 109, at 435 ("It therefore appears to be the case that once an entity has established itself in international society as a state, it does not lose statehood by losing its territory or effective control over that territory. To be sure, the Montevideo Convention was concerned with whether an entity *became* a state, not with how an entity might cease to be a state" (emphasis in original)); UNHCR, Bellagio Roundtable Summary, *supra* note 39, at 7, ¶ 30; UNHCR, *Climate Change and Statelessness*, *supra* note 106, at 1; Burkett, *Nation* Ex-Situ, *supra* note 108, at 354–55. *But see* Alexander & Simon, *Sinking Into Statelessness*, *supra* note 110, at 22–25 (arguing that without a habitable territory, small island States cannot continue to exist).

State's nationals so as to render them *de jure* stateless within the meaning of the 1954 Convention.[118]

Some small island States and scholars have envisaged solutions which would, in theory, allow the State to meet the Montevideo Indicia by, for example, acquiring land which could serve as new territory of the State should the islands become uninhabitable or submerged.[119] Others have theorized that the State could continue to exist with a government operating "in exile", or *ex situ*.[120] Whether any of these strategies would be feasible or successful, or would be welcomed by nationals of small island States,[121] is uncertain.

In light of the uncertainty surrounding the fate of small island States and the legal status of their nationals, reliance on the protection provided by the 1954 Convention to climate change mobility—particularly at this stage where adaptive measures may still be taken—is uncompelling. Although it may prove worthwhile to test these legal questions at a later time when and if small island States do become submerged or uninhabitable, the 1954 Convention will likely not provide protection for all of their inhabitants and citizens.[122] Even should it apply, the 1954 Convention is not widely ratified[123]

118   *See* Alexander & Simon, *Sinking Into Statelessness*, *supra* note 110, at 21; UNHCR, *Climate Change and Statelessness*, *supra* note 106, at 1–2; Park, *supra* note 109, at 8; UNHCR, Prato Conclusions, *supra* note 100, at 2, ¶ 7; MCADAM, FORCED MIGRATION, *supra* note 78, at 139.

119   For an analysis of the challenges associated with this potential solution, see MCADAM, FORCED MIGRATION, *supra* note 78, at 143–53. *See also* UNHCR, *Climate Change and Statelessness*, *supra* note 106, at 2; Rayfuse, *supra* note 101, at 8–10.

120   *See* Piquet, *supra* note 102, at 875–76; Burkett, *Nation* Ex-Situ, *supra* note 108, at 363–71; Rosemary Rayfuse, *W(h)ither Tuvalu? International Law and Disappearing States* 10–13 (UNSW Law Research Paper No. 2009–9, Apr. 2009), *available at* https://papers.ssrn.com/sol3/papers.cfm?abstract_id=1412028. It has also been suggested that other self-governing options that would not equate to statehood but other independent forms of governance that have been recognized internationally could be explored. See MCADAM, FORCED MIGRATION, *supra* note 78, at 153–158; Wannier & Gerrard, *Disappearing States*, *supra* note 101, at 623–27.

121   *See, e.g.*, Autumn Skye Bordner, *Climate Migration & Self-Determination*, 51(1) COLUM. HUM. RTS. L. REV. 183, 192–203 (2019) (explaining that for many Marshallese, moving away from the islands would not be an acceptable adaptation option).

122   *See* McAdam et al., *Sea-Level Rise*, *supra* note 33, at 36, ¶ 92.

123   The Refugee Convention has 146 parties; the Refugee Protocol has 147. By contrast, the 1954 Convention currently has only 95 parties. *Depository, Status of Treaties, Chapter V, 2. Convention relating to the Status of Refugees*, UN TREATY COLLECTION, https://treaties.un.org/Pages/ViewDetailsII.aspx?src=TREATY&mtdsg_no=V-2&chapter=5&Temp=mtdsg2&clang=_en (last visited 22 May 2021); *Depository, Status of Treaties, Chapter V, 5. Protocol relating to the Status of Refugees*, UN TREATY COLLECTION,

and, even where ratified, is often poorly implemented on the national
level.[124]


## C    Protection for Migrant Workers

The International Convention on the Protection of the Rights of All Migrant
Workers and Members of Their Families (Convention on Migrant Workers)
was adopted on 18 December 1990 and entered into force on 1 July 2003.[125]
One of the nine so-called "core" international human rights instruments, the
Convention on Migrant Workers compiles applicable human rights and establishes minimum standards of treatment for migrant workers and their families.[126] The Convention on Migrant Workers defines a "migrant worker" as "a
person who is to be engaged, is engaged or has been engaged in a remunerated
activity in a State of which he or she is not a national".[127]

---

https://treaties.un.org/Pages/ViewDetails.aspx?src=TREATY&mtdsg_no=V-5&chap
ter=5&clang=_en (last visited 22 May 2021); *Depository, Status of Treaties, Chapter V,
3. Convention relating to the Status of Stateless Persons*, UN TREATY COLLECTION,
https://treaties.un.org/PAGES/ViewDetailsII.aspx?src=TREATY&mtdsg_no=V-3&chap
ter=5&Temp=mtdsg2&clang=_en (last visited 22 May 2021).

124   *See* McAdam et al., *Sea-Level Rise, supra* note 33, at 36, ¶ 92; Jane McAdam, Side Event to
the High Commissioner's Dialogue on Protection Challenges in Geneva, Switz.: Climate
Change Displacement and International Law 7 (8 Dec. 2010), http://www.unhcr.org/pro
tection/hcdialogue%20/4d05ecf49/side-event-high-commissioners-dialogue-protect
ion-challenges-2010-climate.html ("most countries do not have any formal procedures for
determining the legal status of stateless persons. Thus, there is no clear means by which
the treaty's benefits could be accessed"). For a summary of the status of national implementation as of 2013, see GÁBOR GYULAI, STATELESSNESS: DETERMINATION AND THE
PROTECTION STATUS OF STATELESS PERSONS 6–7 (2013), *available at* https://www.
refworld.org/pdfid/53162a2f4.pdf.

125   International Convention on the Protection of the Rights of All Migrant Workers and
Members of Their Families, 18 Dec. 1990, 2220 U.N.T.S. 3 [hereinafter 'Convention on
Migrant Workers'].

126   *See* OHCHR, THE INTERNATIONAL CONVENTION ON MIGRANT WORKERS AND ITS
COMMITTEE: FACT SHEET NO. 24 (REV.1) 4–10 (2005), *available at* https://www.ohchr.
org/documents/publications/factsheet24rev.1en.pdf (reviewing the contents of the
Convention on Migrant Workers); MARIETTE GRANGE, STRENGTHENING PROTECTION
OF MIGRANT WORKERS AND THEIR FAMILIES WITH INTERNATIONAL HUMAN RIGHTS
TREATIES: A DO-IT-YOURSELF KIT 36–49, tbls.III, IV (2006), *available at* https://www.
iom.int/sites/default/files/our_work/ICP/IDM/ICMC-Strengthening-Protection-of-
Migrant-Workers-and-Their-Families.pdf (comparing provisions of the Convention on
Migrant Workers to those contained in other international human rights instruments).

127   Convention on Migrant Workers, *supra* note 125, art. 2(1).

For human mobility in the context of climate change, the Convention on Migrant Workers potentially provides protection to persons who move abroad to escape slow onset degradation or sea level rise, although it only provides specific protection in cases where such persons, or a member of their families,[128] engage in paid work.[129] Its potential applicability is further limited by its poor ratification: the Convention on Migrant Workers currently has only 56 parties.[130] Even where the Convention on Migrant Workers does apply, the protection it offers is modest; it does not require States to grant entry to migrant workers or to allow them to stay within the country. The Convention on Migrant Workers does prohibit collective expulsion and requires that individual expulsions follow process of law.[131] As Roger Zetter has observed, however, the Convention does not provide any guidance as to the criteria which States should consider when making a decision on expulsion; it is therefore unclear to what extent, if any, States would take into account climate change impacts in a migrant worker's home State when deciding on expulsion.[132]

---

128    Under the Convention on Migrant Workers, " 'members of the family' refers to persons married to migrant workers or having with them a relationship that, according to applicable law, produces effects equivalent to marriage, as well as their dependent children and other dependent persons who are recognized as members of the family by applicable legislation or applicable bilateral or multilateral agreements between the States concerned". Convention on Migrant Workers, *supra* note 125, art. 4.

129    Some of the rights set forth in the Convention on Migrant Workers are specific to migrant workers, whilst others restate human rights that are contained in other universal human rights treaties or that are considered *jus cogens*, such as the rights to life and prohibition on slavery. *See* Beatriz Felipe Pérez, *Beyond the Shortcomings of International Law, in* 'CLIMATE REFUGEES': BEYOND THE LEGAL IMPASSE?, *supra* note 2, at 214, 217.

130    Depository, Status of Treaties, Chapter IV, 13. International Convention on the Protection of the Rights of All Migrant Workers and Members of Their Families, UN TREATY COLLECTION, https://treaties.un.org/Pages/ViewDetails.aspx?src=TREATY&mtdsg_no=IV-13&chapter=4&clang=_en (last visited 22 May 2021). On the number of parties to other instruments discussed herein, see *supra* note 122. Moreover, as Beatriz Felipe Pérez observes, most States Parties to this treaty are countries of origin and not generally "receiving" States. Pérez, *supra* note 129, at 217.

131    Convention on Migrant Workers, *supra* note 125, arts. 22–24.

132    Roger Zetter, *Protecting Environmentally Displaced People: Developing the Capacity of Legal and Normative Frameworks* 22–23 (Univ. of Oxford, Refugee Studies Ctr. Research Report, Feb. 2011), *available at* https://www.refworld.org/pdfid/4da579792.pdf [hereinafter 'Zetter, *Protecting Environmentally Displaced People*'].

## D      Protection for Internally Displaced Persons

### 1)      *The Guiding Principles on Internal Displacement*

The Guiding Principles on Internal Displacement (Guiding Principles) are a compilation, restatement, and interpretation of existing human rights and humanitarian law relating to the rights of persons displaced internally.[133] The Guiding Principles were elaborated under the supervision of the United Nations Representative to the Secretary-General on Internally Displaced Persons with the assistance of a team of legal experts and in consultation with international organizations and intergovernmental agencies.[134] Although the Guiding Principles are not binding,[135] they are widely recognized as being authoritative.[136] Moreover, the principles expressed in the

---

133     Guiding Principles on Internal Displacement, UN Doc. E/CN.4/1998/53/Add.2 (11 Feb. 1998) [hereinafter 'Guiding Principles']. On the content and legal nature of the Guiding Principles, see generally Walter Kälin, *Guiding Principles on Internal Displacement: Annotations* (ASIL, Studies in Transnational Legal Policy No. 38, 2008), *available at* https://www.brookings.edu/wp-content/uploads/2016/06/spring_guiding_princip les.pdf [hereinafter 'Kälin, *Annotations*']; Walter Kälin, *How Hard is Soft Law? The Guiding Principles on Internal Displacement and the Need for a Normative Framework*, in RECENT COMMENTARIES ABOUT THE NATURE AND APPLICATION OF THE GUIDING PRINCIPLES ON INTERNAL DISPLACEMENT 1 (2002) [hereinafter 'Kälin, *How Hard is Soft Law?*'].

134     For an account of the development of the Guiding Principles, see Roberta Cohen, *The Guiding Principles on Internal Displacement: An Innovation in International Standard Setting*, 10 GLOBAL GOVERNANCE 459, 465–67 (2004); *International Standards*, OHCHR, http://www.ohchr.org/EN/Issues/IDPersons/Pages/Standards.aspx (last visited 22 May 2021).

135     On the legal character of the Guiding Principles, see Kälin, *How Hard is Soft Law?*, *supra* note 133, at 7–10; Robert K. Goldman, *Internal Displacement, the Guiding Principles on Internal Displacement, the Principles Normative Status, and the Need for their Effective Domestic Implementation in Colombia*, 2 COLOMBIAN Y.B. INT'L L. 59, 70–74 (2009); Bartram Brown, *Reconciling State Sovereignty and Protections for the Internally Displaced*, in INVISIBLE REFUGEES: INTERNALLY-DISPLACED PERSONS AND THE NEW UNDERSTANDINGS OF PROTECTION AND SOVEREIGNTY 21, 26–27 (J. Williams ed., 2003).

136     The UN General Assembly has recognized "the Guiding Principles on Internal Displacement as an important international framework for the protection of internally displaced persons, welcome[d] the fact that an increasing number of States, United Nations organizations and regional and non-governmental organizations are applying them as a standard, and encourage[d] all relevant actors to make use of the Guiding Principles when dealing with situations of internal displacement". G.A. Res. 68/180, ¶ 16, UN Doc. A/RES/68/180 (18 Dec. 2003). *See also* G.A. Res. 70/165, ¶¶ 7, 21, UN Doc. A/RES/ 70/165 (17 Dec. 2015); H.R.C. Res. 2004/55, ¶¶ 6, 7, UN Doc. E/CN.4/RES/2004/55 (20 Apr.

Guiding Principles restate and reflect existing, binding international legal principles.[137]

The Guiding Principles comprise thirty principles on the rights of internal displacees at three stages: pre-displacement (prevention/planning), during displacement, and post-displacement (return/relocation/resettlement).[138] Underlying these principles is the fundamental duty of governments to protect their people, including those displaced within their borders.[139]

Application of the Guiding Principles to climate change mobility is of particular importance because it is expected that most of the displacement driven by environmental disasters and climate change impacts will occur within national borders.[140] The Guiding Principles describe internally displaced persons (IDPs) as those:

> who have been forced or obliged to flee or to leave their homes or places of habitual residence, in particular as a result of or in order to avoid the effects of armed conflict, situations of generalized violence, violations of human rights or natural or human-made disasters, and who have not crossed an internationally recognized State border.[141]

---

2004); H.R.C. Res. 2005/46, ¶¶ 7, 8, UN Doc. E/CN.4/RES/2005/46 (20 Apr. 2005); 2005 World Summit Outcome, G.A. Res. 60/1, ¶ 132, UN Doc. A/RES/60/1 (16 Sept. 2005). Wide support has also been given at the regional level and some States have implemented provisions derived from the principles domestically. *See* Goldman, *supra* note 135, at 72–73.

137 *See* Kälin, *Annotations*, *supra* note 133, at 3–5; Kälin, *How Hard is Soft Law?*, *supra* note 133, at 7–10; Goldman, *supra* note 135, at 70–74.

138 For a more detailed description of the contents of the Guiding Principles, see MCADAM, FORCED MIGRATION, *supra* note 78, at 250–52; Goldman, *supra* note 135, at 67–70.

139 Goldman, *supra* note 135, at 67; UNHCR, UNHCR, ENVIRONMENT & CLIMATE CHANGE 9 (Volker Türk et al. eds., updated version, 2015) [hereinafter 'UNHCR, ENVIRONMENT & CLIMATE CHANGE']; Roberta Cohen, *Lessons Learned from the Development of the Guiding Principles on Internal Displacement* 9–10 (Working Paper, Crisis Migration Project, Georgetown University, Oct. 2013), *available at* https://www.brookings.edu/wp-cont ent/uploads/2016/06/Lessons_Learned_GPs_Cohen_Oct2013.pdf [hereinafter 'Cohen, *Lessons Learned*']. This sovereign responsibility is enshrined in the Guiding Principles, *supra* note 133, art. 3(1) ("National authorities have the primary duty and responsibility to provide protection and humanitarian assistance to internally displaced persons within their jurisdiction.") and art. 25(1) ("The primary duty and responsibility for providing humanitarian assistance to internally displaced persons lies with national authorities").

140 *See, e.g.*, UNHCR, ENVIRONMENT & CLIMATE CHANGE, *supra* note 139, at 8, 16; Zetter, *Protecting Environmentally Displaced People*, *supra* note 132, at 21; McAdam et al., *Sea-Level Rise*, *supra* note 33, at 20, ¶ 50.

141 Guiding Principles, *supra* note 133, Introduction, ¶ 2. This is a "descriptive identification" of IDPs and not a legal definition. Being an IDP falling within this description does not,

This description explicitly contemplates natural or human-made disasters as possible triggers for internal displacement. Given this inclusion, there is broad agreement[142] that the Guiding Principles apply to movement within national borders relating to rapid onset hazards, such as hurricanes, earthquakes, and floods, including when such disasters may be attributable to climate change.[143] There is, however, currently no consensus as to whether internal movement relating to slow onset hazards also falls within the scope of the Guiding Principles. Some have questioned whether slow onset hazard impacts can be considered "disasters" falling within the meaning of the explicit text.[144] Even if

in itself, confer any specific legal status or concomitant rights. Kälin, *Annotations, supra* note 133, at 3–5; *see also* Goldman, *supra* note 135, at 67.

142     *But see* Roberta Cohen & Megan Bradley, *Disasters and Displacement: Gaps in Protection*, 1 INT'L HUMANITARIAN LEGAL STUDIES 95, 102–3 (2010) ("In the case of governments, some have been reluctant to call persons uprooted by natural disasters IDPs because they basically perceive IDPs as those displaced by conflict"). This reluctance directly conflicts with the language contained in the Guiding Principles, but such language is ultimately not binding. *See also* Robin Bronen, *Climate-Induced Community Relocations: Creating an Adaptive Governance Framework Based in Human Rights Doctrine*, 35 N.Y.U. REV. L. & SOC. CHANGE 357, 395–96 (2011) [hereinafter 'Bronen, *Climate-Induced Community Relocations*'] (noting that the Guiding Principles "are based primarily on population displacement caused by ethnic and political violence").

143     *See, e.g.,* Kälin, *Conceptualising, supra* note 115, at 87; Margareta Wahlström, *Chairperson's Summary, in* The Nansen Conference, Oslo, Norway, 6–7 June 2011, *Climate Change and Displacement in the 21st Century*, at 18, 19, ¶ 19 (*text by* Christian Gahre), *available at* https://www.unhcr.org/4ea969729.pdf; UNHCR, Bellagio Roundtable Summary, *supra* note 39, at 5, ¶ 19; Fabrice G. Renaud et al., *A Decision Framework for Environmentally Induced Migration*, 49 INT'L MIGRATION e5, e14 (2011); MCADAM, FORCED MIGRATION, *supra* note 78, at 99, n.2 (noting that the Kampala Convention (discussed *infra*) explicitly addresses movement related to climate change and opining that this is essentially an elaboration of the criteria under the Guiding Principles).

144     *See* UNHCR, Bellagio Roundtable Summary, *supra* note 39, at 5, ¶ 19 (considering that the Guiding Principles apply to slow onset hazard impacts and there is therefore no gap in this respect); Khaled Hassine, *Implementation, in* REPAIRING DOMESTIC CLIMATE DISPLACEMENT: THE PENINSULA PRINCIPLES 153, 157 (Scott Leckie & Chris Huggins eds., 2016) ("[T]his is one of the major lacunae of the Guiding Principles as a framework applicable to climate displacement, they do not apply to internal displacement as a result of slow-onset disasters, but are limited to internally displaced persons (IDPs) uprooted by sudden-onset disasters."); Renaud et al., *supra* note 143, at e15 (opining that the Guiding Principles may be applicable to movement related to slow onset impacts); European Commission, *Commission Staff Working Document: Climate Change, Environmental Degradation, and Migration*, at 17, SWD (2013) 138 final (16 Apr. 2013) ("even if the list of persons covered by the principles is not exhaustive, it is not clear whether those who migrate due to gradual processes of degradation can be included"); Kälin, *Conceptualising, supra* note 115, at 89–90 (considering that slow onset mobility in connection with slow onset hazards may fall within the scope of the Guiding Principles if and when it becomes

slow onset hazard impacts cannot be considered "disasters", the list of potential triggers included in the IDP description is demonstrative and not exhaustive in nature.[145] Although the drafters did not explicitly contemplate slow onset hazards as a potential trigger, their intent was to create a flexible description which would encompass displacement triggers they had not anticipated.[146] To the extent that the Guiding Principles address displacement triggered by certain climate change impacts, slow onset or otherwise,[147] they generally restate and reflect universally applicable rights. There is therefore little reason to artificially narrow the scope of the Guiding Principles to exclude categorically movement relating to slow onset hazards or other unspecified environmental triggers.

Another key factor in the IDP description is that the movement must be involuntary;[148] thus, the Guiding Principles describe IDPs as persons who "have been *forced* or *obliged to flee* or to leave their homes".[149] As discussed earlier, there is little common ground as to how the nature of movement as voluntary or involuntary in such cases can be discerned, particularly in relation to slow onset hazards; the Guiding Principles do not themselves provide any guidance in this respect.

At the same time and notwithstanding the criterion of forced movement, the Guiding Principles contain guidance which applies even prior to displacement. In particular, principles five through nine on "Protection from Displacement" set forth rights relevant to the prevention of displacement and affirm procedural rights for those who must be displaced. Amongst other applications, these procedural rights may be pertinent to planned relocations (in relation to climate change impacts or otherwise), such as rights

forced); Roger Zetter, *Protecting People Displaced by Climate Change: Some Conceptual Challenges, in* CLIMATE CHANGE AND DISPLACEMENT: MULTIDISCIPLINARY PERSPECTIVES, *supra* note 6, at 143 (noting that it is "yet to be fully accepted" that slow onset hazard impacts can be called disasters).

145 Kälin, *Annotations, supra* note 133, at 4; Cohen, *Lessons Learned, supra* note 139, at 9.

146 Cohen, *Lessons Learned, supra* note 139, at 9.

147 This is not to say that the Guiding Principles are substantively sufficient to address all potential aspects of mobility related to slow onset hazard events, given that the drafters did not anticipate this as a driver of internal displacement.

148 *See* Cohen & Bradley, *supra* note 142, at 104; Kälin, *Conceptualising, supra* note 115, at 89–90; Koko Warner et al., *Changing Climate, Moving People: Framing Migration, Displacement and Planned Relocation* 40 (UNU-EHS Publication Series, Policy Brief No. 8, June 2013), *available at* https://i.unu.edu/media/migration.unu.edu/publication/229/Policybrief_8_web.pdf.

149 Guiding Principles, *supra* note 133, ¶ 2 (emphasis added).

to participation and access to information during the planning stages of a relocation.[150]

## 2)    *The Kampala Convention*

The African Union Convention for the Protection and Assistance of Internally Displaced Persons in Africa (Kampala Convention) was adopted on 23 October 2009 and entered into force on 6 December 2012.[151] The Kampala Convention draws and in some ways expands upon the Guiding Principles.[152] Like the Guiding Principles, the Kampala Convention provides for protection at three stages: pre-displacement, during displacement, and post-displacement.[153] Unlike the Guiding Principles, the Kampala Convention is binding on States Parties.[154]

The Kampala Convention is noteworthy, amongst other reasons, for being commonly considered the first international instrument to link explicitly displacement to climate change.[155] Article 5(4) of the Kampala Convention requires that "States Parties shall take measures to protect and assist persons who have been internally displaced due to natural or human made disasters, *including climate change*".[156] This is in contrast to the Guiding Principles, which refer to "natural or human made disasters" but do not explicitly include climate change impacts in the scope of disasters which trigger protection obligations. The Kampala Convention's definition of IDP s, however, is identical to the description of IDP s contained in the Guiding Principles and does not itself make explicit reference to climate change.[157]

---

150    *Id.* art. 7(3). This is not to say, however, that the Guiding Principles provide sufficient operational guidance in the case of planned relocations. In this respect, see McAdam et al., *Sea-Level Rise, supra* note 33, at 29, ¶ 78; Bronen, *Climate-Induced Community Relocations, supra* note 142, at 395–98 (setting forth reasons as to why the Guiding Principles are inadequate to address planned relocation in the context of climate change).

151    African Union, Kampala Declaration on Refugees, Returnees and Internally Displaced Persons in Africa (Kampala Convention), 23 Oct. 2009, Ext/Assembly/AU/PA/Draft/Decl. (I) Rev.1 [hereinafter 'Kampala Convention'].

152    *See* Maria Stavropoulou, *The Kampala Convention and Protection from Arbitrary Displacement*, 36 FORCED MIGRATION REV. 62, 63 (2010).

153    *Id.* at 62–63. The Guiding Principles are discussed *supra.*

154    States Parties must incorporate their obligations under the Convention into domestic law. Kampala Convention, *supra* note 151, art. 3(2)(a).

155    However, the United Nations Convention to Combat Desertification (UNCCD), discussed *infra*, pre-dates the Kampala Convention and can also be considered to link climate change and displacement. *See* Michelle Leighton, *Desertification and Migration, in* GOVERNING GLOBAL DESERTIFICATION: LINKING ENVIRONMENTAL DEGRADATION, POVERTY AND PARTICIPATION 43, 49 (Pierre Marc Johnson et al. eds., 2006).

156    Emphasis added.

157    Kampala Convention, *supra* note 151, art. 1(k); Guiding Principles, *supra* note 133, ¶ 2.

Notwithstanding the reference to climate change in Article 5(4) and the significance of this explicit acknowledgement of the link between climate change and internal displacement, the language of the Kampala Convention arguably does not provide for a wider scope of application than the Guiding Principles. According to its definition of IDPs in Article 1(k) and the language of Article 5(4), the Kampala Convention applies in the context of internal displacement caused by "natural or human made disasters". The Guiding Principles also apply in the context of "natural or human made disasters", which is generally understood to include those related to climate change. There is widespread agreement that rapid onset hazard impacts such as hurricanes, earthquakes, and floods (including those that are climate change driven) are "disasters" within the meaning of the Guiding Principles and also, presumably, the Kampala Convention. As noted above in relation to the Guiding Principles, whether slow onset hazard impacts, including sea level rise, can be considered "disasters" falling within the explicit language—or otherwise fall within the scope—of the Guiding Principles (or the Kampala Convention) is an open question. The text of the Kampala Convention does not completely resolve this ambiguity: it confirms that disasters are covered when they are caused by climate change but does not clarify which kinds of climate change impacts fall within the scope of "disasters". Nor does the Kampala Convention clarify whether climate change impacts that may not be considered "disasters", but that trigger displacement, may nevertheless give rise to protection. The significance of including express reference to climate change in Article 5(4) of the Kampala Convention therefore lies in its explicit acknowledgement of the connection between displacement and climate change and not necessarily in the scope of protection it offers.

∴

The Guiding Principles and the Kampala Convention address internal displacement on international and regional levels, respectively. Forced movement following rapid onset hazards falls within the scope of both the Guiding Principles and the Kampala Convention, whereas their application in the case of slow onset hazard events is debatable and has been identified by some as a potential "gap". The Kampala Convention is noteworthy for its explicit mention of the role of climate change in driving internal displacement, although this does not necessarily broaden the scope of its application. The Kampala Convention is binding on States Parties and must be incorporated into their national laws. The Guiding Principles reflect and restate existing international principles, but are non-binding and do not themselves confer any enforceable rights or protection to IDPs. They could not therefore act as the singular basis for legal action, although they remain highly influential.

## E     The Human Rights Framework

Climate change impacts threaten to interfere with enjoyment of the most fundamental human rights, including the rights to life, adequate food and water, health, adequate housing, and self-determination.[158] Vulnerable populations, such as women, children, indigenous persons, disabled persons, and those living in poverty, will suffer the effects of climate change impacts most intensely.[159] Affected persons may move in response to the threats to their rights. At the same time, challenges arising in connection with mitigation and adaptation efforts—including human mobility—may themselves contribute to interference with some of these human rights. It is therefore essential that any mitigation and adaptation efforts be undertaken in a manner that ensures the protection of fundamental human rights.

Fundamental human rights are enshrined in a number of international instruments, including the Universal Declaration of Human Rights, the International Covenant on Civil and Political Rights, and the International Covenant on Economic, Social and Cultural Rights, as well as a number of regional instruments, such as the American Convention on Human Rights, the African Charter on Human and Peoples' Rights, the European Convention for the Protection of Human Rights and Fundamental Freedoms, and the Arab Charter on Human Rights.[160] In addition to these human rights

---

158     A 2009 report by the United Nations High Commissioner for Human Rights details the potential implications that climate change will have on the enjoyment of human rights and the instruments in which those rights are contained. OHCHR, *Report on the Relationship Between Climate Change and Human Rights*, ¶¶ 20–41, Human Rights Council, 10th Sess., UN Doc A/HRC/10/61 (15 Jan. 2009) [hereinafter 'OHCHR Climate Change Report']. *See also* Siobhán McInerney-Lankford, *Climate Change and Human Rights: An Introduction to Legal Issues*, 33(2) HARV. ENVTL L. REV. 431, 436 (2009).

159     OHCHR Climate Change Report, *supra* note 158, ¶¶ 42–54; McInerney-Lankford, *supra* note 158, at 436.

160     Universal Declaration of Human Rights, G.A. Res. 217 (III) A, UN Doc. A/RES/217(III) (10 Dec. 1948) [hereinafter 'UDHR']; International Covenant on Civil and Political Rights, 19 Dec. 1966, 999 U.N.T.S. 171 [hereinafter 'ICCPR']; International Covenant on Economic, Social and Cultural Rights, 16 Dec. 1966, 993 U.N.T.S. 3 [hereinafter 'ICESCR']; American Convention on Human Rights "Pact of San Jose, Costa Rica", 22 Nov. 1969, 1144 U.N.T.S. 123 [hereinafter 'ACHR']; African Charter on Human and Peoples' Rights, 27 June 1981, 1520 U.N.T.S. 217 [hereinafter 'African Charter']; Convention for the Protection of Human Rights and Fundamental Freedoms, 4 Nov. 1950, 213 U.N.T.S. 221 [hereinafter 'ECHR'];

instruments—which are not restricted to a defined group of persons—some instruments aim to protect the human rights of specific groups of vulnerable persons, such as the United Nations Convention on the Rights of the Child, the Convention on the Rights of Persons with Disabilities, the Convention on the Elimination of All Forms of Discrimination against Women, and the Declaration on the Rights of Indigenous Peoples.[161] Many of these instruments are legally binding on States Parties and may be enforced before international decision-making bodies, whilst others are declaratory in nature, nonetheless forming part of the general body of international law.

Unlike, for example, asylum treaties, which aim to protect defined groups of persons under specific circumstances, the fundamental rights protected by universal human rights treaties (i.e., those which are not limited geographically or restricted to a defined group of persons), such as the International Covenants on Civil and Political Rights and on Economic, Social and Cultural Rights, apply universally to persons within the territory of States Parties, excepting only legitimate derogations, exceptions, or limitations.[162] The rights protected by these general treaties therefore apply to persons who move in connection with climate change, internally or internationally, within the territory of States Parties.

The protection of all human rights is crucial in the context of climate change impacts and responses. For the purposes of examining the scope of protection that may be provided by human rights law for climate change mobility, this chapter will focus on three foundational human rights. Although certainly far from the only applicable rights, these three human rights may have particular relevance to persons moving in the context of

League of Arab States, Arab Charter on Human Rights, 22 May 2004 (entered into force 15 Mar. 2008), reprinted in 12 INT'L HUM. RTS. REP. 893 (2005).

161   Convention on the Rights of the Child, 20 Nov. 1989, 1577 U.N.T.S. 3; Convention on the Rights of Persons with Disabilities, G.A. Res 61/106, UN Doc. A/RES/61/106 (24 Jan. 2007); Convention on the Elimination of All Forms of Discrimination against Women, 18 Dec. 1979, 1249 U.N.T.S. 13; Declaration on the Rights of Indigenous Peoples, G.A. Res. 61/295, UN Doc. A/RES/61/295 (2 Oct. 2007).

162   See UDHR, supra note 160, art. 29(2) ("In the exercise of his rights and freedoms, everyone shall be subject only to such limitations as are determined by law solely for the purpose of securing due recognition and respect for the rights and freedoms of others and of meeting the just requirements of morality, public order and the general welfare in a democratic society."); see also Benoît Mayer & Christel Cournil, Climate Change, Migration and Human Rights: Towards Group-Specific Protection?, in CLIMATE CHANGE AND HUMAN RIGHTS: AN INTERNATIONAL LAW PERSPECTIVE 173, 176 (Ottavio Quirico & Mouloud Boumghar eds., 2015).

climate change: the rights to self-determination, freedom of movement, and life.[163]

### 1)    *Self-Determination*

The right to self-determination is a fundamental human right, enshrined in several international treaties. The substantive nature of self-determination and the rights it may ensure have evolved over time and will vary depending upon the circumstances. Climate change impacts may threaten self-determination rights, particularly for inhabitants of small island States and indigenous populations who risk losing their native lands. In such cases, climate change mobility as an adaptation strategy may itself impact self-determination rights. The pathways to enforcing self-determination rights in this context are, as of now, untested and uncertain.

a          From Political Principle to Universal Human Right

With historic roots in political principles dating back to the American Declaration of Independence (1776) and the French Revolution (1789),[164] the right to self-determination has undergone significant development since its appearance as a legal principle in Article 1(2) of the 1945 Charter of the United Nations, which states that one of "[t]he Purposes of the United Nations" is "[t]o develop friendly relations among nations based on respect for the principle of equal rights and self-determination of peoples, and to take other appropriate measures to strengthen universal peace".[165] The right to self-determination became a cornerstone for decolonization in the 1960s.[166] Its status as a

---

163    For a discussion of other human rights which may be impacted by climate change and human mobility, see generally OHCHR Climate Change Report, *supra* note 158.

164    On the historical origins of self-determination, see Joshua Castellino, INTERNATIONAL LAW AND SELF-DETERMINATION: THE INTERPLAY OF THE POLITICS OF TERRITORIAL POSSESSION WITH FORMULATIONS OF POST-COLONIAL 'NATIONAL' IDENTITY 11–18 (2000); Michael Freeman, *The Right to Self-Determination: Philosophical and Legal Perspectives*, 31(2) NEW ENG. J. PUB. POL'Y, Art. 4 (2019).

165    A similar notion appears in Article 55 of the UN Charter: "With a view to the creation of conditions of stability and well-being which are necessary for peaceful and friendly relations among nations based on respect for the principle of equal rights and self-determination of peoples, the United Nations shall promote: 1. higher standards of living, full employment, and conditions of economic and social progress and development; 2. solutions of international economic, social, health, and related problems; and international cultural and educational cooperation; and 3. universal respect for, and observance of, human rights and fundamental freedoms for all without distinction as to race, sex, language, or religion."

166    *See* Matthew Saul, *The Normative Status of Self-Determination in International Law: A Formula for Uncertainty in the Scope and Content of the Right?*, 11(4) HUM. RTS L. REV.

universal human right extending to all peoples, and not only to those subject to external domination, was confirmed by its inclusion in the 1966 International Covenant on Civil and Political Rights (ICCPR) and International Covenant on Economic, Social and Cultural Rights (ICESCR).[167] Notwithstanding, debate as to whether the right to self-determination applies beyond the colonial context, and in what way, persisted for decades after the completion of the ICCPR and the ICESCR.[168] The practical application of self-determination rights continues to be the subject of academic discussion and legal uncertainty today.

Self-determination is enshrined in Article 1 of both the ICCPR and the ICESCR, in identical fashion:

1. All peoples have the right of self-determination. By virtue of that right they freely determine their political status and freely pursue their economic, social and cultural development.

2. All peoples may, for their own ends, freely dispose of their natural wealth and resources without prejudice to any obligations arising out of international economic co-operation, based upon the principle of mutual benefit, and international law. In no case may a people be deprived of its own means of subsistence.

3. The States Parties to the present Covenant, including those having responsibility for the administration of Non-Self-Governing and Trust Territories, shall promote the realization of the right of self-determination, and shall respect that right, in conformity with the provisions of the Charter of the United Nations.

---

609, 613–614 (2011); Declaration on the Granting of Independence to Colonial Countries and Peoples, G.A. Res. 1514 (XV), ¶ 2, UN Doc. A/RES/1514(XV) (14 Dec. 1960), ("All peoples have the right to self-determination; by virtue of that right they freely determine their political status and freely pursue their economic, social and cultural development."); Declaration on Principles of International Law Concerning Friendly Relations and Co-operation Among States in Accordance with the Charter of the United Nations, Annex, G.A. Res. 2625 (XXV), UN Doc. A/RES/2625(XXV) (24 Oct. 1970) ("Every State has the duty to refrain from any forcible action which deprives peoples referred to in the elaboration of the principle of equal rights and self-determination of their right to self-determination and freedom and independence." [...] "Every State has the duty to promote, through joint and separate action, realization of the principle of equal rights and self-determination of peoples, in accordance with the provisions of the Charter, and to render assistance to the United Nations in carrying out the responsibilities entrusted to it by the Charter regarding the implementation of the principle").

167   ICCPR, *supra* note 160; ICESCR, *supra* note 160.

168   *See* Robert McCorquodale, *Self-Determination: A Human Rights Approach*, 43(4) INT'L & COMP. L.Q. 857, 859–863 (1994) ("There is less consensus as to whether this right [to self-determination] can be applied to non-colonial situations." (quotation at 860)).

Self-determination is the only right included in both the ICCPR and ICESCR and is also the only collective (as opposed to individual) right expressed in either Covenant.[169] Its inclusion in both Covenants confirms that the right to self-determination comprises both political as well as economic, social, and cultural dimensions. Self-determination is also understood as having "external" and "internal" aspects, i.e., the right to independence from external domination and the right to choose one's government, respectively. Abdulqawi Yusuf, former President of the International Court of Justice, argues that the UN Charter also introduced a "third strand" of self-determination—the right to socio-economic self-determination: "This is the right of peoples freely to pursue their economic, social, and cultural development, and to participate, contribute to, and enjoy such development."[170] The position of the principles of self-determination as the first article in each Covenant reflects its fundamental importance as a gateway to the enjoyment of other, individual human rights.[171]

The Human Rights Committee, the body responsible for monitoring implementation of the ICCPR, has clarified that paragraph 3 of Article 1 imposes positive obligations on States Parties to promote self-determination of all peoples, regardless of whether such peoples are dependent upon the State.[172] The International Court of Justice has also confirmed that the right to self-determination is an *erga omnes* obligation, i.e., one that is owed by all States "towards the international community as a whole".[173] Self-determination is also arguably a peremptory, or *jus cogens*,[174] norm, although this is still the

---

169   James Summers, *The Right of Peoples to Self-Determination in Article 1 of the Human Rights Covenants as a Claimable Right*, 31(2) NEW ENG. J. PUB. POL'Y, art. 5, 2 (2019).

170   Abdulqawi A. Yusuf, *The Role that Equal Rights and Self-Determination of Peoples can Play in the Current World Community, in* REALIZING UTOPIA: THE FUTURE OF INTERNATIONAL LAW 375, 377 (Antonio Cassese ed., 2012).

171   UN Human Rights Committee, *CCPR General Comment No. 12: Article 1 (Right to Self-Determination): The Right to Self-determination of Peoples*, ¶ 1, UN Doc. HRI/GEN/1/Rev.6 (13 Mar. 1984) [hereinafter 'HRC General Comment 12'].

172   *Id.* ¶ 6.

173   The International Court of Justice explained the nature of *erga omnes* obligations in Barcelona Traction, Light and Power Company Limited (Belg. v Spain), 1970 I.C.J. 1, at 32, ¶ 33 (5 Feb. 1970). For a discussion on the *erga omnes* status of the right to self-determination and the consequences flowing from this, see Saul, *supra* note 166, at 631–633.

174   "[A] peremptory norm of general international law [*jus cogens*] is a norm accepted and recognized by the international community of States as a whole as a norm from which no derogation is permitted and which can be modified only by a subsequent norm of general international law having the same character." Vienna Convention on the Law of Treaties art. 53, 23 May 1969, 1155 U.N.T.S. 331. *Jus cogens* are also "hierarchically superior to other rules" of international law. International Law Commission, *Second Report on* Jus Cogens, at 12, ¶ 23, UN Doc A/CN.4/706 (16 Mar. 2017) (*by* Dire Tladi, Special Rapporteur).

subject of some debate.[175] At the same time, and despite its essential nature, the right to self-determination is subject to limitation. Any exercise of the right to self-determination must not impinge on the rights of others.[176] Outside of the decolonization paradigm, the exercise of the right to self-determination will generally not, absent exceptional circumstances (which have been found in some cases), justify disturbing territorial integrity and is not tantamount to a right to secession.[177] Any action taken by States Parties to promote or respect self-determination must be consistent with other obligations under the Charter of the United Nations and international law.[178]

The right to self-determination also appears in later human rights instruments, including in the 1981 African Charter on Human and Peoples' Rights (African Charter) as Article 20:

> 1.  All peoples shall have the right to existence. They shall have the unquestionable and inalienable right to self-determination. They shall freely determine their political status and shall pursue their economic and social development according to the policy they have freely chosen.

---

175   Self-determination has been referred to as a peremptory norm by authoritative voices. *See, e.g.*, International Law Commission, *Fourth Report on Peremptory Norms of General International Law* (jus cogens), at 63, ¶ 137, UN Doc. A/CN.4/727 (31 Jan. 2019) (*by* Dire Tladi, Special Rapporteur) ("the most widely recognized examples of peremptory norms of general international law (*jus cogens*) are: [...] the right to self-determination [...]"). For a discussion on whether self-determination is a peremptory norm and the consequences thereof, see Hector Gros Espiell, *Self-Determination and Jus Cogens, in* UN LAW, FUNDAMENTAL RIGHTS: TWO TOPICS IN INTERNATIONAL LAW 167, 167–171 (Antonio Cassese ed., 1979); Saul, *supra* note 166, at 634–641.

176   *See* McCorquodale, *supra* note 168, at 876–878.

177   *See id.* at 879–880 ("[T]he territorial integrity limitation cannot be asserted in all situations. [...] [A] government of a State which does not represent the whole population on its territory without discrimination [...] cannot succeed in limiting the right of self-determination on the basis that it would infringe that State's territorial integrity."); *see also* Katangese Peoples' Congress v. Zaire, African Commission on Human & People's Rights, Communication No. 75/92 (1995), ¶¶ 5–6 [hereinafter 'Katanga Decision'] ("The Commission is obligated to uphold the sovereignty and territorial integrity of Zaire [...]. In the absence of concrete evidence of violations of human rights to the point that the territorial integrity of Zaire should be called to question and in the absence of evidence that the people of Katanga are denied the right to participate in government as guaranteed by Article 13(1) of the African Charter, the Commission holds the view that Katanga is obliged to exercise a variant of self-determination that is compatible with the sovereignty and territorial integrity of Zaire.").

178   ICCPR, *supra* note 160, art 1(3). HRC General Comment 12, *supra* note 171, ¶ 6.

2.   Colonized or oppressed peoples shall have the right to free them-
     selves from the bonds of domination by resorting to any means rec-
     ognized by the international community.
3.   All peoples shall have the right to the assistance of the States par-
     ties to the present Charter in their liberation struggle against foreign
     domination, be it political, economic or cultural.[179]

Unlike the ICCPR and ICESCR, the African Charter specifically states in paragraph 2 of Article 20 that the right to self-determination includes freedom
from colonization or foreign domination. Also, the language in paragraph
3 of Article 20 suggests that, under the African Charter, the positive obligations incumbent on States Parties require the provision of assistance to
those subject to foreign domination, and not necessarily to protecting and
promoting self-determination in general. Finally, Article 1(2) in the ICCPR/
ICESCR includes the provision that "all peoples may, for their own ends,
freely dispose of their natural wealth and resources". Under the African
Charter, similar language is included, in elaborated fashion, as a separate
Article—Article 21.

The 2007 United Nations Declaration on the Rights of Indigenous Peoples
includes the right to self-determination under Articles 3 and 4:

3.   Indigenous peoples have the right to self-determination. By virtue of
     that right they freely determine their political status and freely pur-
     sue their economic, social and cultural development.
4.   Indigenous peoples, in exercising their right to self-determination,
     have the right to autonomy or self-government in matters relating to
     their internal and local affairs, as well as ways and means for financ-
     ing their autonomous functions.

Unlike the ICCPR, ICESCR, and African Charter, the United Nations Declaration
on the Rights of Indigenous Peoples provides that the exercise of self-determination includes autonomy or self-government for internal and local affairs.
Also unlike the ICCPR, ICESCR, and African Charter, the United Nations
Declaration on the Rights of Indigenous Peoples is declaratory in nature and
not binding.

---

179   African Charter, *supra* note 160, art. 20.

b        Climate Change Mobility and Self-Determination

Human mobility in the context of climate change can threaten both political and socio-economic aspects of self-determination.[180] As discussed above
in the context of protection for stateless persons, it is uncertain whether a
nation that has lost most or all of its habitable territory can continue to exist
as a "State". Climate change impacts that threaten the territorial integrity of
nations, such as small island developing States, therefore also threaten the
right to political self-determination.[181] A people may not be able to freely dispose of their natural wealth and resources, nor freely pursue their economic,
social, or cultural development, if they are deprived of their territory and must
move.[182] Loss of territory is all the more detrimental to self-determination
where the cultural identity and livelihood of indigenous peoples and inhabitants of small island States tend to be inextricably tied to the land.[183] Losing
this land to climate change impacts or leaving this land may therefore hinder
the political, cultural, and socio-economic self-determination of such peoples.

---

180  *See, e.g.*, Bordner, *supra* note 121, at 224–229 (arguing that, by losing their territory through
     collective migration, Marshallese islanders would lose territorial sovereignty and, con-
     sequently, their political self-determination, as well as their sovereignty over natural
     resources); Tekau Frere et al., *Climate Change and Challenges to Self-Determination: Case
     Studies from French Polynesia and the Republic of Kiribati*, THE YALE LAW JOURNAL
     FORUM 648, 667–671 (24 Feb. 2020), https://www.yalelawjournal.org/forum/climate-cha
     nge-and-challenges-to-self-determination (arguing that Kiribati, not wishing its people
     to "lose connections with their ancestral land", has embraced adaptation policies that will
     allow its citizens to continue to live on their land and that this approach is consistent with
     self-determination (quotation at 667)); D. Kapuaʻala Sproat, *An Indigenous People's Right
     to Environmental Self-Determination: Native Hawaiians and the Struggle Against Climate
     Change Devastation*, 35(2) STAN. ENVTL. L.J. 157, 165 (2016) ("The decision to stay or move
     raises significant political, legal, and cultural issues and, for some, neither adaptation nor
     migration is an option because indigenous identity and entire cultures and ways of life
     are inextricably bound to specific lands and resources."); Rights of Indigenous People in
     Addressing Climate Forced Displacement, Complaint submitted by the Alaska Institute
     for Justice on behalf of Tribes of Alaska and Louisiana to the UN Special Rapporteur on
     the Human Rights of Internally Displaced Persons et al., at 12 (15 Jan. 2020) [hereinaf-
     ter 'Rights of Indigenous People Complaint'] ("The right to self-determination is the
     most important principle to protect, promote and fulfill in the context of climate-forced
     displacement.").
181  *See* Bordner, *supra* note 121, at 224–229. *See also* Frank Dietrich & Joachim Wündisch,
     *Territory Lost—Climate Change and the Violation of Self-determination Rights*, 2(1) MORAL
     PHIL. & POL. 83, 85–86, 103 (2015) (arguing, from a philosophical perspective, that "terri-
     tory is a necessary condition for exercising the right to political self-determination").
182  Bordner, *supra* note 121, at 224–229.
183  *Id.*; Sproat, *supra* note 180, at 164–166.

Inhabitants of small island States and indigenous persons are therefore faced with options of staying on land that eventually may be destroyed by climate change impacts or trying to leave to resettle on non-native lands—which may also threaten their political, cultural, and economic self-determination.[184] Moving away from their homes could deprive indigenous populations of lands tied to their culture and identity, potentially disperse communities, and/or subject inhabitants to political rule not of their choosing. In the face of these choices, some peoples are committed to *in situ* adaptation.[185] Others have decided to move, attempted to move, or have already moved.[186]

The choice of inhabitants of threatened lands to attempt *in situ* adaptation measures or to move will impact their political and cultural identity, as well as their socio-economic opportunity, and therefore falls within the scope of their self-determination rights. These threats to self-determination may raise obligations for the entire international community, as States have positive obligations, under the ICCPR and ICESCR,[187] to promote and respect self-determination for all peoples, including those outside their territories.

---

184    *See* Sproat, *supra* note 180, at 165.

185    *See* Bordner, *supra* note 121, at 198–200; Frere et al., *supra* note 180, at 667–671.

186    *See, e.g.*, Sarah M. Munoz, *Understanding the Human Side of Climate Change Relocation*, THE CONVERSATION (6 June 2019), https://theconversation.com/understanding-the-human-side-of-climate-change-relocation-115887 (discussing the plight of the inhabitants of the Carteret Islands, who face severe climate change impacts as well as political struggles: "The autonomous government [of the Region of Bougainville] did make a few relocation attempts in 1984 and 1997, but poor planning and a lack of resources contributed to their failure. Local communities now have little trust in their governments, which they perceive as an 'alien external force.'"); Scott Leckie, *Using Human Rights to Resolve the Climate Displacement Problem: The Promise of the Peninsula Principles*, *in* REPAIRING DOMESTIC CLIMATE DISPLACEMENT: THE PENINSULA PRINCIPLES, *supra* note 144, at 1, 2 (giving examples of population movements or relocation planning already underway: "Thousands of members of the Guna indigenous group in Panama are moving from their Caribbean island homes to the mainland as their traditional villages are slowly inundated. People in the Solomon Islands have begun evacuating long-inhabited settlements for safer areas. Inhabitants of Newtok village in the US state of Alaska have begun their trek to nearby Nelson Island because of severe erosion making their home village no longer habitable. The Carteret Islanders in Papua New Guinea have slowly begun their relocation to the larger island of Bougainville, while the Fijian government has identified 676 villages in need of relocation. Small island states such as Kiribati, the Maldives, the Marshall Islands and Tuvalu which rightfully receive the lion's share of media attention on the looming demise of their islands and atolls, of course, are already putting plans into place which ultimately envisage the entire evacuation of their beloved island homes.").

187    As noted *supra*, it is unclear whether the provisions on self-determination included in the African Charter impose a positive obligation on States Parties to promote self-determination beyond the context of decolonization.

Interpreting these obligations broadly, States have a duty, pursuant to the right to self-determination, to mitigate climate change impacts and to assist with adaptation measures that might protect the right to self-determination.[188] The international community therefore has a positive duty, pursuant to the ICCPR and ICESCR, to respect and assist *in situ* adaptation or relocation measures, as decided by and in consultation with affected peoples, as fundamental to their right to self-determination.[189] Any relocation measures would also have to be undertaken in consultation with affected peoples and in view of their rights to self-determination.[190] The extent of these State obligations and the limitations thereon are, however, currently untested and undefined. There is therefore some uncertainty as to what precisely these obligations may require in practice.

c        Enforcing Self-Determination Rights

The right to self-determination includes positive obligations for States Parties that are relevant to human mobility in the context of climate change, particularly under the ICCPR and ICESCR. Insofar as members of the international community do not respect and promote the right to self-determination, these obligations are, at least in theory, enforceable in some venues. Adjudication could also prove utile insofar as the extent of State obligations in connection with self-determination and climate change mobility are, at present, undefined.

The self-determination rights presented in the ICCPR, the ICESCR, and the African Charter are essential and binding on States Parties. The Human Rights Committee; the Committee on Economic, Social and Cultural Rights; and the African Commission on Human and People's Rights (African Commission) oversee the implementation of these treaties, respectively. These bodies may consider and decide upon, under some circumstances, allegations of rights violations by States Parties. Thus far none of these mechanisms has considered the intersection between self-determination rights, human mobility, and climate change.

---

188    OHCHR Climate Change Report, *supra* note 158, at 14–15, ¶ 41 ("While there is no clear precedence to follow, it is clear that insofar as climate change poses a threat to the right of peoples to self-determination, States have a duty to take positive action, individually and jointly, to address and avert this threat. Equally, States have an obligation to take action to avert climate change impacts which threaten the cultural and social identity of indigenous peoples.").

189    *See id.*; Robin Bronen, *Climate Displacement: Preparation and Planning, in* REPAIRING DOMESTIC CLIMATE DISPLACEMENT: THE PENINSULA PRINCIPLES, *supra* note 144, at 89, 93–94 [hereinafter 'Bronen, *Climate Displacement*'].

190    Bronen, *Climate Displacement, supra* note 189, at 93–94.

Under the first Optional Protocol to the ICCPR, the Human Rights Committee may "receive and consider communications from individuals subject to its jurisdiction who claim to be victims of a violation by that State Party of any of the rights set forth in the Covenant", provided that the State in question is a party to the Optional Protocol.[191] The Human Rights Committee, however, has firmly taken the position that individuals may not transmit communications alleging violations of the right to self-determination contained in Article 1, which is a collective right.[192] Given its repeated affirmation of this position, the Human Rights Committee does not seem to be a fertile avenue for enforcing self-determination rights in connection with climate change mobility.

The Committee on Economic, Social and Cultural Rights is the body that monitors implementation of the ICESCR. It may receive and consider communications "by or on behalf of individuals or groups of individuals, under the jurisdiction of a State Party, claiming to be victims of a violation of any of the economic, social and cultural rights set forth in the Covenant by that State Party," again provided that the State in question is a party to the ICESCR's Optional Protocol.[193] The ICESCR's 2008 Optional Protocol is more recent than the ICCPR's 1966 Optional Protocol. The drafters of the ICESCR Optional Protocol therefore had the opportunity to consider issues that had already been put before the Human Rights Committee. Considering a draft of the ICESCR's Optional Protocol, the Committee on Economic, Social and Cultural Rights recommended "that the optional protocol should apply in relation to all of the economic, social and cultural rights set forth in the Covenant and that this would include all the rights contained in articles 1 to 15 [i.e., including self-determination]", provided, "however, that the right to self-determination should be dealt with under this procedure only in so far as economic, social and cultural rights dimensions of that right are involved."[194] The Committee

---

191   Optional Protocol to the International Covenant on Civil and Political Rights art. 1, 16 Dec. 1966, 999 U.N.T.S. 171.

192   Ivan Kitok v. Sweden, Human Rights Committee, Communication No. 197/1985, CCPR/ C/33/D/197/1985 (1988), ¶ 6.3; E. P. et al. v. Colombia, Human Rights Committee, Communication No. 318/1988, CCPR/C/39/D/318/1988 (1990), ¶ 8.2; A. B. et al. v. Italy (South Tyrol), Human Rights Committee, Communication No. 413/1990, CCPR/C/40/D/ 413/1990 (1990), ¶ 3.2; R. L. et al. v Canada, Human Rights Committee, Communication No. 358/1989, CCPR/C/43/D/358/1989 (1991), ¶ 6.2. For a discussion of this jurisprudence, see Summers, supra note 169, at 2–3.

193   Optional Protocol to the International Covenant on Economic, Social and Cultural Rights arts. 1 & 2, G.A. Res. 63/117, UN Doc. A/RES/63/117 (10 Dec. 2008).

194   UN Secretary-General, Note: Status of the International Covenants on Human Rights: Draft Optional Protocol to the International Covenant on Economic, Social and Cultural Rights, at 13, ¶ 25, UN Doc. E/CN.4/1997/105, Commission on Human Rights, 53rd Sess. (18 Dec.

on Economic, Social and Cultural Rights has therefore left the door open, at least in theory, for individuals or groups of individuals to communicate alleged violations of economic, social, or cultural self-determination rights.[195]

The African Commission may also consider communications regarding alleged human rights violations of the African Charter by States. Under the ICCPR and ICESCR Optional Protocols, only individuals claiming to be victims of such violations may transmit communications. Under Article 55 of the African Charter, anyone may transmit a communication to the African Commission alleging human rights violations by a State.[196] The African Commission then has discretion to determine which of these communications it will address.[197]

The African Commission has considered communications alleging both political and economic self-determination—although not with respect to climate change or climate mobility. The African Commission has, in its jurisprudence, given deference to existing governments and territories, and has thus far limited its enquiry to whether the peoples in question have had representation and participation in existing government (finding, in all cases, that they did).[198] In particular, the African Commission has clarified that, absent egregious rights violations and a denial of participation in government, the right to self-determination under the African Charter does not include a right to secession: "the right to self determination can be enjoyed within the existing territories and with full respect for the sovereignty and territorial integrity of State Parties to the [African] Charter".[199] Nor does the right to economic and

---

1996). For an overview of discussions regarding self-determination during the drafting process, *see* Summers, *supra* note 169, at 3.

195    As this pathway has not yet been tested, it is unclear how individuals will be able to establish a valid claim for violations of the collective right to self-determination. One hurdle to overcome is establishing the link between individual rights and the collective rights of "peoples". James Summers has proposed two potential theories by which such a link may be established; for the moment, their efficacy remains theoretical. *See* Summers, *supra* note 169, at 4–6.

196    African Charter, *supra* note 160, art. 55(1).

197    *Id.* art. 55(2).

198    *See* Stefan Salomon, *Self-Determination in the Case Law of the African Commission: Lessons for Europe*, 50(3) VRÜ VERFASSUNG UND RECHT IN ÜBERSEE 217, 238 (2017) (concluding, following a review of African Commission jurisprudence, that "[s]elf-determination should less be understood as a substantive right in its own sense, but as a procedural right that enables the claiming of other rights. [...] By being linked to other rights, self-determination, like nationality or refugee status, enables claiming the violation of other rights.").

199    Front for the Liberation of the State of Cabinda v Angola, African Commission on Human & People's Rights, Communication No. 328/06 (2013), ¶ 126 [hereinafter 'Cabinda Decision']; Kevin Mgwanga Gunme et al. v. Cameroon, African Commission on Human & People's Rights, Communication No. 266/03 (2009), ¶¶ 199 & 200 ("Going by the Katanga

social development in Article 20, or to freely dispose of wealth and natural resources in Article 21, create any enforceable property rights.[200] Rather, the African Commission has opined that the right to economic and social development in Article 20 "imposes a duty on the Respondent State to ensure that resources are effectively managed for the sole and equal benefit of the entire peoples of the state."[201]

The African Commission has not considered any cases concerning climate change and human mobility in connection with self-determination rights. As noted above, the language of the African Charter itself does not appear to impose a positive obligation on States to promote the self-determination rights of peoples outside of their territories (excepting cases of colonization), but this nevertheless remains open for interpretation by the African Commission.

The United Nations Declaration on the Rights of Indigenous Peoples is not binding and does not have a designated enforcement mechanism. It does, however, form part of the body of international law on self-determination rights, potentially supporting enforcement in other venues. An example of this has already emerged: the Alaska Institute for Justice has submitted a complaint concerning the "Rights of Indigenous People in Addressing Climate-Forced Displacement" to a number of United Nations Special Rapporteurs, including those devoted to the Human Rights of Internally Displaced Persons and to the Rights of Indigenous Peoples. The complaint relies in part on the self-determination provisions of the United Nations Declaration on the Rights of Indigenous Peoples to support its allegations that the United States has violated the human rights of five different tribes located in Louisiana and Alaska.[202]

The United Nations Special Rapporteurs may receive complaints alleging human rights violations. If these complaints fall within their mandate, the

---

decision, the right to self-determination cannot be exercised, in the absence of proof of massive violation of human rights under the Charter. [...] The Commission states that the various forms of governance or self-determination such as federalism, local government, unitarism, confederacy, and self-government can be exercised only subject to conformity with state sovereignty and territorial integrity of a State party. It must take into account the popular will of the entire population, exercised through democratic means, such as by way of a referendum, or other means of creating national consensus. Such forms of governance cannot be imposed on a State Party or a people by the African Commission. [...] The African Commission finds that the people of Southern Cameroon cannot engage in secession, except within the terms expressed hereinabove, since secession is not recognised as a variant of the right to self-determination within the context of the African Charter."); *see also* Katanga Decision, *supra* note 177, ¶¶ 5, 6.

200  Salomon, *supra* note 198, at 237; Cabinda Decision, *supra* note 199, ¶¶ 130–132.
201  Cabinda Decision, *supra* note 199, ¶ 131.
202  Rights of Indigenous People Complaint, *supra* note 180, at 40.

Special Rapporteurs will investigate the allegations and communicate with the State concerned to attempt to resolve any alleged rights violations. This is not a judicial or quasi-judicial procedure, and the Special Rapporteurs will not issue an opinion or decision on the merits of the allegations. The communications between the Rapporteurs and the State should, however, be published in a publicly available report to the Human Rights Council.

Submitted on 15 January 2020, the complaint alleges that, "[d]espite their geographic differences, the Tribes in Louisiana and Alaska are facing similar human rights violations as a consequence of the US government's failure to protect, promote and fulfill each tribe's right to self-determination to protect Tribal members from climate impacts."[203] Amongst other allegations in connection with the right to self-determination, the complaint alleges that the United States "failed to engage, consult, acknowledge and promote the self-determination of these Tribes as they identify and develop adaptation strategies, including resettlement".[204]

This petition on behalf of the indigenous tribes in Louisiana and Alaska is reminiscent of a 2005 petition submitted to the Inter-American Commission on Human Rights, alleging that the United States was in violation of the human rights of the Inuit people.[205] The Inuit petition also relied in part on the provisions of the United Nations Declaration on the Rights of Indigenous Peoples, which was then still in the drafting stage. Amongst other allegations, the Inuit petition alleged that the United States is the world's largest contributor to global warming and has failed to reduce greenhouse gas emissions. By its acts and omissions, the petition alleged, the United States has violated the Inuit people's right to their own means of subsistence, freedom of movement and residence, right to life, and their right to use their traditional lands.[206]

---

203 *Id.* at 3.

204 *Id.* at 9.

205 The Inter-American Commission on Human Rights can receive petitions alleging violations of human rights by Member States of the Organization of American States and issue a report thereon. The Inter-American Commission may also refer cases to the Inter-American Court for judicial consideration if the State in question has recognized the contentious jurisdiction of the Court. *See generally* INTER-AMERICAN COMMISSION ON HUMAN RIGHTS, PETITION AND CASE SYSTEM INFORMATIONAL BROCHURE (2010), *available at* https://www.oas.org/es/cidh/docs/folleto/CIDHFolleto_eng.pdf.

206 Petition to the Inter American Commission on Human Rights Seeking Relief from Violations Resulting from Global Warming Caused by Acts and Omissions of the United States, Submitted by Sheila Watt-Cloutier on Behalf of All Inuit of the Artic Regions of the United States and Canada (7 Dec. 2005), *available at* https://earthjustice.org/sites/default/files/library/legal_docs/petition-to-the-inter-american-commission-on-human-rights-on-behalf-of-the-inuit-circumpolar-conference.pdf [hereinafter 'Inuit Petition'].

The Inuit petition did not rely on the self-determination provisions of the (then draft) United Nations Declaration on the Rights of Indigenous Peoples. Instead, the Inuit petition alleged a violation of their right to "their own means of subsistence", which they connected to self-determination.[207] In support of these allegations, the Inuit petition relied on the provision that is now Article 20 of the United Nations Declaration on the Rights of Indigenous Peoples (UNDRIP): "[i]ndigenous peoples have the right to maintain and develop their political, economic and social systems or institutions, to be secure in the enjoyment of their own means of subsistence and development, and to engage freely in all their traditional and other economic activities."[208]

The Inuit petition did not, however, culminate in an opinion or report on the merits. The Inter-American Commission on Human Rights declined to consider the 167-page petition, on the grounds that "the information provided does not enable [the Commission] to determine whether the alleged facts would tend to characterize a violation of rights protected by the American Declaration."[209] The Inter-American Commission did agree to hear testimony on the issue without considering the petition,[210] although the Inter-American Commission still did not render guidance concerning the United States' obligations with respect to climate change and human rights law.

The recent petition filed on behalf of the five indigenous tribes of Alaska and Louisiana, currently pending, comes over a decade after the Inuit petition and invokes a different complaint mechanism. Although the Special Rapporteur procedure will not result in an opinion or decision, communications on the

207   *Id.* at 94 ("The United States' acts and omissions with regard to climate change, done without consultation or consent of the Inuit, violate the Inuit's human rights to self-determination and to their own means of subsistence.").

208   This provision is Article 20 in the final and adopted version of the United Nations Declaration on the Rights of Indigenous Peoples. At the time the Inuit petition was filed, this provision was Article 21 in a draft version of the United Nations Declaration on the Rights of Indigenous Peoples. Draft United Nations Declaration on the Rights of Indigenous Peoples art. 21, *in* Report of the Sub-Commission on Prevention of Discrimination and Protection of Minorities, Commission on Human Rights, 46th Sess., 1–26 Aug. 1994, Annex, at 111, UN Doc. E/CN.4/Sub.2/1994/56 (28 Oct. 1994) (*rapporteur* Osman El-Hajjé).

209   Letter from Ariel E. Dulitzky, Assistant Executive Secretary of the Inter-American Commission on Human Rights, to Sheila Watt-Cloutier et al., Petition No. P-1413-05 (16 Nov. 2006), *available at* http://blogs2.law.columbia.edu/climate-change-litigation/wp-content/uploads/sites/16/non-us-case-documents/2006/20061116_na_decision.pdf.

210   Letter from Ariel E. Dulitzky, Assistant Executive Secretary of the Inter-American Commission on Human Rights, to Sheila Watt-Cloutier et al. (1 Feb. 2007), *available at* https://earthjustice.org/sites/default/files/library/legal_docs/inter-american-commission-on-human-rights-inuit-invite.pdf.

nexus between self-determination, climate change, and human mobility may open further avenues for advocacy and dialogue on State obligations with respect to self-determination rights, climate change mobility, and adaptation.

Untested avenues for enforcement of self-determination rights in connection with climate change and human mobility include the International Court of Justice, which may decide disputes between States under general international law. Until now, its jurisprudence on self-determination is in large part concerned with decolonization disputes. Small island nations could, in theory, explore this venue in attempting to enforce the positive obligations of other States vis-à-vis the self-determination rights that are threatened by climate change impacts and human mobility.[211] The International Court of Justice may also give a non-binding advisory opinion on questions concerning general international law put before it by the United Nations General Assembly.[212] The General Assembly could therefore potentially request the International Court of Justice to make a determination concerning the position of international law on State obligations vis-à-vis self-determination and climate change mobility.

Bringing climate change litigation before the International Court of Justice is not a new idea: small island States have contemplated both State-to-State litigation and seeking an advisory opinion before the International Court of Justice with respect to State obligations to reduce carbon emissions.[213] There are, however, significant jurisdictional and substantive hurdles to bringing climate change claims before the International Court of Justice.[214] In addition, small island developing States may fear economic retaliation should they bring legal

---

211   For the basis on which the International Court of Justice may have jurisdiction over a State-to-State dispute, see *Basis of the Court's Jurisdiction*, INTERNATIONAL COURT OF JUSTICE, https://www.icj-cij.org/en/basis-of-jurisdiction (last visited 24 May 2021).

212   *See Advisory Jurisdiction*, INTERNATIONAL COURT OF JUSTICE, https://www.icj-cij.org/en/advisory-jurisdiction (last visited 24 May 2021).

213   *See, e.g.*, Rebecca Elizabeth Jacobs, *Treading Deep Waters: Substantive Law Issues in Tuvalu's Threat to Sue the United States in the International Court of Justice*, 14(1) WASH. INT'L L.J. 103 (2005); *Palau Seeks UN World Court Opinion on Damage Caused by Greenhouse Gases*, UN NEWS (22 Sept. 2011), https://news.un.org/en/story/2011/09/388202#:~:text=The%20Paci fic%20island%20nation%20of,do%20not%20harm%20other%20States; Dana Drugmand, *Pacific Islands Group Pushes for International Court Ruling on Climate and Human Rights*, THE CLIMATE DOCKET (13 Aug. 2019), https://www.climatedocket.com/2019/08/13/pacific-islands-climate-change-human-rights/.

214   For a discussion of these hurdles, see Andrew L. Strauss, *Climate Change Litigation: Opening the Door to the International Court of Justice, in* ADJUDICATING CLIMATE CHANGE: STATE, NATIONAL, AND INTERNATIONAL APPROACHES 334, 338–350 (William G.C. Burns & Hari M. Osofsky eds., 2009).

action against other, more powerful, States.[215] Also, in order to obtain an advisory opinion, small island developing States would need the support of other States for the General Assembly to request an advisory opinion from the International Court of Justice. If these hurdles can be overcome, however, a legal decision on climate change mitigation or adaptation could be a powerful catalyst to move forward negotiations and action on mitigation and adaptation measures.[216]

## 2)    *Freedom of Movement*

Freedom of movement is vital for persons to be able to move away from climate change impacts, either in response to rapid onset hazard impacts or as a form of long-term adaptation, and for persons to return to their homes if this is possible in light of climate change impacts.[217] Freedom of movement under human rights law includes the right to move freely within the borders of a State and choose a residence therein, the right to leave any country, and the right to return to one's own country. It does not, however, contain any rights to enter or remain in any country except for one's own. Nor does the right to freedom of movement entail any *non-refoulement* obligations, as discussed more fully below.

a          Freedom of Movement as a Human Right

Freedom of movement is included in the Universal Declaration of Human Rights (UDHR) as Article 13:

(1)   Everyone has the right to freedom of movement and residence within the borders of each State.

---

215   *See* Lisa Friedman, *Island States Mull Risks and Benefits of Suing Big Emitters*, E&E NEWS (16 Nov. 2012), https://www.eenews.net/stories/1059972615.

216   *See* Maxine Burkett, *A Justice Paradox: On Climate Change, Small Island Developing States, and the Quest for Effective Legal Remedy*, 35 U. HAW. L. REV. 633, 657–59 (2013); Aaron Korman & Giselle Barcia, *Rethinking Climate Change: Towards an International Court of Justice Advisory Opinion*, 37 YALE J. INT'L L. ONLINE 37, 39–40, 42 (2012).

217   "Freedom of movement" as discussed herein refers to a universal human right. Outside the scope of human rights law, some States have concluded agreements for free movement of persons between those States. For a view as to the role that these kinds of agreements may play in connection with disaster displacement and with climate-induced migration, see generally TAMARA WOOD, THE ROLE OF FREE MOVEMENT OF PERSONS AGREEMENTS IN ADDRESSING DISASTER DISPLACEMENT: A STUDY OF AFRICA (2019), *available at* https://disasterdisplacement.org/wp-content/uploads/2019/06/52846_PDD_FreeMovement_web-single_compressed.pdf; Ama Francis, *Free Movement Agreements & Climate-Induced Migration: A Caribbean Case Study* (Columbia Law School, Sabin Center For Climate Change Law, Sept. 2019), *available at* http://columbiaclimatelaw.com/files/2019/09/FMAs-Climate-Induced-Migration-AFrancis.pdf.

(2)   Everyone has the right to leave any country, including his own, and to return to his country.

The UDHR, which is declaratory in nature, specifies that freedom of movement includes liberty of movement and residence within a State, as well as the right to leave any country and return to own's own.

The 1948 American Declaration on the Rights and Duties of Man also contains a freedom of movement provision as Article VIII: "Every person has the right to fix his residence within the territory of the state of which he is a national, to move about freely within such territory, and not to leave it except by his own will." This provision only grants rights to free movement to persons in the State of which they are a national and is therefore more restrictive than Article 13 of the UDHR and similar provisions in other treaties. Like the UDHR, the American Declaration on the Rights and Duties of Man is declaratory and not binding in nature.

A more elaborate freedom of movement provision is included in the ICCPR as Article 12:

1.   Everyone lawfully within the territory of a State shall, within that territory, have the right to liberty of movement and freedom to choose his residence.
2.   Everyone shall be free to leave any country, including his own.
3.   The above-mentioned rights shall not be subject to any restrictions except those which are provided by law, are necessary to protect national security, public order (ordre public), public health or morals or the rights and freedoms of others, and are consistent with the other rights recognized in the present Covenant.
4.   No one shall be arbitrarily deprived of the right to enter his own country.

ICCPR Article 12 specifies the potential limitations that may be legitimately placed upon the right to freedom of movement. Paragraph 3 of ICCPR Article 12 confirms that any limitations must be "provided by law" and "consistent with the other rights" included in the ICCPR. Such limitations must be necessary for national security, public order, public health or morals, or to protect the rights of others. In addition to being necessary for any of the specified reasons, any limitations must satisfy the overarching principle of proportionality and must not nullify the right to freedom of movement itself.[218]

---

218   UN Human Rights Committee, CCPR *General Comment No. 27: Freedom of Movement, Article 12*, ¶¶ 2, 13–15, UN Doc. CCPR/C/21/Rev.1/Add.9 (2 Nov. 1999) [hereinafter 'HRC

Paragraph 1 of ICCPR Article 12 also limits freedom of movement and residence to those *lawfully* in the territory. It does not apply to persons unlawfully in a territory and therefore does not apply to persons who may have crossed an international border in contravention of State entry laws. This provision highlights that the freedom of movement does not include a right to enter any country, except for one's own.

One's "own country" includes, but is not restricted to, the country of nationality; "it embraces, at the very least, an individual who, because of his or her special ties to or claims in relation to a given country, cannot be considered to be a mere alien."[219] Paragraph 4 of Article 12 indicates that States may not *arbitrarily* deprive the right to return to one's own country. This wording suggests that there may be legitimate reasons—provided by law—to prevent return to one's own country. The Human Rights Committee has cautioned, however, "that there are few, if any, circumstances in which deprivation of the right to enter one's own country could be reasonable."[220] The right to return also "implies the right to remain in one's own country."[221] Article 12 of the ICCPR does not otherwise contain any *non-refoulement* obligations or prohibition on expulsion. Article 13 of the ICCPR does prohibit *arbitrary* expulsion of persons lawfully within a territory; expulsion is therefore potentially permissible when it is not arbitrary and/or when a person is not lawfully within a State.[222]

The African Charter also includes as Article 12 a provision on the right to freedom of movement:

1.  Every individual shall have the right to freedom of movement and residence within the borders of a State provided he abides by the law.

---

General Comment 27'] (The principle of proportionality requires that restrictive measures "must be appropriate to achieve their protective function; they must be the least intrusive instrument amongst those which might achieve the desired result; and they must be proportionate to the interest to be protected." (quotation ¶ 14)).

219   *Id.* ¶ 20. *See also* Stefan Lars Nystrom v. Australia, Human Rights Committee, Communication No. 1557/2007, CCPR/C/102/D/1557/2007 (2011), ¶¶ 7.4–7.6 (confirming that one's "own country" is not restricted to nationality).

220   HRC General Comment 27, *supra* note 218, ¶ 21.

221   *Id.* ¶ 19.

222   ICCPR, *supra* note 160, art. 13 ("An alien lawfully in the territory of a State Party to the present Covenant may be expelled therefrom only in pursuance of a decision reached in accordance with law and shall, except where compelling reasons of national security otherwise require, be allowed to submit the reasons against his expulsion and to have his case reviewed by, and be represented for the purpose before, the competent authority or a person or persons especially designated by the competent authority.").

2.  Every individual shall have the right to leave any country including his own, and to return to his country. This right may only be subject to restrictions, provided for by law for the protection of national security, law and order, public health or morality.

3.  Every individual shall have the right, when persecuted, to seek and obtain asylum in other countries in accordance with the law of those countries and international conventions.

4.  A non-national legally admitted in a territory of a State Party to the present Charter, may only be expelled from it by virtue of a decision taken in accordance with the law.

5.  The mass expulsion of non-nationals shall be prohibited. Mass expulsion shall be that which is aimed at national, racial, ethnic or religious groups.

Paragraphs 1 and 2 of Article 12 in the African Charter designate "[e]very individual" as holding the rights to freedom of movement and residence, the right to leave a country, and the right to return to her own. Unlike the ICCPR, the right to freedom of movement and residence applies to all persons, and is not restricted to individuals lawfully within a territory.[223] The African Charter does not specify what limitations may legitimately be placed upon the right to freedom of movement and residence within a country. Paragraph 2 of Article 12 specifies that any legitimate restrictions of the right to *leave* any country or return to one's own must be provided by law and may only be for reasons of "national security, law and order, public health or morality". The African Charter also includes in the same Article, in paragraphs 4 and 5, a prohibition on arbitrary or mass expulsion. Paragraph 3 states that individuals have the right to seek asylum in another country, but that this is subject to the law of those countries and international law. Thus, although individuals have the freedom to seek asylum, there is no State duty, pursuant to the freedom of movement, to grant entry or asylum.

b        Climate Change Mobility and Freedom of Movement

In the context of climate change, the right to freedom of movement and residence is critical for all persons who must move, either temporarily or permanently. For persons moving internally, the relevance of the freedom of movement is elucidated in the Guiding Principles on Internal Displacement as

---

223    African Commission on Human & Peoples' Rights, *General Comment No. 5 on the African Charter on Human and Peoples' Rights: The Right to Freedom of Movement and Residence (Article 12(1))*, ¶ 8 (10 Nov. 2019).

Principles 14 and 15, which clarify that internally displaced persons "have the right to move freely in and out of camps or other settlements", "to seek safety in another part of the country", "to leave their country", or "to seek asylum in another country".[224] The right to the freedom of movement embodied in the UDHR, ICCPR, and African Charter is broader than the Guiding Principles, however, in that they apply to *all* persons moving internally, and not only those who may be considered as being "displaced". At the same time, States may limit such movement for reasons of national security or public order, issues which may become increasingly relevant in the context of severe climate change impacts and mass internal or international movements.

For persons moving to another country, they have the right to leave any country and, in theory, the right to choose their country of destination. Once lawfully in another territory (or even unlawfully for persons within the jurisdiction of the African Charter), persons moving once again have the right to freedom of movement and residence, which prohibits the host State from imposing arbitrary or unlawful restrictions on such movement.[225] However, the right to freedom of movement alone will not grant them entry or the right to stay in another country unless it is considered to be "their own".

Because the right to freedom of movement lacks a corresponding right of entry, Morai Paz, a scholar in the field of human rights, has referred to this right as being "incomplete". Paz centers her discussion on the plight of refugees who can leave their country but may not be able to gain entry to another.[226] Her arguments are relevant to persons moving in the context of climate change, who have the right to leave any country in response to climate change impacts but no corresponding right to gain entry to another country. This includes persons living on land or in nations that may become uninhabitable due to sea level rise. Paz provides an evocative description of the plight of such persons who cannot gain entry to another country:

> This frame leaves without protection those who are stranded between states—whose state of nationality either is the source of their harm (positive violation) or is unable to remedy their harm (negative violation).

---

224    Guiding Principles, *supra* note 133, arts. 14, 15.

225    HRC General Comment 27, *supra* note 218, ¶ 4 ("Once a person is lawfully within a State, any restrictions on his or her rights guaranteed by article 12, paragraphs 1 and 2, as well as any treatment different from that accorded to nationals, have to be justified under the rules provided for by article 12, paragraph 3.").

226    Many instruments under asylum law prohibit *refoulement* but do not grant right of entry without territorial presence. Moria Paz, *The Incomplete Right to Freedom of Movement*, 111 AM. J. INT'L L. UNBOUND 514, 516–17 (2017).

They can exit their state, but no state has a corresponding duty to allow them in. [...]

So long as we live in a state system, with territory limiting the responsibility of states such that states have no duties to engage in unilateral humanitarian intervention, a better way to effect change is by putting pressure on states to voluntarily permit more entry. Alas such entry rights would not be universal, dependent as they would be on the political will of each state. [...]

And the remaining refugees who are unable to secure entry? Whether they chose or were forced to leave their state, human rights law guarantees them only a point of departure but no point of arrival. Marooned on land and adrift at sea, they carry suitcases full of meaningless human rights.[227]

Paz concludes in the above that, in light of the existing international legal framework, political pressure on States to voluntarily admit more persons is "a better way to effect change".[228]

The ICCPR and the African Charter do create binding and enforceable obligations for States Parties to ensure the right to freedom of movement within their territories and to grant entry to persons who establish that State as their "own country". As discussed above in the context of the right to self-determination, the Human Rights Committee and the African Commission oversee the implementation of the ICCPR and the African Charter, respectively. These bodies may therefore consider and decide upon, under some circumstances, allegations of rights violations by States Parties. Also as discussed above, the International Court of Justice may decide disputes between States or provide an advisory opinion, including concerning the right to freedom of movement under general international law. Thus far none of these mechanisms has considered the intersection between freedom of movement, human mobility, and climate change.

The 2005 Inuit Petition (discussed above), submitted to and rejected by the Inter-American Commission on Human Rights, was a missed opportunity to have an international body opine on State obligations to protect freedom of movement in the context of climate change. To recall, the petition alleged that the United States, by failing to reduce greenhouse gas emissions, was violating the Inuit people's rights. Amongst other rights, the Inuit petition alleged

227    *Id.* at 517–518.
228    *Id.* at 518.

violations of their freedom of movement and residence.[229] In support of its allegations with respect to freedom of movement, the Inuit petition relied on Article VIII of the American Declaration on the Rights and Duties of Man. Freedom of movement has, however, not been included as an issue in recent climate change related petitions submitted to other international bodies. As climate change impacts increasingly render lands uninhabitable, however, the right to freedom of movement may be seen as progressively relevant to climate change mobility.

### 3)    *The Right to Life*

The right to life is a fundamental and non-derogable right, referred to by the Human Rights Committee as the "supreme" human right.[230] The right to life is not only intimately intertwined with other human rights; it is a prerequisite for the enjoyment of all other rights.[231] Domestic and international bodies have affirmed the direct link between environmental conditions, including climate change impacts, and the right to life. Recent case law has confirmed that States have a positive obligation to protect the right to life by taking action to miti-gate climate change and its impacts. In some cases the right to life entails *non-refoulement* obligations for States, which may apply to persons that have left territories confronting perilous climate change impacts.

### a        The Supreme Human Right: Treaty Provisions

The right to life is enshrined in many international declarations and trea-ties, in varying forms. UDHR Article 3 sets forth the right to life in its simplest form: "Everyone has the right to life, liberty and security of person." The ICCPR, in Article 6(1), expounds on the right to life, providing that "[e]very human being has the inherent right to life. This right shall be protected by law. No

---

229    Inuit Petition, *supra* note 206, at 94–96.
230    UN Human Rights Committee, *CCPR General Comment No. 36, Article 6: Right to Life*, ¶ 2, UN Doc. CCPR/C/GC/36 (3 Sept. 2019) [hereinafter 'HRC General Comment 36'].
231    *Id.*; The Environment and Human Rights (State Obligations in Relation to the Environment in the Context of the Protection and Guarantee of the Rights to Life and to Personal Integrity: Interpretation and Scope of Articles 4(1) and 5(1) in relation to Articles 1(1) and 2 of the American Convention on Human Rights), Advisory Opinion OC-23/17, Inter-Am. Ct. H.R., (ser. A) No. 23, ¶ 108 (15 Nov. 2017) [hereinafter 'Inter-American Court Opinion OC-23/17'] ("The Court has affirmed repeatedly that the right to life in the American Convention is essential because the realization of the other rights depends on its protec-tion."); Case of the Yakye Axa Indigenous Community v. Paraguay, Inter-Am. Ct. H.R. (ser. C) No. 125, ¶ 161 (17 June 2005) [hereinafter 'Yakye Axa v. Paraguay'] ("When the right to life is not respected, all the other rights disappear, because the person entitled to them ceases to exist.").

one shall be arbitrarily deprived of his life." Subsequent paragraphs in ICCPR Article 6 clarify the conditions and limitations on the use of capital punishment. These paragraphs on capital punishment underscore that, in some jurisdictions, the right to life is fundamental and non-derogable, but it is not absolute. There is an international movement towards abolishing the death penalty entirely.[232] However, at present, in some circumstances and under the terms of certain treaties, a person may be deprived of life in accordance with capital punishment measures provided by law and strictly applied.[233] With respect to State obligations under the ICCPR, the Human Rights Committee has clarified that abolishment of the death penalty is "legally irrevocable".[234] Similarly, a State may not introduce or reintroduce capital punishment for crimes that did not entail the death penalty at the time it ratified the ICCPR, or apply capital punishment retroactively.[235] Where States still use the death penalty, it must be reserved for only the most serious crimes involving intentional killing.[236]

Certain regional treaties also include provisions clarifying that, under some circumstances, deprivation of life may not contravene the right to life. Article 4(1) of the American Convention on Human Rights (ACHR) states: "Every person has the right to have his life respected. This right shall be protected by law and, in general, from the moment of conception. No one shall be arbitrarily deprived of his life." Like the ICCPR, ACHR Article 4 includes in subsequent paragraphs the conditions under which capital punishment may (or may not) be used in accordance with the right to life.[237] The European Convention on Human Rights (ECHR) Article 2(1) provides that "[e]veryone's right to life shall be protected by law. No one shall be deprived of his life intentionally save in the execution of a sentence of a court following his conviction of a crime for which this penalty is provided by law." The ECHR goes on to clarify in a subsequent paragraph that deprivation of life will not contravene the convention when

---

232 UN Secretary-General, *Capital Punishment and the Implementation of Safeguards Guaranteeing Protection of the Rights of Those Facing the Death Penalty: Yearly Supplement of the Secretary-General to His Quinquennial Report on Capital Punishment*, ¶ 3, Human Rights Council, 42nd Sess., 9–27 Sept. 2019, UN Doc. A/HRC/42/28 (28 Aug. 2019) [hereinafter 'HRC, Capital Punishment']; OHCHR, DEATH PENALTY, https://www.ohchr.org/EN/Issues/DeathPenalty/Pages/DPIndex.aspx (last visited 7 June 2021).

233 HRC General Comment 36, *supra* note 230, ¶¶ 10–17. ICCPR, *supra* note 160, arts. 6(2), (4)–(5).

234 HRC General Comment 36, *supra* note 230, ¶ 34; HRC, Capital Punishment, *supra* note 232, ¶ 4.

235 HRC General Comment 36, *supra* note 230, ¶ 34; HRC, Capital Punishment, *supra* note 232, ¶ 5.

236 HRC, Capital Punishment, *supra* note 232, ¶¶ 8, 12.

237 ACHR, *supra* note 160, arts. 4(2)–(6).

it results from force that was not more than absolutely necessary in defense against unlawful violence, to make a lawful arrest or prevent escape from lawful detention, or used in a lawful action to stop a riot or insurrection.[238]

All other binding regional treaties include provisions on the right to life as well. The African Charter includes the right to life as Article 4: "Human beings are inviolable. Every human being shall be entitled to respect for his life and the integrity of his person. No one may be arbitrarily deprived of this right." The Arab Charter on Human Rights contains as its Article 5 a provision similar to the UDHR right to life: "Everyone has the right to life, liberty, and security of person; these rights are protected by law."

The United Nations Convention on the Rights of the Child includes a right to life provision as Article 6(1): "States Parties recognize that every child has the inherent right to life." The Convention on the Rights of the Child specifies in paragraph 6(2) that the right to life not only requires States Parties to ensure survival, but also development of the child: "States Parties shall ensure to the maximum extent possible the survival and development of the child." This provision makes explicit what is implicit in the provisions of other treaties: the right to life entails more than the right to be alive.

In connection with the ICCPR and regional treaties, the right to life has been interpreted and applied broadly as the right to enjoy a life with dignity.[239] The dignity inherent in human life is a tenet underlying all of human rights law.[240] The preamble to the ICCPR states that the rights therein "derive from the inherent dignity of the human person". Some instruments have separate provisions on the right to human dignity, such as the UDHR and the African Charter.[241] Notwithstanding, even in treaties including separate provisions on

---

238    ECHR, *supra* note 160, art. 2(2).

239    HRC General Comment 36, *supra* note 230, ¶ 3; African Commission on Human & Peoples' Rights, *General Comment No. 3 on the African Charter on Human and Peoples' Rights: The Right to Life (Article 4)*, at 7, ¶ 3 (18 Nov. 2015) [hereinafter 'African Commission General Comment 3']; Case of the "Street Children" (Villagran-Morales et al.) v. Guatemala, Inter-Am. Ct. H.R. (ser. C) No. 63, ¶ 144 (19 Nov. 1999); Norma Portillo Cáceres et al. v. Paraguay, Human Rights Committee, Communication No. 2751/2016, CCPR/C/126/D/2751/2016 (2019), ¶ 7.3 [hereinafter 'Cáceres v. Paraguay']; Yakye Axa v. Paraguay, *supra* note 231, ¶ 161.

240    *See* UDHR, *supra* note 160, art. 1 ("All human beings are born free and equal in dignity and rights."); UN Charter, preamble ("We the peoples of the United Nations determined [...] to reaffirm faith in fundamental human rights, in the dignity and worth of the human person [...].").

241    UDHR, *supra* note 160, art. 1 ("All human beings are born free and equal in dignity and rights. They are endowed with reason and conscience and should act towards one another in a spirit of brotherhood."); African Charter, *supra* note 160, art. 5 ("Every individual shall have the right to the respect of the dignity inherent in a human being and to the recognition of his legal status. All forms of exploitation and degradation of man particularly

human dignity, the right to life must be understood as ensuring the right to life *with dignity*.[242]

A State is not merely prohibited from arbitrarily depriving persons of life (with dignity) within their territory. States are obligated to take measures to protect against deprivation of life with dignity within their territory from foreign or non-State actors.[243] Recent jurisprudence, discussed later in this chapter, confirms that States must also take measures to protect the right to life in the face of environmental—or climate change—threats.

State obligations to protect the right to life within national territory also prohibit a State from sending or returning an individual to another country where she may be arbitrarily deprived of life.[244] The Human Rights Committee has clarified that this *non-refoulement* obligation in connection with the right to life may be broader than *non-refoulement* obligations under refugee law, as States must protect the right to life of all foreign individuals in their territory, and not only those entitled to refugee status.[245] This is particularly significant for climate change mobility, where individuals will, in many cases, not fall within the protection of the Refugee Convention.

b      The Right to Life and the Environment

The profound connection between the right to life and the environment is well-established and has been acknowledged in the jurisprudence of the International Court of Justice, the European Court of Human Rights, the Inter-American Court of Human Rights, the Human Rights Committee, and Dutch domestic courts.[246] Recent jurisprudence has confirmed that climate change is

---

slavery, slave trade, torture, cruel, inhuman or degrading punishment and treatment shall be prohibited.").

242  For example, the African Charter contains as its Article 5 protection of "the right to the respect of the dignity inherent in a human being". The African Commission has nevertheless clarified that Article 4 on the right to life "envisages the protection not only of life in a narrow sense, but of dignified life." African Commission General Comment 3, *supra* note 239, at 7, ¶ 3.

243  HRC General Comment 36, *supra* note 230, ¶¶ 18–29.

244  *Id.* ¶ 30.

245  *Id.* ¶ 31.

246  *See, e.g.,* MCADAM, FORCED MIGRATION, *supra* note 78, at 58–60 (reviewing jurisprudence on the right to life and the environment); Gabcíkovo-Nagymaros Project (Hungary v. Slovakia), 1997 I.C.J. 7, 91 (25 Sept. 1997) (separate opinion of Vice-President Weeramantry) ("The protection of the environment is likewise a vital part of contemporary human rights doctrine, for it is a *sine qua non* for numerous human rights such as the right to health and the right to life itself."); Inter-American Court Opinion OC-23/17, *supra* note 231, ¶ 66 ("The Court considers that the rights that are particularly vulnerable to environmental impact include the right[] to life [...].."); *Urgenda Foundation v. The*

one of the environmental factors connected to the right to life and that States have positive obligations to protect the right to life by addressing environmental—and climate change—risk factors.

In November 2017, at the request of the Republic of Colombia, the Inter-American Court of Human Rights gave an Advisory Opinion on the Environment and Human Rights and, in particular, on State obligations in relation to the environment in the context of the rights to life and to personal integrity under the American Convention on Human Rights. Colombia requested the Inter-American Court to clarify State protection obligations "in the context of the construction of major new infrastructure projects" in the Wider Caribbean Region "that, owing to their dimensions and permanence, may cause significant harm to the marine environment and, consequently, to the inhabitants of the coastal areas and islands located in this region who depend on this environment for their subsistence and development."[247] Although Colombia's request did not include any further factual context, its submission coincided with maritime boundary disputes between Nicaragua and Colombia, as well as Nicaragua's plans to conduct off-shore drilling and to construct a 170-mile canal linking the Caribbean Sea to the Pacific Ocean.[248] In this respect, the opinion focuses largely on State obligations to prevent environmental harm caused by development projects. Although its opinion was not focused on climate change impacts, the Inter-American Court acknowledged climate change as an environmental factor that may impact the enjoyment of human rights, including (amongst others) the rights to life and self-determination.[249]

The Inter-American Court confirmed that States have a positive obligation to "use all the means at their disposal to avoid activities under their jurisdiction causing significant harm to the environment"[250] and specified some of the particular obligations this would entail:

---

*State of the Netherlands* [2019] HR 19/00135 (Supreme Court, 20 Dec. 2019) (Neth.), unofficial English translation, at 4–5, *available at* https://www.urgenda.nl/wp-content/uploads/ENG-Dutch-Supreme-Court-Urgenda-v-Netherlands-20-12-2019.pdf       [hereinafter 'Urgenda Decision'].

247     Inter-American Court Opinion OC-23/17, *supra* note 231, ¶ 2.

248     *See* Monica Feria-Tinta & Simon C. Milnes, *International Environmental Law for the 21st Century: The Constitutionalization of the Right to a Healthy Environment in the Inter-American Court of Human Rights Advisory Opinion 23*, 12 ANUARIO COLOBIANO DE DERECHO INTERNACIONAL 43, 49–50 (2019); Maria L. Banda, *Inter-American Court of Human Rights' Advisory Opinion on the Environment and Human Rights*, 22(6) AM. SOC'Y INT'L L. INSIGHT (2018), https://www.asil.org/insights/volume/22/issue/6/inter-american-court-human-rights-advisory-opinion-environment-and-human.

249     Inter-American Court Opinion OC-23/17, *supra* note 231, ¶ 54.

250     *Id.* ¶ 142.

a. States have the obligation to prevent significant environmental damage within or outside their territory [...].

b. To comply with the obligation of prevention, States must regulate, supervise and monitor the activities within their jurisdiction that could produce significant environmental damage; conduct environmental impact assessments when there is a risk of significant environmental damage; prepare a contingency plan to establish safety measures and procedures to minimize the possibility of major environmental accidents, and mitigate any significant environmental damage that may have occurred, even when it has happened despite the State's preventive actions [...].

c. States must act in keeping with the precautionary principle in order to protect the rights to life and to personal integrity in the case of potential serious or irreversible damage to the environment, even in the absence of scientific certainty [...].

d. States have the obligation to cooperate, in good faith, to protect against environmental damage [...].

e. To comply with the obligation of cooperation, States must notify other potentially affected States when they become aware that an activity planned under their jurisdiction could result in a risk of significant transboundary harm and also in cases of environmental emergencies, and consult and negotiate in good faith with States potentially affected by significant transboundary harm [...].

f. States have the obligation to ensure the right of access to information, established in Article 13 of the American Convention, concerning potential environmental impacts [...];

g. States have the obligation to ensure the right to public participation of the persons subject to their jurisdiction [...] in policies and decision-making that could affect the environment [...], and

h. States have the obligation to ensure access to justice in relation to the State obligations with regard to protection of the environment set out in this Opinion[...].[251]

Paragraph (a) specifies that States are obliged to prevent environmental damage *outside* as well as within their territory. Paragraph (c) confirms that the precautionary principle applies to these State obligations—i.e., action to prevent potentially serious or irreversible damage cannot be postponed even

---

251   *Id.* ¶ 242.

without full scientific certainty that such damage will occur.[252] States must also act in cooperation with other potentially impacted States (paragraph e), and ensure public participation in decision-making (paragraphs f and g). This opinion thus underscores that the right to life establishes positive obligations for States, both within their territory and extraterritorially, vis-à-vis persons within their jurisdiction and with other States.

In 2018, shortly after the 2017 Inter-American Court of Human Rights gave its Advisory Opinion on the Environment and Human Rights, the Human Rights Committee issued General Comment No. 36 on the Right to Life, which further clarifies State protection obligations with respect to the environment, including climate change mitigation and response. The Human Rights Committee addresses environmental and climate change factors relating to the right to life in complementary paragraphs 26 and 62 of General Comment No. 36.[253]

Paragraph 26 is situated in Section III, which expands on the duty to protect life pursuant to the requirement in ICCPR Article 6(1) that the right to life "shall be protected by law". The Human Rights Committee affirmed that the positive obligations associated with the right to life require States to address societal conditions that may threaten the right to life with dignity, including environmental degradation and deprivation of indigenous lands:

> The duty to protect life also implies that States parties should take appropriate measures to address the general conditions in society that may give rise to direct threats to life or prevent individuals from enjoying their right to life with dignity. These general conditions may include high levels of criminal and gun violence, pervasive traffic and industrial accidents, *degradation of the environment* (see also para. 62 below), *deprivation of indigenous peoples' land, territories and resources*, the prevalence of life-threatening diseases, such as AIDS, tuberculosis and malaria, extensive substance abuse, widespread hunger and malnutrition and extreme poverty and homelessness.[254]

---

252    United Nations Framework Convention on Climate Change art. 3.3, 9 May 1992, 1771 U.N.T.S. 107; United Nations Conference on Environment and Development, Rio de Janiero, Brazil, 3–14 June 1992, *Rio Declaration on Environment and Development*, Annex II, UN Doc. A/CONF.151/26/Rev.1 (Vol. I) (12 Aug. 1992), Principle 15.

253    For a drafting history of paragraphs 26 and 62 in General Comment No. 36, see Ginevra Le Moli, *The Human Rights Committee, Environmental Protection and the Right to Life*, 69 INT'L & COMP. L.Q. 726, 740–745 (2020).

254    HRC General Comment 36, *supra* note 230, ¶ 26 (citations omitted, emphasis added).

In addition, the Human Rights Committee gives its view in paragraph 26 that, amongst other steps that States must take in fulfillment of their obligation to protect the right to life, States should develop disaster management and preparedness strategies to address rapid onset hazard events:

> Furthermore, *States parties should also develop, when necessary, contingency plans and disaster management plans designed to increase preparedness and address natural and manmade disasters that may adversely affect enjoyment of the right to life, such as hurricanes, tsunamis, earthquakes,* radioactive accidents and massive cyberattacks resulting in disruption of essential services.[255]

Paragraph 62 of General Comment No. 36 is found in Section v on the "[r]elationship of article 6 with other articles of the Covenant and other legal regimes". In paragraph 62, the Human Rights Committee identifies "[e]nvironmental degradation, climate change and unsustainable development" as "some of the most pressing and serious threats to the ability of present and future generations to enjoy the right to life."[256] The Committee explains that obligations under international environmental law and the right to life are intertwined and must be understood in conjunction with one another:

> The obligations of States parties under international environmental law should thus inform the content of article 6 of the Covenant, and the obligation of States parties to respect and ensure the right to life should also inform their relevant obligations under international environmental law. *Implementation of the obligation to respect and ensure the right to life, and in particular life with dignity, depends, inter alia, on measures taken by States parties to preserve the environment and protect it against harm, pollution and climate change caused by public and private actors.* States parties should therefore ensure sustainable use of natural resources, develop and implement substantive environmental standards, conduct environmental impact assessments and consult with relevant States about activities likely to have a significant impact on the environment, provide notification to other States concerned about natural disasters and emergencies and cooperate with them, provide appropriate access

---

255   *Id.* (emphasis added).
256   *Id.* ¶ 62 (citations omitted).

to information on environmental hazards and pay due regard to the pre-cautionary approach.[257]

The Human Rights Committee thus was of the clear view that State obligations to protect the right to life include preserving and protecting the environment against climate change.[258]

In its August 2019 decision in the *Portillo Cáceres v Paraguay* case, the Human Rights Committee confirmed that the environmental protection pro-visions set forth in General Comment No. 36 are not aspirational in nature, but reflect positive obligations on States to protect individuals from environmen-tal harm.[259] In *Cáceres*, a private actor's misuse of agrochemicals resulted in the death of Mr. Portillo Cáceres and pesticide poisoning of other complain-ants. The Human Rights Committee found that the State had violated the right to life by failing to take action when it was aware of, and had acknowledged, the "reasonably foreseeable" danger posed to the complainants by the use of agrochemicals by a private party.[260] In addition, the complainants had already obtained a decision in a State court that the State had failed to enforce.[261] Not only had the State violated the right to life of Mr. Cáceres, who was deceased, but also the right to life of the other living complainants. As the decision notes, a State may be in breach of the right to life even if the threats do not result

---

257  *Id.* (citations omitted, emphasis added); *see also* M. Özel et al. v. Turkey, 14350/05, 15245/05 & 16051/05, Eur. Ct. H.R. (Section II) (Revised Judgment of 2 May 2016), ¶ 173.

258  Ginevra Le Moli observes that the terms "protect" and "preserve" reflect environmental law terminology and expand "the spatial scope of the obligation to prevent and therefore highlights the extraterritorial scope of the obligations arising from the right to life." She further observes that such an "approach is consistent with the interpretation of the right to life given by the Inter-American Court in its 2017 *Advisory Opinion on Human Rights and the Environment*". Le Moli, *supra* note 253, at 746.

259  In the *Cáceres* decision, the Human Rights Committee relies on paragraph 26 in establish-ing the State's duty to address environmental pollution to protect the right to life. Cáceres v. Paraguay, *supra* note 239, ¶ 7.3. Paragraphs 26 and 62 of General Comment No. 36 use the term "should" when referring to State obligations to protect against, inter alia, envi-ronmental harm. Although the word "should" could be understood in a soft, aspirational, or optional sense, the decisions in the *Cáceres* and *Teitiota* cases (discussed *infra*) dispel any potential ambiguity and confirm that these paragraphs reflect positive obligations. Jefferi Hamzah Sendut, *Climate Change as a Trigger of Non-Refoulement Obligations Under Human Rights Law*, EJIL:TALK! (6 Feb. 2020), https://www.ejiltalk.org/climate-change-as-a-trigger-of-non-refoulement-obligations-under-international-human-rights-law/ (citing Sarah Joseph, *Extending the Right to Life Under the International Covenant on Civil and Political Rights: General Comment 36*, 19(2) HUM. RTS. L. REV. 347, 357 (2019)).

260  Cáceres v. Paraguay, *supra* note 239, ¶ 7.5.

261  *Id.*

in loss of life.[262] In other words, one need not lose her life before bringing a valid claim.

The *Cáceres* case did not concern climate change impacts, but rather harm to the environment directly caused by identifiable non-State actors. It did, however, confirm the connection between environmental protection and the right to life:

> The Committee also takes note of developments in other international tribunals that have recognized the existence of an undeniable link between the protection of the environment and the realization of human rights and that have established that environmental degradation can adversely affect the effective enjoyment of the right to life. Thus, severe environmental degradation has given rise to findings of a violation of the right to life.[263]

The Human Rights Committee thus notes that its findings in *Cáceres* were consistent with international jurisprudence and were not novel.

c           The Right to Life and Emerging Climate Change Case Law

Against this background, a new case, concerning government obligations to prevent climate change and protect the right to life, is currently pending before the Human Rights Committee. In May 2019, the Human Rights Committee received a communication on behalf of Torres Strait Islanders, indigenous inhabitants of the Torres Strait Islands off the coast of Queensland, Australia.[264] The Torres Strait islands and their inhabitants are particularly vulnerable to climate change impacts (including sea level rise) given their location and the islanders' cultural connections with the land.[265] The communication alleges that Australia failed to sufficiently mitigate greenhouse gas emissions and to fund resilience and adaptation measures for the Torres Strait Islands and thus is in breach of its right to life obligations under ICCPR Article 6, as well

---

262   *Id.* ¶ 7.3. *See also* HRC General Comment 36, *supra* note 230, ¶ 7; Nell Toussaint v. Canada, Human Rights Committee, Communication No. 2348/2014, CCPR/C/123/D/2348/2014 (2018), ¶ 11.3.

263   Cáceres v. Paraguay, *supra* note 239, ¶ 7.4 (citations omitted).

264   *Climate Threatened Torres Strait Islanders Bring Human Rights Claim Against Australia*, CLIENTEARTH (12 May 2019), https://www.clientearth.org/press/climate-threatened-tor res-strait-islanders-bring-human-rights-claim-against-australia/.

265   *See Adapting to Climate Change*, AUSTRALIAN GOVERNMENT, TORRES STRAIT REGIONAL AUTHORITY, http://www.tsra.gov.au/the-tsra/programmes/env-mgt-prog ram/adapting-to-climate-change (last visited 25 May 2020).

as in breach of Article 17 (the right to privacy, family, and home) and Article 27 (the right to culture).[266] The communication seeks to have the Australian Government invest at least 20 million in emergency and long-term adaptation measures, to reduce emissions by 65% in the next 10 years, to achieve zero net emissions by 2050, and to phase out the use of thermal coal.[267]

In August 2020, Australia asked the Human Rights Committee to dismiss the pending complaint on the basis that the allegations concern future risks rather than current impacts.[268] Australia also contends that, because it is not the only, nor indeed the primary, contributor to climate change, it cannot be held responsible for climate change under human rights law.[269] Several months prior to requesting dismissal, however, Australia announced that it would invest 25 million dollars for Torres Strait to construct seawalls, repair jetties, and to re-establish ferry services.[270] ClientEarth, who filed the communication on behalf of the Torres Strait Islanders, has recognized this measure as fulfilling a "key ask" of the communication.[271]

---

266   Miriam Cullen, *Climate Change and Human Rights: The Torres Strait Islanders' Claim to the UN Human Rights Committee,* INTERNATIONAL LAW UNDER CONSTRUCTION: SHAPING SUSTAINABLE SOCIETIES, BLOG OF THE GRONINGEN JOURNAL OF INTERNATIONAL LAW (27 June 2019), https://grojil.org/2019/06/27/climate-change-and-human-rights-the-torres-strait-islanders-claim-to-the-un-human-rights-committee/; Sophie Marjanac & Sam Hunter Jones, *Are Matters of National Survival Related to Climate Change Really Beyond a Court's Power,* OPEN GLOBAL RIGHTS (28 June 2020), https://www.openglobalrights.org/matters-of-national-survival-climate-change-beyond-courts/.

267   Marjanac & Jones, *supra* note 266; *Our Story,* OUR ISLANDS OUR HOME, https://ourislandsourhome.com.au/about-the-campaign/about-the-campaign-copy/ (last visited 25 May 2021); Katharine Murphy, *Torres Strait Islanders Take Climate Change Complaint to the United Nations* (12 May 2019), https://www.theguardian.com/australia-news/2019/may/13/torres-strait-islanders-take-climate-change-complaint-to-the-united-nations.

268   Katharine Murphy, *Australia Asks UN to Dismiss Torres Strait Islanders' Claim Climate Change Affects Their Human Rights,* THE GUARDIAN (13 Aug. 2020), https://www.theguardian.com/australia-news/2020/aug/14/australia-asks-un-to-dismiss-torres-strait-islanders-claim-climate-change-affects-their-human-rights [hereinafter 'Murphy, *Australia Asks UN to Dismiss*']; ClientEarth, *Australian Government Denies Responsibility for Climate-Threatened Torres Strait* (14 Aug. 2020), https://www.clientearth.org/latest/latest-updates/news/australian-government-denies-responsibility-for-climate-threatened-torres-strait/ [hereinafter 'ClientEarth, *Australian Government Denies Responsibility*'].

269   Murphy, *Australia Asks UN to Dismiss, supra* note 268; ClientEarth, *Australian Government Denies Responsibility, supra* note 268.

270   Shahni Wellington, *Funding to Build Seawalls in the Torres Strait, Amidst Calls for Climate Change Action,* NITV NEWS (22 Dec. 2019), https://www.sbs.com.au/nitv/article/2019/12/22/funding-build-seawalls-torres-strait-amidst-calls-climate-change-action.

271   *Torres Strait Islanders Win Key Ask After Climate Complaint,* CLIENTEARTH (19 Feb. 2020), https://www.clientearth.org/torres-strait-islanders-win-key-ask-after-climate-complaint/.

To recall, the 2005 Inuit Petition, discussed earlier, similarly included allegations that the United States had, by failing to reduce its greenhouse gas emissions, violated the Inuits' right to life (amongst other human rights violations).[272] Although the Inuit petition failed to yield a decision on the merits, the Dutch *Urgenda* case has since upheld an obligation for the State to reduce emissions in light of its right to life obligations, potentially paving the way for the Torres Strait Islander petition, as well as other similar actions.

In *Urgenda*, a domestic case, the Dutch Supreme Court found that, pursuant to ECHR Articles 2 (right to life) and 8 (respect for private and family life), the Dutch government is obliged to reduce its greenhouse gas emissions, irrespective of its comparatively low emissions on a global scale. In the words of the Dutch Supreme Court:

> Each country is thus responsible for its own share. That means that a country cannot escape its own share of the responsibility to take measures by arguing that compared to the rest of the world, its own emissions are relatively limited in scope and that a reduction of its own emissions would have very little impact on a global scale. The State is therefore obliged to reduce greenhouse gas emissions from its territory in proportion to its share of the responsibility. This obligation of the State to do 'its part' is based on Articles 2 and 8 ECHR, because there is a grave risk that dangerous climate change will occur that will endanger the lives and welfare of many people in the Netherlands.[273]

The *Urgenda* decision—that the State must do "its part" to reduce emissions, although not binding in international *fora*—is at odds with Australia's argument that it cannot be held accountable for reducing its emissions because it

---

272    Miriam Cullen draws a link between the Torres Strait Islanders' communication to the Human Rights Committee, the Inuit petition (discussed *supra*), and the *Urgenda* case (discussed *infra*). She is optimistic about the timing of this new claim brought by the Torres Strait Islanders in relation to these two precedents. Cullen, *supra* note 266 ("It has been more than a decade since a comparable claim [i.e. the Inuit Petition] was made before the Inter-American Court of Human Rights which was declined. Legal thinking has moved on since, both in terms human rights and in terms of state responsibility for contributions to climate change. The *Urgenda* decision in the District Court of The Hague in 2015 (and upheld on appeal in 2018) did away with the traditional objection that the inability to prove direct causation from specific emission to each specific impact is enough to avoid responsibility under human rights law.").

273    Urgenda Decision, *supra* note 246, at 4. In addition to the right to life under ECHR Article 2, the Court refers to Article 8 of the ECHR, which protects the right to private family life, home, and correspondence.

is not the only or even primary polluter on the world stage.[274] It demonstrates also that the right to life can form the basis for successful action in climate change mitigation.[275]

Despite the success of the *Urgenda* claim and its probable impact on future litigation, human rights-based claims to compel governments to take stronger mitigation measures have not always proven successful in other jurisdictions. For example, in *Union of Swiss Senior Women for Climate Protection et al. v. Swiss Federal Council and others*, the Union of Swiss Senior Women, along with four individual complainants, sought a ruling compelling government entities to

---

274   *See supra* note 272.

275   Fundamental rights have also formed the basis for successful actions against government and private actors where they are reflected in domestic law, such as national constitutions. For example, the German Federal Constitutional Court recently struck down provisions of the Federal Climate Protection Act as being incompatible with fundamental rights under the German Constitution (the "Basic Law"), on the grounds that it did not sufficiently address emissions reductions beyond 2030. In particular, the Court found that the State's obligation to protect life applied also to future generations, entailing "the necessity to treat the natural foundations of life with such care and to leave them to posterity in such a condition that subsequent generations cannot continue to preserve them only at the price of their own radical abstinence". *Luisa Neubauer et al. v. Federal Republic of Germany* [2021] 1 BvR 2656/18, 1 BvR 96/20, 1 BvR 78/20, 1 BvR 288/20, 1 BvR 96/20, 1 BvR 78/20 (Federal Constitutional Court, 29 Apr. 2021) (Ger.), unofficial English translation, ¶¶ 191–93, *available at* http://climatecasechart.com/climate-change-litigation/wp-content/uploads/sites/16/non-us-case-documents/2021/20210429_11817_judgment-2.pdf. The Lahore High Court of Pakistan found that "the delay and lethargy of the State in implementing the [National Climate Change Policy] Framework offends the fundamental rights of the citizens which need to be safeguarded", as reflected in Articles 9 (the right to life) and 14 (the right to human dignity) of Pakistan's constitution. In so deciding, the Court observed that fundamental rights formed the foundation for judicial intervention on government climate change response. *Ashgar Leghari v. Federation of Pakistan* [2015] W.P. No. 25501/2015, ¶¶ 7, 8 (Lahore High Court, 4 Sept. 2015) (Pak.). Also, the Colombian Supreme Court decided in favor of a group of 25 plaintiffs comprising children and young adults, who alleged that the Colombian government, by failing to reduce to zero the net rate of deforestation in the Colombian Amazon, had violated the plaintiffs' fundamental rights. The Colombian Supreme Court, overturning the decision of the lower court, considered that "[t]he increasing deterioration of the environment is a serious attack on current and future life and on other fundamental rights; it gradually depletes life and all its related rights." In addition, given the importance of the Amazon to the ecosystem, the Court declared the Colombian Amazon to be a " 'subject of rights', entitled to protection, conservation, maintenance and restoration led by the State and the territorial agencies". *Future Generations v. Ministry of the Environment et al.* [2018] STC 4360-2018 (Supreme Court, 14 Apr. 2018) (Colom.), unofficial English translation of excerpts by Dejusticia, at 13, 45, *available at* https://www.dejusticia.org/wp-content/uploads/2018/04/Tutela-English-Excerpts-1.pdf [hereinafter 'Future Generations Decision'].

take specific measures that would limit global warming to below two degrees Celsius. In support of their petition, the Union of Swiss Senior Women relied on fundamental rights in the Swiss Constitution, as well as ECHR Articles 2 and 8—the same provisions which formed the basis for the *Urgenda* decision. The Swiss Federal Supreme Court, in line with the opinions of the lower Swiss authorities, decided that the Union of Swiss Senior Women and the individual complainants did not have a valid claim based on the Swiss Constitution or the ECHR. Rather, the Court held that any alleged failure of the Swiss authorities to take action against climate change did not pose a sufficiently relevant or specific threat to the Swiss Senior Women.[276] The Court also considered relevant in this respect that exceeding two degrees of global warming "will only occur in the medium to more distant future".[277] The Swiss Federal Supreme Court went on to say that the same reasoning applied to claims under ECHR Article 2 and 8.[278] Because the Union of Swiss Senior Women failed to prevail on the merits of the case, they were ordered to pay court costs in the amount of 4,000 Swiss Francs.[279]

In *Friends of the Irish Environment v. The Government of Ireland*, an Irish non-profit organization sought to overturn the government's National Mitigation

---

276    *Union of Swiss Senior Women for Climate Protection v. Swiss Federal Council et al.* [2020] A-2992/2017, Judgment 1C_37/2019 (Federal Supreme Court, Public Law Division 1, 5 May 2020), unofficial English translation, ¶ 5.4, *available at* https://klimaseniorinnen. ch/wp-content/uploads/2020/06/Judgment-FSC-2020-05-05-KlimaSeniorinnen-Engl ish.pdf [hereinafter 'Swiss Senior Women Decision']. *See also Armando Ferrão Carvalho et al. v. The European Parliament and the Council of the European Union* [2019] T-330/18 (General Court, 2nd Chamber, 8 May 2019) (E.U.) [hereinafter 'Carvalho Decision'] (dismissing an application, based in part on fundamental rights, to nullify three EU legal acts for inadequate GHG emissions targets and to compel more stringent reduction targets, on the grounds that "the applicants have not established that the contested provisions of the legislative package infringed their fundamental rights and distinguished them individually from all other natural or legal persons concerned by those provisions just as in the case of the addressee.").

277    Swiss Senior Women Decision, *supra* note 276, ¶ 5.4; *see also* ¶ 5.5 ("Accordingly, their request to the above-mentioned authorities for issuance of a ruling on real acts does not serve to ensure their individual legal protection. Rather, it aims to have the climate protection measures at the federal level existing today and planned up to the year 2030 examined in the abstract for their compatibility with state obligations to protect. Indirectly— through the requested action of state authorities—it aims to initiate the tightening of these measures. Such a procedure or *actio popularis* is inadmissible in terms of Art. 25a APA, which guarantees the protection of individual rights only.").

278    *Id.* ¶ 7.

279    *Id.* at 20, ¶ 2. *See also* Carvalho Decision, *supra* note 276, ¶¶ 109, 110 (ordering the unsuccessful applicants to bear their own costs as well as those of the defendants, the European Parliament, and the Council of the European Union).

Plan, based in part on its alleged failure to protect fundamental rights under the Irish Constitution as well as Articles 2 and 8 of the ECHR (again, the same provisions which formed the basis for the *Urgenda* opinion). The Friends of the Irish Environment ultimately prevailed on their claim before the Supreme Court of Ireland, solely on the basis that the National Mitigation Plan was *ultra vires* the 2015 Irish Climate Action and Low Carbon Development Act.[280] However, the Supreme Court of Ireland opined, in *obiter* remarks, that Friends of the Irish Environment did not have standing to bring any of its rights-based claims, under the Irish Constitution or the ECHR, as those rights belonged to individuals and not corporate entities.[281] In this respect it is worth recalling that in the case of the *Union of Swiss Senior Women*, the complaint had been joined by four individuals. The Swiss Courts nevertheless found that their individual rights were not impacted in a "legally relevant way". The *Union of Swiss Senior Women* outcome also highlights the risk for adverse costs awards in unsuccessful claims. In response to concerns over "possible exposure to the costs of unsuccessful proceedings" for individuals bringing rights-based claims under the Irish Constitution or the ECHR, the Irish Supreme Court noted that a corporate entity could still provide support for those individuals "in whatever manner it considered appropriate."[282]

The claimants in *Notre Affaire á Tous v. France* also relied in part on Articles 2 and 8 of the ECHR, as well as a number of other international legal instruments (including the UNFCCC and the Paris Agreement) and national laws, to support their allegations that the French government had failed to take sufficient action on climate change. In its recent decision, the Administrative Court of Paris did not take any express position on the ECHR claims or provisions.[283]

---

280   *Friends of the Irish Environment v. Government of Ireland et al.* [2020] IESC 49, ¶ 6.48 (Supreme Court, 31 July 2020) (Ir.).

281   *Id.* ¶¶ 7.22–7.24.

282   *Id.* ¶ 7.22. *See also* Orla Kelleher, *The Supreme Court of Ireland's Decision in Friends of the Irish Environment v Government of Ireland ("Climate Case Ireland")*, EUROPEAN JOURNAL OF INTERNATIONAL LAW, EJIL:TALK! (9 Sept. 2020), https://www.ejiltalk.org/the-supr eme-court-of-irelands-decision-in-friends-of-the-irish-environment-v-government-of-ireland-climate-case-ireland/. ("The Court said that the risk of exposure to costs for an individual from unsuccessful proceedings (which could be several hundred thousand euros) was 'no real explanation' for the case not being brought by an individual rather than an NGO. These obiter remarks are hard to reconcile with the prohibitive legal costs regime in Ireland.").

283   *Notre Affaire à Tous et al. v. France* [2021] Decision No. 1904967-1904968-1904972-1904976/ 4-1 (Administrative Court of Paris, 3 Feb. 2021) (Fr.), unofficial English translation, ¶ 29, *available at* http://climatecasechart.com/climate-change-litigation/wp-content/uplo ads/sites/16/non-us-case-documents/2021/20210203_NA_decision-1.pdf.

The Court held, taking into consideration provisions of European and national laws (which referred also to commitments under the UNFCCC and Paris Agreement), that the French government was in a position to reduce greenhouse gas emissions and could be found responsible, but only for failing to meet its own targets:

> [I]n line with the commitments it has set itself and the timetable it has established, the State has recognised that it is in a position to take direct action on greenhouse gas emissions. [...]
>
> Moreover, the fact that the State could achieve the objectives of reducing greenhouse gas emissions by 40% in 2030 compared with their 1990 level and achieving carbon neutrality by 2050 does not exonerate it from its liability where failure to comply with the path it has set itself to achieve those objectives results in additional greenhouse gas emissions, which will accumulate with the previous emissions and produce effects throughout the lifetime of these gases in the atmosphere, i.e. around 100 years, thus aggravating the ecological damage claimed.[284]

The Court ordered the State, for its failure to meet its commitments, to pay symbolic moral damages of one Euro to each of the claimants.[285] The Court denied, however, compensatory damages as the claimants had not shown that the government would be unable to repair the ecological harm caused.[286] The Court also found that the ecological damage was not directly aggravated by any potential discrepancy between renewable energy or energy efficiency objectives set by the government and the results achieved.[287] The Court deferred its decision on whether to issue an injunction requiring the government to take stronger action against emissions, pending additional submissions by the French government.[288]

The Court reserved the possibility to rule, later in the proceedings, on the rights and means of the parties not expressly decided,[289] which includes the allegations from the claimants that the French State has a duty to fight climate change pursuant to its obligations under Articles 2 and 8 of the ECHR. The Court

---

284   *Id.* ¶¶ 29, 31.
285   *Id.* ¶¶ 40–45.
286   *Id.* ¶¶ 35–39.
287   *Id.* ¶¶ 25, 28.
288   *Id.* at 33, art. 4.
289   *Id.* at 33, art. 6 ("All rights and means of the parties which are not expressly ruled on by the present judgment are reserved until the end of the proceedings.").

is, however, unlikely to pronounce any decision on these particular claims since it has already acknowledged the French State's liability on other grounds and the only pending issue is that of the injunction requested by the claimants. The issue may therefore remain open for future cases before the French courts.

These examples demonstrate that actions relying on fundamental rights, such as the right to life, may face legal hurdles, such as standing and justiciability. Even so, where legal action to support mitigation may not succeed on the basis of human rights, it may nevertheless triumph on the basis of national or (other) international laws and instruments. In either case, the *Urgenda* decision will influence future litigation efforts and has already been cited in other actions, before domestic and international *fora*, against States to enforce emissions reductions, based in part on the right to life and other fundamental rights.[290] The decision of the Human Rights Committee in the Torres Strait case—on admissibility and/or the merits—will indicate whether international bodies like the Human Rights Committee may now be prepared, like the Dutch courts, to interpret the right to life to include positive State obligations to reduce greenhouse gas emissions in order to mitigate climate change. Future cases may, like the Torres Strait petition, extend the focus beyond greenhouse gas emissions to other adaptive measures.

d        *Non-Refoulement* and Climate Change Mobility: The *Teitiota* Case
As explored earlier in this chapter, jurisprudence increasingly establishes that the right to life imposes positive obligations on States to mitigate climate change and its impacts. Disaster management and mitigation fall within the scope of those obligations, as should other adaptation measures, including human mobility.[291] In addition to imposing obligations on States to protect, the right to life entails a *non-refoulement* obligation for States; they may not send or return an individual to another State where there is a foreseeable risk to her right to life. The right to life could, therefore, also prevent States from returning individuals to a territory where their right to life is threatened by climate change impacts. Although no decision-making body has yet upheld a *non-refoulement* obligation based on the right to life in the context climate

---

290    *See, e.g.*, Duarte Agostinho et al. v. Portugal & 32 other States, 39371/20, Eur. Ct. H.R. (complaint of 2 Sept. 2020, pending), ¶¶ 9, 36, 37, *available at* https://youth4climatejustice. org/wp-content/uploads/2020/12/Application-form-annex.pdf.

291    As noted *supra*, the Human Rights Committee has already said that States should develop disaster management plans in response to rapid onset hazard events. HRC General Comment 36, *supra* note 230, ¶ 26. Such plans may provide for temporary or long-term mobility should it become necessary.

change impacts, the issue was recently considered and the scope of obligations clarified by the Human Rights Committee in the *Teitiota* case.

As discussed earlier, Mr. Ioane Teitiota, a national of the Republic of Kiribati, a low-lying Pacific island State, unsuccessfully applied for refugee status in New Zealand based on the climate change impacts in his home State. In support of his petition, Mr. Teitiota demonstrated that:

- violent land disputes (sometimes involving fatalities) had erupted on Tarawa—capital of the Republic of Kiribati and Mr. Teitiota's home island—due to the increasing scarcity of habitable land;
- sea level rise had contaminated fresh water lenses, depriving Mr. Teitiota and his family of access to potable water;
- salt deposits from sea level rise made it difficult to grow crops, depriving Mr. Teitiota's subsistence; and
- increasingly intense flooding and sea wall breaches posed a risk to the lives of Mr. Teitiota and his family.[292]

The New Zealand Immigration and Protection Tribunal, although accepting the veracity of his pleadings, found that Mr. Teitiota had not demonstrated that the threats were personal and specific to him in particular; that there was a real risk of physical harm; that obtaining land, growing crops, or accessing potable water was impossible; or that the government of Kiribati had failed to take remedial measures to address these issues.[293]

In addition to examining the issue under the refugee framework, the New Zealand courts considered whether there were other grounds under the ICCPR, including the right to life, for granting Mr. Teitiota protected status.[294] The Tribunal found that Mr. Teitiota's case did not trigger New Zealand's *non-refoulement* obligation in connection with the right to life for two reasons:

---

292   *AF (Kiribati)* [2013] NZIPT 800413, ¶¶ 15–19, 25–28, 72–74 (New Zealand Immigration and Protection Tribunal, 25 June 2013) (N.Z.) [hereinafter 'Teitiota Immigration Tribunal Decision']; Ioane Teitiota v. New Zealand, Human Rights Committee, Communication No. 2728/2016, UN Doc. CCPR/C/127/D/2728/2016 (23 Sept. 2020), ¶¶ 9.7–9.10 [hereinafter 'Teitiota v. New Zealand'].

293   Teitiota Immigration Tribunal Decision, *supra* note 292, ¶¶ 72–75; Teitiota v. New Zealand, *supra* note 292, ¶ 9.6.

294   The New Zealand Immigration and Protection Tribunal also briefly examined and dismissed the possibility that the prohibition on cruel, inhuman, or degrading treatment under ICCPR Article 7 might raise *non-refoulement* obligations. Article 7 was not one of the grounds for relief considered by the Human Rights Committee. Teitiota Immigration Tribunal Decision, *supra* note 292, ¶¶ 80–96.

(i) Mr. Teitiota could not show that any act or omission by the Kiribati government caused a risk to arbitrary deprivation of life, and (ii) Mr. Teitiota did not establish that the risk to his life or that of his family was imminent at that time.[295]

The Tribunal observed that the right to life under ICCPR Article 6 protects against arbitrary deprivation of life by State action or as a consequence of its omissions.[296] The Tribunal thus held that New Zealand's *non-refoulement* obligations would only be triggered if Mr. Teitiota could show that an act or omission *by the Kiribati government* threatened arbitrary deprivation of Mr. Teitiota's right to life.[297] In this respect, the New Zealand Immigration and Protection Tribunal observed that Kiribati is attempting to take remedial measures against climate change impacts and therefore was not threatening Mr. Teitiota's right to life through its acts or omissions.[298] The Tribunal therefore followed a strict interpretation of New Zealand's *non-refoulement* obligations, by which any risk of harm to life with dignity would have to flow directly from the home State's action or omission. In following this interpretation, the Tribunal did not specifically take into consideration risks to the right to life that may be beyond the capacity or ability of governments to address, such as sea level rise and climate change impacts.

The Tribunal also considered that the risk to Mr. Teitiota's life was not "imminent".[299] The Tribunal understood establishing imminence to require:

> no more than sufficient evidence to establish substantial grounds for believing the appellant would be in danger. In other words, these standards should be seen as largely synonymous requiring something akin to the refugee 'real chance' standard. That is to say, something which is more than above mere speculation and conjecture, but sitting below the civil balance of probability standard.[300]

---

295    *Id.* ¶¶ 88–89.

296    *Id.* ¶ 85.

297    *Id.* ¶ 88. The High Court restated the Tribunal's reasoning on this point without discussion. Teitiota High Court Decision, *supra* note 18, ¶ 32. The New Zealand Supreme Court, in rejecting Mr. Teitiota's application for leave to appeal, simply stated, without discussion: "Nor do we consider that the provisions of the ICCPR relied on have any application on these facts." Teitiota Supreme Court Decision, *supra* note 22, ¶ 12.

298    Teitiota Immigration Tribunal Decision, *supra* note 292, ¶ 88.

299    *Id.* ¶ 91.

300    *Id.* ¶ 90. On the use of "imminence" in assessing a risk of harm for international protection purposes, see generally Adrienne Anderson et al., *Imminence in Refugee and Human Rights Law: A Misplaced Notion for International Protection*, 68 INT'L & COMP. L.Q. 111 (2019).

The Tribunal accepted that there was some degree of predictability associated with climate change and related sea level rise and natural disasters. It nevertheless found insufficient evidence to show that the situation in Kiribati at that time was "so precarious" as to put Mr. Teitiota or his family's lives at risk, and that any such risk remained "firmly in the realm of conjecture or surmise".[301]

The New Zealand High Court and Supreme Court upheld the decision of the New Zealand Immigration and Protection Tribunal. Notwithstanding, the New Zealand Courts left open the possibility that, in other cases, climate change impacts could "create a pathway into the Refugee Convention or protected person jurisdiction".[302]

Mr. Teitiota and his family were returned to Kiribati in September 2015. Mr. Teitiota transmitted a communication to the Human Rights Committee, alleging that New Zealand had violated his right to life by returning him and his family to Kiribati in light of the threats posed by climate change impacts. Following a highly deferential standard of review, the Human Rights Committee found that New Zealand's assessment of the risk to Mr. Teitiota's right to life was not "clearly arbitrary" and did not "amount[] to a manifest error or denial of justice".[303] Accordingly, the Committee found that New Zealand had not violated its obligations with respect to the right to life in returning Mr. Teitiota to Kiribati.[304]

In its decision, the Human Rights Committee clarified that "the obligation of States parties to respect and ensure the right to life extends to *reasonably foreseeable* threats and life-threatening situations that can result in loss of life", confirming the applicability of a "foreseeability" standard in the *non-refoulement* context.[305] The Human Rights Committee had applied this

---

301   Teitiota Immigration Tribunal Decision, *supra* note 292, ¶ 91.

302   Teitiota Supreme Court Decision, *supra* note 22, ¶ 13. As the New Zealand High Court explained, "there is a complex inter-relationship between natural disasters, environmental degradation and human vulnerability. Sometimes a tenable pathway to international protection under the Refugee Convention can result. Environmental issues sometimes lead to armed conflict. There may be ensuing violence towards or direct repression of an entire section of a population. Humanitarian relief can become politicised, particularly in situations where some group inside a disadvantaged country is the target of direct discrimination." Teitiota High Court Decision, *supra* note 18, ¶ 27 (citations omitted).

303   Teitiota v. New Zealand, *supra* note 292, ¶ 9.13 (The Committee explained its standard of review at paragraph 9.3: "it is generally for the organs of States parties to examine the facts and evidence of the case in order to determine whether such a risk exists, unless it can be established that the assessment was clearly arbitrary or amounted to a manifest error or a denial of justice.").

304   *Id.* ¶ 10.

305   *Id.* ¶ 9.4 (emphasis added). On foreseeability versus imminence, see Anderson et al., *supra* note 300, at 135–139 (noting, amongst other observations, that "[w]here courts

standard inconsistently in prior jurisprudence.[306] The Committee also clarified that to trigger *non-refoulement* obligations pursuant to Articles 6 (right to
life) or 7 (prohibition on cruel, inhuman, or degrading treatment) of the ICCPR:

  – there must be "substantial grounds for believing that there is a real
     risk of irreparable harm such as that contemplated in articles 6 and 7
     of the Covenant";
  – "there is a high threshold for providing substantial grounds to estab-
     lish that a real risk of irreparable harm exists"; and
  – "the risk must be personal, [...] it cannot derive merely from the gen-
     eral conditions in the receiving State, except in the most extreme
     cases".[307]

Although the Committee's decision did not provide any relief for Mr. Teitiota,
the opinion was celebrated as a landmark case that opened the door to protection for climate change mobility pursuant to the right to life.[308] In its decision,
the Human Rights Committee recognized that the right to life could, in other
cases or in the future, trigger *non-refoulement* obligations in the face of climate
change impacts:

  Both sudden-onset events, such as intense storms and flooding, and slow-
  onset processes, such as sea level rise, salinization and land degradation,
  can propel cross-border movement of individuals seeking protection from
  climate change-related harm. The Committee is of the view that without

---

invoke a foreseeability test alone, imminence does not appear to be relevant. But where
the concept of necessity (or similar) is introduced, if the risk is not imminent then it
seems difficult for decision-makers to conclude that a necessary consequence of removal
is the violation of human rights.").

306   Le Moli, *supra* note 253, at 747; Anderson et al., *supra* note 300, at 136–137 (noting also
       at 136 their conclusion that "where foreseeability is the test, a claim is more likely to
       succeed").

307   Teitiota v. New Zealand, *supra* note 292, ¶ 9.3.

308   *See, e.g.*, *Historic UN Human Rights Case Opens Door to Climate Change Asylum Claims*,
       OHCHR, NEWS AND EVENTS (21 Jan. 2020), https://www.ohchr.org/EN/NewsEvents/
       Pages/DisplayNews.aspx?NewsID=25482; *UN Human Rights Body Supports Asylum
       for Climate Change Refugees*, IISD, SDG KNOWLEDGE HUB (30 Jan. 2020), https://sdg.
       iisd.org/news/un-human-rights-body-supports-asylum-for-climate-change-refugees/
       ; Maria Courtoy, *An Historic Decision for "Climate Refugees"? Putting it into Perspective*,
       UCLOUVAIN, CAHIERS DE L'EDEM (25 Mar. 2020), https://uclouvain.be/en/research-ins
       titutes/juri/cedie/news/united-nations-human-rights-committee-views-on-communicat
       ion-no-2728-2016-ioane-teitiota-v-new-zealand-october-24-2019.html.

robust national and international efforts, *the effects of climate change in receiving States may expose individuals to a violation of their rights under articles 6 or 7 of the Covenant, thereby triggering the non-refoulement obligations of sending States.* Furthermore, given that the risk of an entire country becoming submerged under water is such an extreme risk, the conditions of life in such a country may become incompatible with the right to life with dignity before the risk is realized.[309]

Here the Human Rights Committee confirms that *non-refoulement* obligations to protect the right to life with dignity could arise "before the risk is realized", i.e., before climate change impacts render a territory uninhabitable or result in loss of life.

In its decision, the Human Rights Committee acknowledges in its factual background, but does not directly address the merits of, the New Zealand Courts' interpretation that *non-refoulement* obligations are triggered only when the threat to arbitrary deprivation of life flows directly from State acts or omissions.[310] The Human Rights Committee does, however, make clear that climate change impacts, if they pose a risk to arbitrary deprivation of life, can trigger *non-refoulement* obligations.[311]

The Human Rights Committee's decision on Mr. Teitiota's case was accompanied by two dissenting opinions. The dissenting opinions, for differing reasons, considered that returning Mr. Teitiota and his family to the circumstances they faced in Kiribati was already, without the need for those circumstances to become more dire, a violation of their right to life. The author of one opinion, Vasilka Sancin, considered access to safe drinking water to be a pivotal issue.

---

309    Teitiota v. New Zealand, *supra* note 292, ¶ 9.11 (citations omitted, emphasis added). As noted by the Human Rights Committee, Article 7 of the ICCPR, prohibiting cruel, inhuman, or degrading treatment, also entails a *non-refoulement* obligation and could, in theory, apply to cases involving climate change impacts. For a discussion on case law involving *non-refoulement* obligations for cruel, inhuman, or degrading treatment and how this may apply in climate change mobility cases, *see* MCADAM, FORCED MIGRATION, *supra* note 78, at 63–79.

310    Teitiota v. New Zealand, *supra* note 292, ¶ 2.9.

311    *See* Jane McAdam, *Climate Refugees Cannot Be Forced Back Home*, SYDNEY MORNING HERALD (20 Jan. 2020), https://www.smh.com.au/environment/climate-change/clim ate-refugees-cannot-be-forced-back-home-20200119-p53sp4.html [hereinafter 'McAdam, *Climate Refugees Cannot Be Forced Back Home*'] ("This is the first time the UN Human Rights Committee has expressly acknowledged that human rights law prohibits governments from sending people to places where they face a real risk of life-threatening or serious harm from the adverse impacts of climate change. The decision is not legally binding but the international legal obligations on which it is based are.").

She was of the view that the burden should fall upon the State, in accordance with its positive obligations to protect the right to life, to prove that an applicant would have access to it upon return to their home State.[312]

The author of the other dissenting opinion, Duncan Laki Muhumuza, generally considered that New Zealand had "placed an unreasonable burden of proof on the author [Mr. Teitiota] to establish the real risk and danger of arbitrary deprivation of life", given that the circumstances presented by Mr. Teitiota "are significantly grave and pose a real, personal and reasonably foreseeable risk of a threat to his life under article 6 (1)" of the ICCPR.[313] In particular, Mr. Muhumuza considered that the *difficulty*—without any need to show *impossibility* or the regular occurrence of death—in accessing drinking water and growing crops should be sufficient to establish a "reasonably foreseeable risk of a threat to his right to life".[314]

Mr. Muhumuza also considered that the threat to Mr. Teitiota was personal and dire, notwithstanding that many other Kiribati nationals faced similar threats and that Kiribati is taking adaptive measures.[315] In this respect, he likens New Zealand's return of Mr. Teitiota to Kiribati to forcing a drowning person back onto a sinking ship filled with other passengers:

> [W]hile it is laudable that Kiribati is taking adaptive measures to reduce the existing vulnerabilities and address the evils of climate change, it is clear that the situation of life continues to be inconsistent with the standards of dignity for the author, as required under the Covenant. The fact that that is a reality for many others in the country does not make it any more dignified for the persons living in such conditions. The action taken by New Zealand is more like forcing a drowning person back into a sinking vessel, with the "justification" that after all, there are other passengers

---

312    Ms. Sancin also draws a distinction, in paragraph 3 of her opinion, between "potable water" and "safe drinking water": "My concern arises from the fact that the notion of 'potable water' should not be equated with 'safe drinking water'. Water can be designated as potable, while containing microorganisms dangerous for health, particularly for children (all three of the author's dependent children were born in New Zealand and were thus never exposed to water conditions in Kiribati)." Teitiota v. New Zealand, *supra* note 292, Annex II: Dissenting opinion of Vasilka Sancin, ¶¶ 1–5 (quotation ¶ 3).

313    *Id.* Annex I: Dissenting opinion of Duncan Laki Muhumuza, ¶ 1.

314    *Id.* Annex I: Dissenting opinion of Duncan Laki Muhumuza, ¶ 5 ("It would indeed be counter-intuitive to the protection of life to wait for deaths to be very frequent and considerable in number in order to consider the threshold of risk as met. It is the standard upheld in the Committee that threats to life can be a violation of the right, even if they do not result in the loss of life.").

315    *Id.* Annex I: Dissenting opinion of Duncan Laki Muhumuza, ¶ 6.

on board. Even as Kiribati does what it takes to address the conditions, for as long as they remain dire, the life and dignity of persons remains at risk.[316]

Mr. Muhumuza's opinion invokes the notion of dignity, which the Human Rights Committee did not discuss extensively as a distinct issue in its decision.

The opinion rendered by the Human Rights Committee and the two dissenting opinions support an increasingly broad interpretation of *non-refoulement* obligations under Article 6 with respect to climate change impacts. As several commentators have observed, however, precisely what circumstances will eventually trigger these *non-refoulement* obligations remains to be clarified.[317]

∵

As can be discerned from the foregoing international and regional human rights-based legal instruments, as well as the emerging litigation over the issue of climate change, a human rights-based approach to ameliorating the adverse effects of climate change upon human mobility does exist and is being pursued by different actors. Human rights law has increasingly formed the legal basis for bringing climate change related claims, both domestically and internationally.[318] Many climate change cases fall within the scope of climate change mitigation efforts. Climate change mitigation efforts influence climate mobility insofar as they aim to reduce climate change impacts and potentially reduce the need for adaptive measures, such as mobility. Success in some domestic cases seeking emissions reductions must also be considered in the context of other, similar cases that have faced procedural roadblocks. In particular, plaintiffs pleading cases based on fundamental, human, or constitutional rights to compel governments to take climate mitigation action may face hurdles in establishing standing and justiciability. Despite such roadblocks, some of these cases have nevertheless succeeded on the basis of other national and international laws. Legal action to support mitigation will likely continue to

---

316  *Id.*

317  *See* Courtoy, *supra* note 308; McAdam, *Climate Refugees Cannot Be Forced Back Home*, *supra* note 311.

318  For examples of recent, human rights-based climate change litigation, see generally JOANA SETZER & REBECCA BYRNES, GLOBAL TRENDS IN CLIMATE CHANGE LITIGATION: 2020 SNAPSHOT (2020), *available at* https://www.lse.ac.uk/granthamin stitute/wp-content/uploads/2020/07/Global-trends-in-climate-change-litigation_2020-snapshot.pdf.

flourish in the coming decades alongside other advocacy to compel governments to increase their efforts against global warming.

Case law with a more direct influence on preventing, assisting, and protecting climate change mobility is less developed. The existing case law nevertheless suggests that judicial and quasi-judicial action can play a role in climate
change mobility for some individuals. Recent jurisprudence has confirmed
that human rights law can and does apply to climate change adaptation and
mobility. The success of cases brought in support of climate change mitigation
suggests that creative legal thinking and judicial advocacy may yet play a significant role in addressing climate change mobility. At the same time, it is unlikely
that human rights instruments and court cases alone will be able to reduce, to
an appreciable degree, the level of human suffering that is in store for vulnerable populations who are forced to leave their homes, or even entire countries,
in order to sustain their livelihoods—or even their very lives. Even to the extent
that human rights instruments and the ruling of judges on individual cases may
have the potential to eventually alter the domestic foreign policy of States, it is
not prudent to rely solely upon this approach. Efforts to convince States to take
action will take time, and adaptive and energetic State action is needed now as
a matter of urgency. The human rights principles and instruments discussed in
the present chapter are a perfectly valid legal lens through which the problem
of climate change mobility may be viewed and is something that should be
pursued—especially with respect to *non-refoulement* rights. However, such an
approach should not stand alone because it may not be the avenue most fruit-
ful to producing effective and proactive change for those at risk.

It may also be pointed out here that the "right to life" in international law
is, in fact, a right to *human* life. Alongside increasing awareness that protecting fundamental human rights also requires preserving Earth's ecosystems,
some geographic locations are subject to protection and conservation measures in their own right.[319] However, the mass killing of plants and animals is,

---

319    For example, the Colombian Supreme Court has declared the Colombian Amazon rain-
       forest and the Atrato River to be the subject of rights and hence entitled to protection
       and conservation. Future Generations Decision, *supra* note 275, at 13, 45; *Center for Social
       Justice Studies et al. v. Presidency of the Republic et al.* [2016] T-622/16 (Constitutional
       Court, 10 Nov. 2016) (Colom.), unofficial English translation of excerpts by the Dignity
       Rights Project at Delaware Law School (USA), at 114, *available at* http://files.harmonyw
       ithnatureun.org/uploads/upload838.pdf. New Zealand has recognized the Te Urewera
       National Park and the Whanganui River (Te Awa Tupua) as legal persons with all the
       "rights, powers, duties, and liabilities of a legal person". Te Urewera Act 2014 (N.Z.); Te Awa
       Tupua (Whanganui River Claims Settlement) Act 2017 (N.Z.). A recent class action filed
       in the Argentinian Supreme Court also seeks to have the Paraná Delta declared a subject

unfortunately and under most circumstances, still perfectly legal under many domestic and international legal systems. We have been busy in the last few centuries, especially the twentieth century CE, articulating and setting down in law the rights of humans, but there has been less progress to grant such rights to animals and plants. As pointed out by Carl Sagan: "Like it or not, we humans are bound up with our fellows, and with the other plants and animals all over the world. Our lives are intertwined."[320] And yet we still have far to go in respecting the rights of even our fellow humans. Perhaps an accelerated advancement of respect for the human right to life would assist our species in recognizing and honoring the rights of the others with whom we share our planet.

## F    Assessing the Rights-Based Framework

As the above survey of existing international instruments demonstrates, and as has been widely acknowledged in the literature, significant protection gaps exist in international law for human mobility in the context of climate change.[321] The lack of a bespoke instrument or framework means that this existing gap is not simply one characterized by a lack of legal protections, but also of a coherent collective governmental and institutional approach to addressing climate change mobility.[322] That is not to say that there is a complete legal or institutional void in relation to protection for climate change

---

of rights. The case is currently pending. For a summary of the complaint in English, see *Asociación Civil por la Justicia Ambiental v. Province of Entre Ríos, et al.*, CLIMATE CASE CHART, NON-U.S. LITIGATION, http://climatecasechart.com/non-us-case/asociacion-civil-por-la-justicia-ambiental-v-province-of-entre-rios-et-al/ (last visited 26 Mar. 2021).

320    CARL SAGAN, BILLIONS & BILLIONS: THOUGHTS ON LIFE AND DEATH AT THE BRINK OF THE MILLENNIUM 80 (1997).

321    *See, e.g.*, Kälin & Schrepfer, *supra* note 7, at 30–43, 78; Bonnie Docherty & Tyler Giannini, *Confronting a Rising Tide: A Proposal for a Convention on Climate Change Refugees*, 33 HARV. ENVTL. L. REV. 349, 357–58, 361 (2009); Katrina Miriam Wyman, *Responses to Climate Migration*, 37 HARV. ENVTL. L. REV. 167, 175–85 (2013).

322    Mostafa Naser describes an "enduring vacuum" that demonstrates the lack of a collective plan by the international community to address climate change mobility. MOSTAFA M. NASER, THE EMERGING GLOBAL CONSENSUS ON CLIMATE CHANGE AND HUMAN MOBILITY 39 (2021). Avidan Kent and Simon Behrman discuss in detail how existing institutions are attempting to fill the "institutional gap". AVIDAN KENT & SIMON BEHRMAN, FACILITATING THE RESETTLEMENT AND RIGHTS OF CLIMATE REFUGEES: AN ARGUMENT FOR DEVELOPING EXISTING PRINCIPLES AND PRACTICES 122–160 (2018) [hereinafter 'KENT & BEHRMAN, FACILITATING RESETTLEMENT'].

mobility. However, the existing legal framework was not tailored to address climate change mobility, and the limits of its applicability are still being tested. It will not, in any case, cover the entirety of the wide range of potential climate mobility scenarios. As Simon Behrman and Avidan Kent aptly observed:

> As can be seen, there is no shortage in laws that are relevant for the position of climate refugees. But even so, most commentators seem to agree that a certain gap does indeed exist; that the legal landscape is seriously lacking in *specific* and *effective* regulation, as well as lacking an *address*, i.e. institutions that claim responsibility for the lives and future of climate refugees.[323]

For persons moving within national borders, the Guiding Principles may apply in some cases, particularly when movement is driven by rapid onset hazard events. The Guiding Principles are influential, but not binding. The Kampala Convention should also provide protection for persons displaced internally by rapid onset hazard impacts; it is binding but its application does not extend beyond States Parties in the African region. For cross-border movement, the asylum law framework was not designed to offer protection for most instances of climate change mobility. Any potential protection offered by the 1954 Convention (on Stateless Persons) to populations of "sinking" island States is obscured by legal uncertainty. The Convention on Migrant Workers offers limited protection and only to those who find employment; it also lacks provisions that would afford specific protection to climate change mobility. Human rights law has perhaps the greatest potential to protect climate change mobility. It is gaining traction as a legal basis for bringing climate change related claims, both domestically and internationally. Much of this developing case law falls within the scope of climate change mitigation efforts; case law with a more direct influence on preventing, assisting, and protecting climate change mobility is less developed. Recent jurisprudence has, however, confirmed that human rights law can and does apply to climate change adaptation and mobility, suggesting that judicial and quasi-judicial action can play a role in climate change mobility for some individuals.

Advocates therefore should not, after a strict academic reading of the legal framework, rule out the potential role of litigation addressing climate change mobility—under human rights law or other legal frameworks, such as asylum law. Matthew Scott cautions that a strict reading of existing legal instruments may

---

323   Simon Behrman & Avidan Kent, *Overcoming the Legal Impasse?: Setting the Scene, in* 'CLIMATE REFUGEES': BEYOND THE LEGAL IMPASSE?, *supra* note 2, at 7 (emphasis in original).

cause lawyers and potential claimants to self-censor climate change mobility-related claims, thereby effectively widening the existing protection gap under international law.[324] He suggests that a "strategic litigation initiative" could help to:

- further test the scope of States' existing legal protection obligations;
- continue to raise public awareness of the issue;
- generate some degree of political pressure on States to address the issue even where the law does not oblige them to; and
- help potential claimants to view litigation as a potential avenue for protection, "thereby promoting claimant self-identification and ongoing development of the law".[325]

Litigation therefore should still play a role in addressing climate change mitigation and adaptation—even absent modifications to the current legal framework. It will still most likely not, however, provide protection for the vast majority of persons who will be forced to move as climate change advances. As Scott acknowledges, "[t]he international protection framework will not be remade by a strategic litigation initiative."[326] Strategic (or any other) litigation would therefore not be an appropriate stand-alone approach; it must form part of an overarching holistic strategy.

Insofar as significant legal gaps are already apparent, a number of advocates have made detailed proposals for a new bespoke international instrument.[327] The discussion over creating a new instrument to address climate change

---

324    Matthew Scott, *A Role for Strategic Litigation*, 49 FORCED MIGRATION REV. 47, 47 (2015).

325    *Id.* at 47–48.

326    *Id.* at 48.

327    Prominent detailed proposals include the following: David Hodgkinson et al., *'The Hour When the Ship Comes In': A Convention for Persons Displaced by Climate Change*, 36(1) MONASH U. L. REV. 69 (2010); Docherty & Giannini, *supra* note 321; Frank Biermann & Ingrid Boas, *Preparing for a Warmer World: Towards a Global Governance System to Protect Climate Refugees*, 10 GLOBAL ENVTL. POL. 60 (2010); Michel Prieur et al., Draft Convention on the International Status of Environmentally-Displaced Persons (third version, May 2013), https://cidce.org/wp-content/uploads/2016/08/Draft-Convention-on-the-International-Status-on-environmentally-displaced-persons-third-version.pdf. Some of these proposals are discussed *supra* in Chapter 2. For a review and analysis of some existing proposals, see KENT & BEHRMAN, FACILITATING RESETTLEMENT, *supra* note 322, at 31–36; Wyman, *supra* note 321, at 185–190; Sheila C. McAnaney, Note, *Sinking Islands? Formulating a Realistic Solution to Climate Change Displacement*, 87 N.Y.U. L. REV. 1172, 1181–85, 1209, tbl.1 (2012). For a general discussion on the creation of a new treaty, see Jane McAdam, *Swimming Against the Tide: Why a Climate Change Displacement Treaty is Not the Answer*, 23(1) INT'L J. REFUGEE L. 2 (2011) [hereinafter 'McAdam, *Swimming Against the Tide*'].

mobility is not a new one. Compelling proposals for a new binding instrument emerged over a decade ago. Even among those advocates who considered a new, binding agreement to be necessary, little common ground was found on key issues, including what form this new agreement should take: a new, independent international convention; expansion of the Refugee Convention; or a new regime within an existing treaty or framework, such as the UNFCCC.[328] There has also been enduring disagreement as to whom precisely such an instrument should protect (for example, persons moving internally or across borders or both) and whether to include or exclude movement that is perceived as voluntary. Diverse proposals therefore abound, and there is little indication of increasing consensus amongst advocates or expanding political will to adopt any form of new binding legal instrument.

As noted, many of the detailed and compelling proposals for a new instrument are not new ones. These proposals are based on extensive research and deliberation. Their value lies in the ideas that academics and practitioners have continued to build upon that may eventually, one day, form a foundation for expanding rights-based frameworks.[329] Notwithstanding, these proposals, even if adopted, would not eliminate entirely the existing protection gaps because they would exclude significant categories of climate change drivers or categories of persons impacted by climate change. To take one prominent example discussed earlier, Docherty and Giannini proposed a new international treaty which would address only persons moving involuntarily across borders (who also meet other proposed criteria). Their proposed treaty would therefore not provide protection to persons moving internally, despite the fact that most people are expected to be displaced by environmental disasters and climate change impacts within national borders. Docherty and Giannini have also excluded from their proposed treaty persons who are perceived to move

---

328    On proposals to expand the Refugee Convention to encompass climate change mobility, see Benoît Mayer, *The International Legal Challenges of Climate-Induced Migration: Proposal for an International Legal Framework*, 22(3) COLO. J. ENVTL. L. & POL'Y 357, 405–6 (2011); Bruce Burson, *Protecting the Rights of People Displaced by Climate Change: Global Issues and Regional Perspectives, in* CLIMATE CHANGE AND MIGRATION: SOUTH PACIFIC PERSPECTIVES 159, 160–61 (Bruce Burson ed., 2010). For arguments in favor of creating a regime that would function within the UNFCCC framework, see KENT & BEHRMAN, FACILITATING RESETTLEMENT, *supra* note 322, at 73–117; *see also* Biermann & Boas, *supra* note 327, at 75–82. For an argument to create a new, stand-alone convention, see Docherty & Giannini, *supra* note 321, at 350.

329    As Avidan Kent and Simon Behrman put it, "these proposals are valuable as they provide a bank of ideas for decision-makers (and others) to pick and choose from, and to develop those elements that they deem more sensible or politically feasible." KENT & BEHRMAN, FACILITATING RESETTLEMENT, *supra* note 322, at 31.

voluntarily. It is not clear from their proposal how the distinction between vol-untary and involuntary would be made; leaving the criteria to diverse national implementation would increase the discretion of States to circumscribe the scope of the treaty. Additionally, Docherty and Giannini sought to define broadly the climate change drivers which would be included in the scope of their treaty (including gradual onset impacts);[330] however, limiting the treaty to involuntary movement risks unintentionally limiting the drivers within its scope to rapid onset impacts, as movement associated with slow onset impacts is often perceived to be fundamentally voluntary in nature.[331]

Other advocates consider that any treaty must address a broader category of human mobility, namely, internal and cross-border movement and/or volun-tary and involuntary movement, in order to address the problem.[332] Docherty and Giannini explain that their criteria are driven by existing legal frameworks and international principles of State sovereignty, which they have sought to balance with humanitarian aims and the particular character of climate change mobility.[333] Other proposals give less weight to existing frameworks and State sovereignty in their proposals.[334] However, broader mechanisms that ignore existing frameworks and that are perceived as impinging on sovereignty would make it difficult for States and institutions to accept such proposals.

Given the distinct issues raised by the various drivers of human mobility and the conditions in which people will move, it may not be feasible or effec-tive to try to address them all with a single international instrument, or indeed in any legal instrument at all.[335] Attempting to cast a wide net which seeks to encompass all mobility scenarios in one treaty risks creating an instrument so broad as to be potentially ineffective and with such an expansive scope of coverage that no State would accept responsibility for the volume of affected

---

330  Docherty & Giannini, *supra* note 321, at 370.

331  *See* MCADAM, FORCED MIGRATION, *supra* note 78, at 194 ("A particular challenge for any new treaty is adequately accounting for slow-onset movement brought about by gradual environmental deterioration, as opposed to flight from sudden disasters").

332  *See* Biermann & Boas, *supra* note 327, at 65–66; Hodgkinson et al., *supra* note 327, at 80, 83, 87–90; McAnaney, *supra* note 327, at 1190–91.

333  Docherty & Giannini, supra note 321, at 372.

334  For example, the proposal presented by Hodgkinson et al. ambitiously attempts to address movement both within and across national borders. Hodgkinson et al., *supra* note 327, at 82–83. As Wyman observes, this is one of the major distinguishing features between the proposals presented by Docherty and Giannini and Hodgkinson et al., which otherwise have a number of similarities. Wyman, *supra* note 321, at 186–87.

335  *See generally* McAdam, *Swimming Against the Tide, supra* note 327 (responding to propos-als for a new instrument); *see also* Kälin & Schrepfer, *supra* note 7, at 79 (opining that any new instrument should have a "soft law character").

persons that ratifying it would entail.[336] It also risks ignoring the specific needs
and interests of the various groups of persons impacted in different ways by
climate change.[337] The disagreements among advocates as to the scope and
form of a new treaty are symptomatic not only of the significant gaps in protection, but also of the unworkability of a "one-size-fits-all approach".[338]

   Thus, if a treaty is pursued (although it is not an option States are actively
considering at present), any new instrument must, as many existing proposals take into account, strike a balance between humanitarian interests and
State interests and must also present a workable framework for the scope of
mobility it seeks to address.[339] Such a legal instrument may not be able to
present a comprehensive solution to all existing protection gaps.[340] In particular, it would be difficult to craft a palatable proposal for a binding treaty
which encompasses mobility connected with slow onset hazard events, one
of the largest protection gaps,[341] or internal movement, the largest anticipated

---

336   *See* MCADAM, FORCED MIGRATION, *supra* note 78, at 194–95 (opining that States
      would be unlikely to agree to a treaty which covered slow onset hazard impacts). *See
      also* McAnaney, *supra* note 327, at 1190–93 (concluding that "[t]he most effective way of
      distinguishing along the spectrum of voluntary and forced migration seems to be a grad-
      uated scale of protections" based on the kind of climate change impact and the urgency
      of the displacement).

337   *See, e.g.*, McAdam, *Swimming Against the Tide*, *supra* note 327, at 4–5.

338   *See* MCADAM, FORCED MIGRATION, *supra* note 78, at 5.

339   Docherty & Giannini, *supra* note 321, at 372; McAdam, *Complimentary Protection*, *supra*
      note 8, at 48. In this respect, Wyman challenges the feasibility of crafting an instrument
      which would address the population targeted by its drafters due to, inter alia, the limits of
      science and multicausality. Wyman, *supra* note 321, at 196–200.

340   *See* Docherty & Giannini, *supra* note 321, at 361 (acknowledging that a new treaty "should
      be viewed as one piece of a larger solution to the problem of displacement" and opin-
      ing that "it would be a critical step toward mitigating the burgeoning crisis of climate
      change refugees"); Kälin & Schrepfer, *supra* note 7, at 58 ("it is clear that there is no single
      approach that provides the solution to current challenges. Approaches must be multifac-
      eted, containing internal and external components"). *See also* McAdam, *Complimentary
      Protection*, *supra* note 8, at 48 (commenting on the International Law Commission's
      attempt to draft articles on the "Protection of persons in the event of disasters": "This is
      both the difficulty and the danger of tailoring legal norms to a new context. The difficulty
      is in specifying with sufficient clarity a legal definition that is workable and that will get
      buy-in from States. The danger is that the law then responds only to a narrow subset of
      disasters, or does not facilitate a holistic response to disasters but rather one in which
      traditional disciplinary boundaries remain entrenched").

341   The protection paradigm, as currently conceived, may have difficulty addressing move-
      ment associated with the impacts of slow onset hazards, which is often viewed as vol-
      untary. *See* MCADAM, FORCED MIGRATION, *supra* note 78, at 189–90. McAdam also
      observed that "there is a discernable shift in emphasis at the international level, in par-
      ticular, away from 'climate change' displacement, towards viewing climate change as a

category of movement in the context of climate change.[342] If a new treaty cannot address these major categories, the cost of creating it may outweigh its benefits. Even if an effective legal instrument could be concluded, it would still require proper implementation, another significant challenge.

Some have suggested that regional or bilateral instruments would be a preferable approach to a global instrument, as they may be tailored to address local and regional concerns and needs with the bottom-up participation of affected populations and also present a more feasible option than a global instrument based on the current political landscape.[343] Others have suggested the development of soft law principles, possibly modeled after the 1998 Guiding Principles and other existing guidelines such as the Nansen Principles,[344] as a solution that could gain more political traction than binding obligations.[345] However, States may have concerns about the legitimacy of such an instrument if it is not based on existing legal norms (as the 1998 Guiding Principles were) or be wary of accepting soft law norms that may evolve into binding

---

subset of natural disasters [...]. However, if a framework responding to displacement by sudden-onset disasters is developed, it is vital that responses to slow-onset movement do not drop off the agenda." (at 240); *see also* The Nansen Conference, Oslo, Norway, 6–7 June 2011, *Climate Change and Displacement in the 21st Century, supra* note 143, at 5, Principle IX ("A more coherent and consistent approach at the international level is needed to meet the protection needs of people displaced externally owing to sudden-onset disasters. States, working in conjunction with UNHCR and other relevant stakeholders, could develop a guiding framework or instrument in this regard.").

342   *See* Docherty & Giannini, *supra* note 321, at 369. *See also* UNHCR, ENVIRONMENT & CLIMATE CHANGE, *supra* note 139, at 8 ("It is widely agreed that the vast majority of people displaced by disasters and the impacts of climate change will be internally displaced.").

343   *See, e.g.*, Williams, *supra* note 8, at 518–19 (proposing a regional regime under the UNFCCC); McAdam, *Swimming Against the Tide, supra* note 327, at 4–5, 26; Phillip Dane Warren, Note, *Forced Migration After Paris COP21: Evaluating the "Climate Change Displacement Coordination Facility"* 116 COLUM. L. REV. 2103, 2134–35, 2141–42 (2016) (arguing that binding regional instruments should be developed under the UNFCCC as a "primary umbrella organization"). *But see* Mayer, *supra* note 328, at 400 (cautioning that "regional governance may lead to fears that the treatment of climate migrants may differ from one region to another, and that burden-sharing would not be possible on the regional scale, since rich Western States would be separated from needy tropical ones", and suggesting that the potential failure of regional protection should be taken into account and a comprehensive protection regime should therefore include international monitoring and intervention).

344   The Nansen Principles are discussed *infra* in Chapter 5.

345   *See* MCADAM, FORCED MIGRATION, *supra* note 78, at 237–40, 250–56; UNHCR, Bellagio Roundtable Summary, *supra* note 39, at 4–5, ¶ 13; Kälin & Schrepfer, *supra* note 7, at 71–72.

obligations through customary international law or inclusion in future binding instruments.[346]

Even if a new legal instrument has, in theory, the potential to provide (partial) protection as part of a broader approach, concluding such an instrument with the participation of States (be it soft or hard law, regional or global) could siphon scarce political will and economic resources away from the formulation of much needed, preemptive mitigation and adaptation strategies.[347] In addition, such an instrument (be it soft or hard law) would be fiercely negotiated and might fall prey to the least common denominator principle,[348] ultimately serving as a palliative or even eroding existing efforts to help those displaced due to climate change.[349]

In any event, there is currently scant political will for a new multilateral instrument (as has been the case since proposals began to emerge over a decade ago); many States already want to limit protection obligations to individuals falling under existing instruments.[350] The UNHCR, which has been highly involved in this issue, also does not support the creation of a new binding instrument, but instead advocates an adaptive approach "that focuses on the integration of effective practices by States and (sub-) regional organizations into their own normative frameworks and practices in accordance with their specific situations and challenges."[351] In the following chapter, the existing instruments, initiatives, and frameworks that underpin an adaptive approach are explored.

346   See Kälin & Schrepfer, *supra* note 7, at 71–72; MCADAM, FORCED MIGRATION, *supra* note 78, at 238–39.

347   See MCADAM, FORCED MIGRATION, *supra* note 78, at 189–90. *But see* Christine Gibb & James Ford, *Should the United Nations Framework Convention on Climate Change Recognize Climate Migrants?*, 7 ENVTL. RES. LETT. 1, 2 (2012) (arguing that the recognition of human mobility as a valid issue within the UNFCCC process, in particular in the Cancun Adaptation Framework, "indicate[s] a willingness of signatories to address the climate migration issue"). Political will to address human mobility, however, may depend on how the issue is addressed, e.g., as one for adaptation or one which requires a new legal protective framework.

348   See Kälin & Schrepfer, *supra* note 7, at 70.

349   See MCADAM, FORCED MIGRATION, *supra* note 78, at 189–90.

350   Koko Warner, *Human Migration and Displacement in the Context of Adaptation to Climate Change: the Cancun Adaptation Framework and Potential for Future Action*, 30(6) ENV'T & PLAN. C: GOV'T & POL'Y 1061, 1074 (2012); *see also id.* at 197–99; McAnaney, *supra* note 327, at 1202–03; Wyman, *supra* note 321, at 200–02.

351   UNHCR, ENVIRONMENT & CLIMATE CHANGE, *supra* note 139, at 7.

## PART 3

*Implementing an Adaptive Approach
to Climate Change Mobility*

∴

# CHAPTER 5

# The Underpinnings of an Adaptive Approach

> Whoever cannot seek the unforeseen sees nothing, for the known way is an impasse.
> — HERACLITUS

∴

> No one saves us but ourselves. No one can and no one may. We ourselves must walk the path.
> — GAUTAMA BUDDHA

∵

The adaptive approach to climate change mobility builds on cooperative multilateral agreements, non-binding frameworks, and initiatives that attempt to coordinate across sectors and at local, national, regional, and international levels. This adaptive approach has developed through various frameworks aimed at mitigating and adapting to climate change, reducing disaster risk, and developing policy and legal responses to human mobility. This chapter will explore how some of the most prominent international policy and legal instruments in these areas address climate change mobility. Climate change mobility is often—but not always—one of many crucial, interrelated but diverse issues addressed within these frameworks. This examination will show that human mobility was not always an issue included at the outset within climate change mitigation, adaptation, or disaster risk reduction frameworks, but has gained increasing recognition as a vital component therein. Growing awareness of the critical nature of addressing climate change mobility has facilitated the development of new, targeted initiatives and inclusion of climate change mobility in a broader spectrum of frameworks.

© KONINKLIJKE BRILL NV, LEIDEN, 2022 | DOI:10.1163/9789004298880_007

A        **Frameworks for Mitigating and Adapting to Climate Change
         Impacts**

Human mobility is increasingly recognized as a crucial aspect of mitigation
and adaptation to climate change impacts. States already recognized the
interconnected nature of desertification and human mobility in 1994 when
the United Nations Convention to Combat Desertification (UNCCD) was concluded. The nexus between desertification, drought, land degradation, and
human mobility has gained increasing attention as the UNCCD has adapted
and developed evolving implementation strategies. Human mobility was
not initially addressed within the scope of the UNCCD's sister convention,
the United Nations Framework Convention on Climate Change (UNFCCC).
However, increasing recognition that the effects of climate change had already
begun to manifest, and that singular focus on mitigation would not ward off
its impacts, led States to give greater attention to adaptation measures and
to bring human mobility within the scope of State efforts to address climate
change under the UNFCCC.

1)       *The United Nations Convention to Combat Desertification*
Significant areas of the Earth's landmass have oscillated between many different climatic zones throughout the planet's history. The periodic ice ages are a
prime example of the dramatic shifts that can alter the weather and climate
not only in a specific region, but across the entire biosphere. One of the current
extremes in this spectrum can be referred to as a desert ecosystem. However,
the common view of a desert as something barren is far too simplistic, as a
plethora of diverse plant and animal species commonly populate even the
driest and hottest desert landscape. It is only an anthropocentric perspective
that considers such an area unfit for life, which in fact means unfit for *human*
life. And even this is not accurate; one should instead speak of some desert
environments being unfit for *large scale* human settlement, absent significant
alterations to the environment.

   Nevertheless, as the climate in certain areas of the Earth has changed over
the last several decades and as human populations have continued to increase,
it has been increasingly difficult for some communities to support themselves,
especially the ones that depend directly upon the local land for their livelihood. The struggle to combat large-scale desertification and land degradation
thus gained momentum in the last century, as human populations began to
experience ever increasing pressures to either move to regions with greater
food security or remain in place with the assistance of *in situ* adaptation measures. Combatting desertification and land degradation is inextricably linked

to efforts to mitigate climate change, as climate change both contributes to and is exacerbated by desertification and land degradation. The United Nations Convention to Combat Desertification in Those Countries Experiencing Serious Drought and/or Desertification, Particularly in Africa (UNCCD) is one of the international instruments that was developed to facilitate these efforts.

The UNCCD was adopted on 17 June 1994 and entered into force on 26 December 1996.[1] The UNCCD is one of the three Rio Conventions emerging from the United Nations Conference on Environment and Development, held in Rio de Janeiro in June 1992 (Rio Earth Summit), all of which address adaptation to climate change. The UNCCD's sister conventions, the United Nations Framework Convention on Climate Change (UNFCCC) and the United Nations Convention on Biological Diversity (UNCBD), were formulated prior to the Rio Earth Summit and signed during the conference. Unlike its sister conventions, the UNCCD would not be completed for another two years. Instead, at the Rio Earth Summit, United Nations States Parties prompted the creation of the UNCCD in Agenda 21: Programme of Action for Sustainable Development (Agenda 21).[2] As requested by Agenda 21, the United Nations General Assembly established, at its 47th session, an international negotiating committee to finalize the UNCCD by June 1994.[3] When the UNCCD was adopted in 1994, States recognized the link between desertification and human mobility, the need for early warning systems and assistance mechanisms, and the value of a regional and sub-regional approach.[4]

---

1   United Nations Convention to Combat Desertification in Countries Experiencing Serious Drought and/or Desertification, Particularly in Africa art. 10(3)(a) & Annex I, art. 11(f), 14 Oct. 1994, 1954 U.N.T.S. 3 [hereinafter 'UNCCD']. For background and drafting history of the UNCCD, see generally Pamela S. Chasek, *The Convention to Combat Desertification: Lessons Learned for Sustainable Development*, 6(2) J. ENV'T & DEV. 147 (1997).

2   United Nations Conference on Environment and Development, Rio de Janiero, Brazil, 3–14 June 1992, *Rio Declaration on Environment and Development*, ¶ 12.40, UN Doc. A/CONF.151/26/Rev.1 (Vol. I), Annex II (12 Aug. 1992), [hereinafter 'Rio Earth Summit'] ("The General Assembly, at its forty–seventh session, should be requested to establish, under the aegis of the General Assembly, an intergovernmental negotiating committee for the elaboration of an international convention to combat desertification in [] those countries experiencing serious drought and/or desertification, particularly in Africa, with a view to finalizing such a convention by June 1994.").

3   G.A. Res. 47/188, ¶ 2, UN Doc. A/RES/47/188 (12 Mar. 1993).

4   UNCCD, *supra* note 1, art. 10(3)(a) & Annex I, art. 11(f). *See also* Michelle Leighton, *Desertification and Migration, in* GOVERNING GLOBAL DESERTIFICATION: LINKING ENVIRONMENTAL DEGRADATION, POVERTY AND PARTICIPATION 43, 50–51 (Pierre Marc Johnson et al. eds., 2006) [hereinafter 'Leighton, *Desertification and Migration*']; International Symposium on Desertification and Migrations, Almería, Spain, 9–11 Feb 1994, *Declaration of Almería* (11 Feb. 1994) [hereinafter 'Almería Declaration'].

a          Origins of the UNCCD
The origins of the UNCCD date back 20 years prior to the Rio Earth Summit.
In 1972, the United Nations Conference on Human Environment held in
Stockholm gave birth to the United Nations Environment Programme (UNEP),
which would have its headquarters in Nairobi, Kenya.[5] This landmark conference coincided with the latter half of a five-year drought in the Sahel that led
to widespread famine and displacement.

The specter of the Sahel drought raised concerns about the broader implications of desertification that, with the United Nations Environment Programme's
influence, sparked a 1977 Conference on Desertification in Nairobi, Kenya
(1977 Conference on Desertification).[6] The 1977 Conference on Desertification
adopted the United Nations Plan of Action to Combat Desertification (PACD),
which the United Nations Environment Programme would implement.[7] The
PACD, which was not binding, had the ambitious goal of eradicating desertification by the close of the twentieth century CE.[8] Assessments at the end of the
1980s and in the early 1990s, however, reported that the PACD had done little
to stymie desertification and suffered from poor implementation, insufficient
scientific foundations, and a lack of funding.[9] It was against this background
that the United Nations Parties took the decision to establish the UNCCD at the
Rio Earth Summit.

---

5   United Nations Conference on Human Environment, Stockholm, Sweden, 5–16 June 1972,
     *Report of the United Nations Conference on Human Environment*, at 29, UN Doc. A/CONF.48/
     14/Rev.1 (25 July 1972); G.A. Res. 2997, UN Doc. A/Res/2997(XXVII) (15 Dec. 1972).
6   United Nations Conference on Desertification, Nairobi, Kenya, 29 Aug.–9 Sep. 1977, *Report
     of the United Nations Conference on Desertification*, at 2, ¶ 4, UN Doc. A/CONF.74/36 (7
     Sept. 1977) [hereinafter 'UNCOD Report'] ("The Sahelian drought of 1968–1973 and its tragic
     effect on the peoples of that region drew world attention to the chronic problems of human
     survival and development on the desert margins."). *See also* United Nations Environment
     Programme, Desertification Control Programme Activity Centre, *Rolling Back the Desert: Ten
     Years after UNCOD*, at 1 (1987) [hereinafter 'Ten Years After UNCOD'].
7   UNCOD Report, *supra* note 6, at 2–63; G.A. Res. 32/172, ¶ 8, UN Doc. A/RES/32/172 (19
     Dec. 1977).
8   Ten Years After UNCOD, *supra* note 6, at 3.
9   G.A. Res. 44/172, preamble & ¶ 2, UN Doc. A/RES/44/172 (19 Dec. 1989); R.S. Odingo,
     *Implementation of the Plan of Action to Combat Desertification (PACD) 1978–1991*, 21
     DESERTIFICATION CONTROL BULL. 6, 6 (1992); Ten Years After UNCOD, *supra* note 6, at
     3–8; William C. Burns, *The International Convention to Combat Desertification: Drawing a Line
     in the Sand?*, 16 MICH. J. INT'L L. 831, 850–54 (1995); Rio Earth Summit, *supra* note 2, at 150,
     ¶ 12.5.

b        Conceptual Foundations of the UNCCD

At its inception, and consistent with its origins, the main focus of the UNCCD was combatting desertification and mitigating the impacts of drought. This is reflected in the name of the convention and set forth therein as its objective: "The objective of this Convention is to combat desertification and mitigate the effects of drought [...] with a view to contributing to the achievement of sustainable development in affected areas."[10] The framing of this objective also makes explicit the link between the implementation of the UNCCD and sustainable development. The UNCCD requires that States Parties give priority to African countries affected by drought and desertification, in light of the significant challenges facing the region.[11]

Desertification is defined in the UNCCD as a form of "land degradation in arid, semi-arid and dry sub-humid areas resulting from various factors, including climatic variations and human activities".[12] The UNCCD's predecessor, the PACD, had defined desertification and also explained the processes that led to it:

> Desertification is the diminution or destruction of the biological potential of the land, and can lead ultimately to desert-like conditions. It is an aspect of the widespread deterioration of ecosystems, and has diminished or destroyed the biological potential, i.e. plant and animal production, for multiple use purposes at a time when increased productivity is needed to support growing populations in quest of development. Important factors in contemporary society—the struggle for development and the effort to increase food production, and to adapt and apply modern technologies, set against a background of population growth and demographic change—interlock in a network of cause and effect.[13]

The PACD definition signaled a fundamental shift in the perception of desertification, a term which had been used with varying meanings in the early twentieth century CE. In early iterations, desertification was often conceived as a steady encroachment of the desert upon more fertile lands.[14] Preparation for

---

10    UNCCD, *supra* note 1, at 5, art. 2(1).

11    *Id.* at 8, art. 7.

12    *Id.* at 4, art. 1(a).

13    UNCOD Report, *supra* note 6, at 3, ¶ 7.

14    For a review of the evolution of the concept, and the varying definitions, of desertification, see generally Michel M. Verstraete, *Defining Desertification: A Review*, 9 CLIMATIC CHANGE 5 (1986). *See also* Ten Years After UNCOD, *supra* note 6, at 1–2 ("The popular belief had been that desertification was mainly an act of nature, the ravages of unpredictable

the 1977 Conference on Desertification included studies that constituted an unprecedented attempt to synthesize and explore the causes of desertification. The UNCCD, like its predecessor, the PACD, encourages a view of desertification that focuses more on the anthropogenic pressures of unsustainable land use that lead to the fragility and vulnerability of the land.[15]

The UNCCD's more succinct definition of desertification also introduced the term "land degradation", positioning desertification as a sub-category therein.[16] Since the UNCCD's inception, the dialogue surrounding the UNCCD's implementation has shifted to issues of "land degradation" more generally. The abbreviation "DLDD"—referring to "desertification, land degradation and drought"—has become common in UNCCD and broader desertification-related discourse. This gradual conceptual broadening nevertheless remains within the scope of the UNCCD's implementation objectives and has not entailed a modification to the terms of the UNCCD itself. States Parties have approved two strategic plans (discussed further below) that embrace this broadened focus.

Legal scholars have argued that the discourse shift from "desertification" to "land degradation" is due to a frustration with the UNCCD's lack of progress and the desire to tap into the larger funding schemes of its sister conventions, the United Nations Framework Convention on Climate Change (UNFCCC) and the United Nations Convention on Biological Diversity (UNCBD).[17] Nevertheless,

---

climate, drought and 'outrageous fortune.' By the time of the UNCOD in Nairobi, we were beginning to recognize that assumption as naïve at best.").

15    *See* Cheikh Mbow, *The Great Green Wall in the Sahel*, CLIMATE SCIENCE, OXFORD RESEARCH ENCYCLOPEDIA 5 (2017), https://oxfordre.com/climatescience/view/10.1093/acrefore/9780190228620.001.0001/acrefore-9780190228620-e-559; *but see* ANTON IMESON, DESERTIFICATION, LAND DEGRADATION AND SUSTAINABILITY 41–42, 301–302 (2012) (noting that "there has never been a sound scientific conceptual underpinning of what desertification actually is", including after the development of the UNCCD; also opining that "[t]he UNCCD has not really provided governments with the tools that are needed to regulate land use").

16    The Intergovernmental Panel on Climate Change (IPCC) has defined land degradation as "a negative trend in land condition, caused by direct or indirect human-induced processes including anthropogenic climate change, expressed as long-term reduction or loss of at least one of the following: biological productivity, ecological integrity, or value to humans." INTERGOVERNMENTAL PANEL ON CLIMATE CHANGE, CLIMATE CHANGE AND LAND 347 (2019) [hereinafter 'IPCC, CLIMATE CHANGE & LAND'] (emphasis in original omitted).

17    *See* Shelley Welton et al., *Legal and Scientific Integrity in Advancing a "Land Degradation Neutral World"*, 40(1) COLUM. J. ENVTL. L. 39, 55–58 (2015). The UNCCD has been likened to the "poor little sister" of the other Rio Conventions because of the comparative difference the UNCCD has received in funding and attention. Jeremy Smith, *Evaluation of the Effectiveness of National Action Programmes to Implement the United Nations Convention to Combat Desertification* 8 (commissioned by the UNCCD Evaluation Office, March 2015),

the trend in recent years has been one of recalibration in approach in order to move away from linear, Cartesian thinking in favor of a more systems[18] and holistic embrace of the complexities involved in combatting large-scale desertification and land degradation.

Combatting desertification and land degradation is a critical component of mitigating climate change. Climate change, desertification, and land degradation have a circular causal nexus. Climate change both contributes to and is exacerbated by desertification and land degradation. Global warming has already led to an observable increase in the rate, frequency, and magnitude of processes that drive land degradation, including heavy precipitation, heat stress, and sea level rise. In the future, climate change will likely lead to increasing floods, drought, cyclones, and sea level rise, further intensifying land degradation processes.[19] In turn, land degradation exacerbates climate change by increasing the release of greenhouse gases into the atmosphere and reducing carbon uptake.[20]

c        The Desertification-Mobility Nexus

Human mobility in connection with desertification, land degradation, or drought is not a singular phenomenon. It can be international or internal, temporary or permanent, and can fall into varying places on the sliding scale of voluntary versus involuntary movement. Migration expert François Gemenne and his colleagues have identified four related environmental "cycles" that may be linked to varying forms of mobility:

- Very long-term cycles: aridification.[21] This process is linked to climate evolution, and will be aggravated by climate change. It involves

---

available at https://www.unccd.int/sites/default/files/relevant-links/2017-01/NAP%20e valuation_0.pdf [hereinafter '2015 NAP Evaluation'] (citing Anneke Trux & Reinhard Bodemeyer, *The United Nations Convention to Combat Desertification—UNCCD: The Rio Conventions' Poor Little Sister*, 1 AGRIC. & RURAL DEV. 22 (2007)).

18    *See generally* FRITJOF CAPRA & PIER LUISI, THE SYSTEMS VIEW OF LIFE: A UNIFYING VISION (2014); FRITJOF CAPRA, THE TURNING POINT: SCIENCE, SOCIETY, AND THE RISING CULTURE (1988).

19    IPCC, CLIMATE CHANGE & LAND, *supra* note 16, at 347.

20    *Id.*

21    Dr. Katerina Michaelides, a contributing author to publications on desertification by the United Nations Intergovernmental Panel on Climate Change (IPCC), has defined aridification as "a progressive change of the climate towards a more arid state—whereby rainfall decreases in relation to the evaporative demand—as this directly affects water supply to vegetation and soils." Robert McSweeney, *Explainer: 'Desertification' and the Role of Climate Change*, CARBON BRIEF, EXPLAINERS (6 Aug. 2019), https://www.carbonbrief.org/explainer-desertification-and-the-role-of-climate-change.

very slow and progressive population displacements, over several
generations.
– Mid-term cycles: desertification. Migration is here linked to a cumu-
lative process, and often circular. In this case, migration can be a livelihood strategy.
– Short-term cycles: droughts. The displacement, here, is a forced one,
linked to a short-term disaster. A possibility of return exists.
– Seasonal cycles: seasonal migration, which is part of a social routine.[22]

These four cycles provide a sense of how differing forms of mobility may be
linked to desertification, land degradation, or drought. They also underscore
that desertification and drought are not synonymous, drought being a rapid
onset event and desertification a slow onset event.

In some of these contexts, migration can be a positive adaptive strategy,
bringing financial, labor, or environmental benefits for the migrants and their
home communities, as well as for host communities. A UNCCD policy brief
details some of these potential benefits:

Among other opportunities, it has been observed that out-migration alle-
viates demographic burden and allows degraded environments to recu-
perate. This enables emigrants coming back with new skills to diversify

---

22    François Gemenne et al., *Understanding Migration Choices: The UNCCD as a Mechanism for
      Developing Coping Strategies*, at 9 (Prepared for International Symposium: Desertification
      and Migrations 11, 25–27 October 2006, Almeria, Spain, 2006), *available at* http://citeseerx.
      ist.psu.edu/viewdoc/download?doi=10.1.1.116.6511&rep=rep1&type=pdf (citation added).
      *See also* INTERNATIONAL ORGANIZATION FOR MIGRATION (IOM), ADDRESSING
      THE LAND DEGRADATION-MIGRATION NEXUS: THE ROLE OF THE UNITED NATIONS
      CONVENTION TO COMBAT DESERTIFICATION 9–10 (2019) (*prepared by* Sara Vigil under
      the supervision of IOM and the UNCCD), *available at* https://environmentalmigration.
      iom.int/sites/environmentalmigration/files/IOM%20UNCCD%20Desertification%202
      019%20FINAL.pdf [hereinafter 'IOM UNCCD Study'] (explaining possible migration tra-
      jectories and destinations); Michelle Leighton, *Desertification + Migration = Conflict?, in*
      DESERTIFICATION: A SECURITY THREAT? ANALYSIS OF RISKS AND CHALLENGES, 21,
      22 (Conference on the Occasion of the World Day to Combat Desertification, 26 June
      2007, Berlin, Germany, 2007), *available at* https://www.desertifikation.de/fileadmin/user
      _upload/downloads/Desertification_a_security_threat_72dpi.pdf [hereinafter 'Leighton,
      *Desertification + Migration = Conflict?*] (explaining that the forms of movement can
      evolve: "Often, what begins among members of a family (similarly within an entire com-
      munity) as temporary migration, such as to take advantage of seasonal agricultural jobs,
      can evolve into permanent relocation. Networks established between the sending and
      receiving communities can constitute a strong magnet for continued migration, particu-
      larly as desertification or drought continue to impact household income.").

livelihoods and thus reduce their reliance on natural resources, or to return with know-how on innovative land use methods, with savings that allow coping during lean periods. Sending remittances to improve lives of those remaining in villages continues as a major economic factor. Migration also plays an important role in co-development of countries of origin and hosting countries. In 2007 for instance, US$251billion out of the US$ 337 billion worldwide remittances were sent to developing countries (IOM 2009); which represents almost twice as much as the Official Development Assistance received in these countries. From the hosting countries perspective, migrants constitute an important low-wage labour supply, including some highly skilled and qualified workers.[23]

However, migration—particularly when it is forced—can result in heavy costs, raising concerns for human security and national security.[24] For individuals moving, migration can be an expensive, difficult, and dangerous undertaking. Persons moving must have enough funds and sufficient health to make the journey and may encounter hostilities *en route* or at their destination. The physical dangers and hardships are compounded for undocumented travelers moving through trafficking networks.[25] Larger movements of people can

---

23   *See* UNCCD Secretariat, Policy Brief on Migration, *Managing Environmentally-Induced Migration in Drylands: The Win-Win Strategy* 8 (Aug. 2009) (*by* Domoina Randriamiarina), *available at* http://catalogue.unccd.int/844_Migration_policy_brief.pdf [hereinafter 'UNCCD Migration Brief']; *see also* IOM UNCCD Study, *supra* note 22, at 7; Leighton, *Desertification + Migration = Conflict?, supra* note 22, at 24–25; Charles P. Martin-Shields at al., *More Development—More Migration? The "Migration Hump" and Its Significance for Development Policy Co-operation with Sub-Saharan Africa* 2–3 (German Dev. Inst., Briefing Paper 20/2017, 2017), *available at* https://www.die-gdi.de/uploads/media/BP_20.2017. pdf (describing the "migration hump" phenomenon, i.e., "growing per capita income in developing countries is typically accompanied by higher rates of emigration." The paper concludes that "[d]evelopment policy co-operation cannot and should not prevent migration. The migration hump shows that migration and development do not mutually exclude one another, but strengthen one another."); TRANSRE, MIGRATION FOR ADAPTATION: A GUIDEBOOK FOR INTEGRATING MIGRATION AND TRANSLOCALITY INTO COMMUNITY-BASED ADAPTATION 20–21 (2018), *available at* http://www.transre. org/application/files/5715/3296/4247/Migration_for_Adaptation_Guidebook_online_ english.pdf (presenting a brief case study describing how migration practices have benefited one family in Thailand).

24   Leighton, *Desertification + Migration = Conflict?, supra* note 22, at 21–22.

25   *Id.* at 24 ("A potential migrant must not only consider a suitable destination, employment prospects, obtain funds for the trip, and contact friends or relatives that could help along the way, but must have the health needed to endure a long journey. The travel can be perilous for a migrant who has no visa or work papers if crossing international borders. She/he may encounter hostility from the transit or destination community, local ethnic

create conflict over scarce resources; aggravate poverty or political, religious, or social tensions; or exceed the capacities of existing infrastructures and environmental resources.[26]

When the UNCCD was under negotiation, States recognized the significance of the nexus between desertification and human mobility, whilst also perceiving the complexity of the issue and the need for further research.[27] In February 1994, several months prior to the completion of the UNCCD, the UNCCD international negotiating committee organized a symposium in Almería, Spain on desertification and migration, attended by experts and State representatives. The participants of the symposium adopted the Almería Statement on Desertification and Migration (Almería Statement), reflecting the views discussed at the symposium.[28] The Almería Statement recognizes that migration has been an adaptation strategy throughout human history, but asserts that, "fundamental to the issue of desertification and migration is the fact that many people wish to be able to have the freedom to stay at home, on their land, in their own culture."[29] The Symposium concluded that "the corollary of the recognized right of freedom of movement is the right to remain."[30] The Symposium participants recommended that the UNCCD international negotiating committee "give greater attention to the phenomenon of desertification-induced migration, at the local, regional and global levels."[31]

---

group, or government authorities. Hostility may also ensue if migrants are forced to compete with local residents for scarce jobs or resources. The trafficking networks that assist undocumented migrants can themselves be very dangerous, too. Migrants may undergo physical abuse, deprivation of food, water or shelter, and even death at sea in crossing the Atlantic or Mediterranean.").

26 *Id. See also* UNCCD Migration Brief, *supra* note 23, at 6.
27 Almería Declaration, *supra* note 4, at 3 ("The relationship between environmental degradation and migration is important, complex, yet little understood.").
28 For a detailed account of the 1994 Almería symposium, see generally Arthur H. Westing, *International Symposium on 'Desertification and Migration', held in Almería, Spain, during 9–11 February 1994*, 21(1) ENVTL. CONSERVATION 85 (1994). A second conference was convened in Almería in 2006, Almería II, "conceived not only as a sequel and a revision of the former, but also as a reference for [Almería II], which also incorporates new approaches, such as the interaction between physical planning and desertification or the environmental problems inherited from the migrations dynamics, both at source and in the housing places," with a focus on sharing information and evidence with policymakers. *Presentation*, II INTERNATIONAL SYMPOSIUM DESERTIFICATION AND MIGRATIONS, http://www.sidym2006.com/eng/eng_presentacion.asp (last visited 29 May 2021).
29 Almería Declaration, *supra* note 4, at 4.
30 *Id.*
31 *Id.*

The contents of the UNCCD reflect these views. In its preamble, the UNCCD acknowledges the link between desertification/drought, sustainable development, and human mobility: "desertification and drought affect sustainable development through their interrelationships with important social problems such as poverty, poor health and nutrition, lack of food security, and those arising from migration, displacement of persons and demographic dynamics."[32] Under Article 17, States Parties to the UNCCD have undertaken to support research activities that "take into account, where relevant, the relationship between poverty, migration caused by environmental factors, and desertification".[33]

In addition, the UNCCD envisages the formulation of "National Action Programmes" (UNCCD NAPs) as tools for States Parties to identify the factors contributing to desertification and the practical measures necessary to combat it. UNCCD NAPs may include measures to prepare for and mitigate the effects of drought, such as early warning systems and mechanisms for assisting "environmentally displaced persons".[34] In the Regional Implementation Annex for Africa, States Parties are required to take into consideration "the difficult socioeconomic conditions, exacerbated by deteriorating and fluctuating terms of trade, external indebtedness and political instability, which induce internal, regional and international migrations" and "the insufficient institutional and legal frameworks" in place to address these issues.[35] At the sub-regional level, action programmes are required to focus—as a matter of priority—on early warning systems and joint planning for mitigating the effects of drought, including measures to address the problems resulting from "environmentally induced migrations".[36]

The UNCCD NAPs therefore provide an avenue for States Parties to proactively address human mobility issues and to potentially receive funding for projects.[37] They were envisaged to be the "key instrument" for implementation of the UNCCD.[38] However, a 2009 UNCCD policy brief on migration notes that

---

32    UNCCD, *supra* note 1, preamble at 2.

33    *Id.* art. 17(1)(e).

34    *Id.* art. 10(3)(a).

35    *Id.* Annex I, arts. 3(e) & (g).

36    *Id.* Annex I, art. 11(f).

37    *See* Leighton, *Desertification and Migration, supra* note 4, at 52 (opining that the text of the UNCCD opens the door for using this institutional framework to address human mobility in connection with desertification); Welton et al., *supra* note 17, at 54–55 (noting that NAPs can be used to solicit financing, but given that the UNCCD does not have its own financing mechanism for these projects, funds must be sourced from developed countries).

38    2015 NAP Evaluation, *supra* note 17, at 3; *see also* UNCCD, *supra* note 1, art. 10.

several NAPs suffer from a disconnect between combatting desertification/land degradation/drought and the impact of those policies and environmental conditions on affected populations: "Population movements that take place in reaction to increasing desertification are, for example, inaccurately recorded or not even assessed at all with a view to addressing the issue efficiently."[39] Moreover, as explained in a 2015 evaluation commissioned by the UNCCD, the NAP process has generally produced theoretical documents which have received little funding and, consequently, often are not implemented in practice.[40] The NAP evaluation concludes that, rather than allowing political will to become "hamstrung by the rigid NAP process",[41] it is preferable to instead "transform NAPs into a general statement of aims for which top-level support is secured."[42]

d        The 10-Year Strategy

By 2007, the UNCCD was facing challenges to its implementation, not only with respect to the NAPs. Like its PACD predecessor, the UNCCD was suffering from insufficient funding, inadequate scientific foundations, and a lack of advocacy/interest amongst States.[43] In September 2007, in light of these challenges and in view of the evolving operational and policy environment, States Parties adopted a 10-year strategic plan and framework to enhance the implementation of the Convention, extending from 2008 to 2018 (10-Year Strategy).[44]

The 10-Year Strategy refers to migration in the introductory paragraphs, recognizing "growing numbers of environmental refugees and migrants shedding

39    UNCCD Migration Brief, *supra* note 23, at 9.
40    2015 NAP Evaluation, *supra* note 17, at 3–5. *See also* Pamela Chasek et al., *Operationalizing Zero Net Land Degradation: The Next Stage in International Efforts to Combat Desertification?*, 112(A) J. ARID ENV'T. 5, 6 (2015) ("the major tool for on the ground implementation [of the UNCCD], the National Action Plans (NAP), are irrelevant to mainstream policy making and development cooperation, and in many cases donors address land degradation issues bilaterally rather than under the framework of the Convention"): UNCCD Migration Brief, *supra* note 23, at 10 (detailing difficulties in the financing of NAPs).
41    2015 NAP Evaluation, *supra* note 17, at 21–22.
42    UNCCD, Ordos, China, 6–16 Sept. 2017, *Report by the Executive Secretary: Integration of Sustainable Development Goal 15 and Related Target 15.3 which States: "to combat desertification, restore degraded land and soil, including land affected by desertification, drought and floods, and strive to achieve a land degradation-neutral world", into the Implementation of the United Nations Convention to Combat Desertification*, at 6, ¶ 10, UN Doc. ICCD/COP(13)/2 (23 June 2017) [hereinafter 'UNCCD COP13 Executive Secretary Report'].
43    UNCCD, Madrid, Spain, 3–14 Sept. 2007, *Report of the Conference of the Parties on Its Eighth Session*, pt. 2, Annex, at 15, ¶¶ 2, 15, UN Doc. ICCD/COP(8)/16/Add.1 (23 Oct. 2007) [hereinafter 'UNCCD COP8 Report'].
44    *Id.* Decision 3, 8, ¶ 1.

new light on the impacts of poverty and environmental degradation."[45] The objectives of the 10-Year Strategy do not mention human mobility specifically, although a UNCCD leaflet notes that "[o]ne pillar of the UNCCD's new 10-year Strategy directly addresses desertification and migration."[46] This is undoubtedly a reference to the first strategic objective of the 10-Year Strategy, which aims "[t]o improve the living conditions of affected populations".[47] The expected impacts of this objective are that affected populations would have an "improved and more diversified livelihood base and [...] benefit from income generated from sustainable land management", as well as reducing their "socio-economic and environmental vulnerability to climate change, climate variability and drought".[48] Fulfilling this objective would help to reduce forced migration from such areas.[49]

e        The 2018–2030 Strategic Framework
In view of the (then) pending expiry of the 10-Year Strategy, the UNCCD Conference of the Parties adopted, at its 13th session in 2017, a new strategic framework for 2018–2030 (2018–2030 Strategic Framework).[50] The 2018–2030 Strategic Framework sets forth its vision for achieving a "future that avoids, minimizes, and reverses desertification/land degradation and mitigates the effects of drought in affected areas at all levels and strive[s] to achieve a land degradation-neutral world".[51]

The objective of a "land-degradation-neutral world" reflects the language adopted—at the urging of the UNCCD Secretariat[52]—in the 2012 United

---

45    *Id.* Annex, at 15, ¶ 4.
46    UNCCD, MIGRATION AND DESERTIFICATION 2 (UNCCD Thematic Fact Sheet Series No. 3, 2011), *available at* https://catalogue.unccd.int/22_loose_leaf_Desertification_migration. pdf [hereinafter 'UNCCD Factsheet'].
47    UNCCD COP8 Report, *supra* note 43, Annex, ¶ 9.
48    *Id.*
49    As the United Nations General Assembly observed in December 2016, "combating desertification, land degradation and drought, including through sustainable land management, can contribute to easing forced migration flows influenced by a number of factors, including economic, social, security and environmental concerns, which can, in turn, reduce current and potential fighting over resources in degraded areas." G.A. Res. 71/229, at 2, UN Doc. A/RES/71/229 (7 Feb. 2017).
50    UNCCD, Ordos, China, 6–16 Sept. 2017, *Report of the Conference of the Parties on Its Thirteenth Session*, pt. 2, at 18, ¶ 1, UN Doc. ICCD/COP(13)/21/Add.1 (23 Oct. 2017) [hereinafter 'UNCCD COP13 Report'].
51    *Id.* at 19, ¶ 4.
52    *See generally* UNCCD Secretariat, *Towards a Land Degradation Neutral World: Land and Soil in the Context of a Green Economy for Sustainable Development, Food Security and Poverty Eradication* (Submission to the Preparatory Process for the Rio+20 Conference 13,

Nations Conference on Sustainable Development (Rio+20), held on the 20-year anniversary of the 1992 Rio Earth Summit. Rio+20 participants undertook to "strive to achieve a land-degradation-neutral world in the context of sustainable development."[53] At Rio+20, United Nations Member States also committed to develop sustainable development goals, which took form in the 2030 Agenda for Sustainable Development, adopted in 2015.[54] Sustainable Development Goal 15.3 aims to, "[b]y 2030, combat desertification, restore degraded land and soil, including land affected by desertification, drought and floods, and strive to achieve a land degradation-neutral world".[55] At its 12th session, even prior to adopting the 2018–2030 Strategic Framework, the UNCCD Conference of the Parties agreed to integrate Sustainable Development Goal 15.3, considering that it would provide "a strong vehicle for driving implementation of the UNCCD, within the scope of the Convention."[56]

The land degradation-neutral paradigm presents several opportunities that could help to overcome previous difficulties in the UNCCD's implementation. In particular, the UNCCD's Science-Policy Interface developed a scientific conceptual framework "to provide a scientifically sound basis for planning, implementing and monitoring" the land degradation neutral paradigm, as well as to provide indicators for monitoring and reporting.[57] The land degradation-neutral paradigm could provide access to greater funding for implementation of the UNCCD.[58] This paradigm should also provide greater opportunities for

Revised Version, 18 Nov. 2011), *available at* http://catalogue.unccd.int/850_Rio_6_pages_english.pdf; *see also* Welton et al., *supra* note 17, at 58–59 (explaining that this strategy originated with the desertification community and the UNCCD Parties, seeking "new avenues for progress on desertification"; the UNCCD Secretariat's proposal at Rio+20 was in line with this strategy).

53   The Future We Want, G.A. Res. 66/288, at 40, ¶ 206, UN Doc. A/RES/66/288 (11 Sept. 2012).
54   Transforming Our World: the 2030 Agenda for Sustainable Development, G.A. Res. 70/1, UN Doc. A/RES/70/1 (21 Oct. 2015) [hereinafter '2030 Agenda for Sustainable Development'].
55   *Id.* at 24.
56   UNCCD, Ankara, Turkey, 12–23 Oct. 2015, *Report of the Conference of the Parties on Its Twelfth Session*, pt. 2, at 8–9, UN Doc. ICCD/COP (12)/20/Add.1 (21 Jan. 2016) (quotation at 9, ¶ 4); *see also* UNCCD COP13 Executive Secretary Report, *supra* note 42.
57   UNCCD COP13 Executive Secretary Report, *supra* note 42, at 5, ¶ 7(a); *see also* at 10, ¶ 21. The UNCCD's Science-Policy Interface is a group of experts that promotes "dialogue between scientists and policy makers on desertification, land degradation and drought (DLDD)" in order to "provide the Committee on Science and Technology (CST) thematic guidance on knowledge requirements for implementing the UNCCD." *The Science-Policy Interface,* UNCCD, KNOWLEDGE HUB, https://knowledge.unccd.int/science-policy-interface (last visited 29 May 2021).
58   UNCCD COP13 Executive Secretary Report, *supra* note 42, at 6, ¶ 8 ("LDN constitutes a vehicle to ensure greater access to financing for the implementation of the Convention

partnerships and resource mobilization, including but not limited to, the other two Rio Conventions, and help to overcome fragmentation between various frameworks and conventions. Finally, it could provide the impetus for scaling up transformative projects that would contribute to land degradation-neutral goals.[59]

The 2018–2030 Strategic Framework, like its predecessor, includes a strategic objective to "improve the living conditions of affected populations".[60] In the 2018–2030 Strategic Framework, this objective explicitly aims to reduce "forced migration" as its expected impact 2.4: "Migration forced by desertification and land degradation is substantially reduced."[61]

f        Collaborative Research on Human Mobility

In addition to addressing the issue of human mobility through its 10-Year Strategy and 2018–2030 Strategic Framework, the UNCCD has initiated collaborations with other organizations in order to further research and knowledge concerning the link between desertification, land degradation, drought, and human mobility. In the last decade, the UNCCD has cooperated with the United Nations University Institute on Environment and Human Security to further joint research on the linkages between human mobility and desertification.[62] In November 2014, the UNCCD launched a formal collaboration with the International Organization for Migration (IOM) to "increase understanding of challenges and opportunities related to the interlinkages between human mobility and land degradation and create political momentum to bring these questions across global policy agendas."[63]

It was shortly thereafter that the 13th Conference of the UNCCD Parties—the same session that adopted the 2018–2030 Strategic Framework—invited States Parties to "[p]romote the positive role that measures taken to implement the Convention can play to address desertification/land degradation and

---

[...] LDN has the potential to become a vehicle to catalyse substantial amounts of sustainable development financing for the implementation of the Convention, including climate finance" (citation omitted)); at 7, ¶ 11 ("Therefore, countries should decide whether and how to integrate the voluntary LDN targets into their NAPs as part of their overall discussion on the implementation of the SDGs. What counts most is to create leverage for LDN implementation and access to additional resources, including climate and restoration finance.").

59    *Id.* at 8–10, ¶¶ 19, 20.
60    UNCCD COP13 Report, *supra* note 50, at 20, Strategic Objective 2.
61    *Id.* at 20, Strategic Objective 2, Expected Impact 2.4.
62    UNCCD Factsheet, *supra* note 46, at 2.
63    *Human Mobility in the UNCCD*, ENVIRONMENTAL MIGRATION PORTAL, https://environmentalmigration.iom.int/human-mobility-unccd (last visited 29 May 2021).

drought as one of the drivers that causes migration".[64] The Conference of the Parties also requested the UNCCD Secretariat to commission "a study on the role that measures taken to implement the Convention can play to address desertification/land degradation and drought as one of the drivers that causes migration so as to promote the objectives of the Convention".[65]

IOM, in view of its collaboration with the UNCCD and in partnership with the Stockholm Environment Institute,[66] completed the study, entitled "Addressing the Land Degradation-Migration Nexus: The Role of the United Nations Convention to Combat Desertification" (IOM-UNCCD Study).[67] The IOM-UNCCD Study seeks "to leverage IOM's expertise in migration issues to contribute to the evidence base on migration-DLDD nexus and advance policy thinking on this topic."[68]

The IOM-UNCCD Study explores further the nexus between land degradation and migration. The IOM-UNCCD Study differentiates "forced migration", which should be reduced, from adaptive or beneficial migration, which will (and should) continue even with successful *in situ* adaptation and which can contribute to sustainable land management:

> Although it is critical to develop measures that reduce forced migration, it is important to note that migration is not a phenomenon that can, or should, be avoided. It is widely acknowledged that migration can bring benefits to individuals, as well as communities of origin and destination.

---

64    UNCCD COP13 Report, *supra* note 50, at 82, ¶ 1(a). The decision also invites States Parties to "enhance international cooperation that aims to promote the positive role sustainable land management can play to address desertification/land degradation and drought as one of the drivers that causes migration" (at 82, ¶ 1(b)) and requests the secretariat to "[s]upport regional and international cooperation and initiatives that aim to promote the positive role sustainable land management can play to address desertification/land degradation and drought as one of the drivers that causes migration" (at 83, ¶ 2(c)), and to "[s]trengthen cross-sectoral cooperation with other United Nations agencies and programmes, regional and international organizations, and stakeholders to share information on the linkages between desertification/land degradation and drought and migration." (at 83, ¶ 2(d)).

65    *Id*. at 82, ¶ 2(b).

66    The Stockholm Environment Institute, named after the Stockholm Declaration on the Environment adopted at the 1972 United Nations Conference on the Human Environment, is a non-profit research institute focusing on issues relating to environment and development. *About*, STOCKHOLM ENVIRONMENT INSTITUTE, https://www.sei.org/about-sei/ (last visited 29 May 2021); *Origins*, STOCKHOLM ENVIRONMENT INSTITUTE, https://www.sei.org/about-sei/origins/ (last visited 29 May 2021).

67    IOM UNCCD Study, *supra* note 22.

68    *Id*. at 3. The study also notes here that its completion "takes place within the framework of a cooperation agreement signed between IOM and the UNCCD in 2014."

[...] [I]t is important to underline that, even when successful adaptation
to environmental stressors does take place in situ, this does not necessarily mean that migration will or should stop. Very often the opposite
happens. [...] [I]t is possible for migrants to contribute to sustainable
land management in their areas of destination, but also of origin; and
that migration can represent an adaptation strategy to the adverse effects
of DLDD [desertification, land degradation, and drought]. It is therefore
important to acknowledge that alongside policy efforts to address DLDD
drivers of forced migration, it is critical to promote the rights of people
on the move,—including land-related rights—and provide migrants
with opportunities that maximize benefits for all.[69]

The IOM-UNCCD Study then reviews a collection of sustainable land management and restoration practices that could beneficially impact social and environmental conditions in a way that could avert or reduce migration. The IOM-UNCCD
Study identifies three key characteristics of successful sustainable land management practices: (i) participatory approaches to protection and restoration of fragile ecosystems; (ii) creation of ample and "dignified" employment opportunities;
and (iii) addressing "pre-existing vulnerabilities and inequalities."[70] Successful
practices tended to include the following, additional characteristics:

  · They strive to secure land rights and access to natural resources for
    those most vulnerable;
  · They are gender sensitive and empower the most marginalized;
  · They support local knowledge;
  · They reinforce local institutional capacities;
  · They take into account specific local migration dynamics.[71]

The IOM-UNCCD Study provides an overview of other policy processes that
address issues relating to environment and human mobility and concludes
with recommendations to States Parties to the UNCCD and other relevant
stakeholders. These recommendations include measures to prioritize "community focused sustainable land management and restoration efforts", developing and implementing "migration policy and practice", and "maximizing
synergies across policy areas".[72]

---

69    *Id.* at 26.
70    *Id.* at 28.
71    *Id.*
72    *Id.* at 33–34.

g          Support for External Initiatives
The UNCCD's objectives are also implemented through support of external initiatives, including those that aim to address migration issues related to desertification, land degradation, and drought. For example, the UNCCD Secretariat
acts as the Secretariat for the Task Force of the Sustainability, Stability, and
Security Initiative (3S Initiative), an intergovernmental action initiated by
Morocco and Senegal.[73] The 3S Initiative focuses on the interaction between
natural resources and instability in Africa; it aims to combat "migration and
conflict related to the degradation of natural resources" by restoring land to
create jobs, improving early warning systems for disasters that could cause displacement, and improving "land access and tenure rights".[74]

The UNCCD also supports the Great Green Wall Initiative, a project to con-
struct 8,000 kilometers of trees and vegetation across the Sahel region of the
African continent. By restoring degraded land, the Great Green Wall Initiative
seeks to combat "climate change, drought, famine, conflict and migration."[75]
The UNCCD initiated a public awareness campaign for the Great Green Wall
with the aim of inspiring public and private investment. The UNCCD's Global
Mechanism, tasked with mobilizing financial resources to implement the
UNCCD, supports the Great Green Wall Initiative by implementing invest-
ments by various stakeholders and donors.[76] The Great Green Wall Initiative is
discussed further in the next chapter, which explores this project through the
conceptual lens of complexity theory.

∵

Climate change both contributes to and is exacerbated by desertification and land degradation. Combatting desertification and land degradation is therefore crucial to mitigating climate change (and vice versa).
Desertification and land degradation are directly linked to human mobility,
encompassing a wide spectrum ranging from adaptive migration to environmental displacement. States Parties to the UNCCD recognized the interconnected relationship between desertification and human mobility even

---

73    *Sustainability, Stability, Security (3S Initiative)*, ACTIONS, UNCCD, https://www.unccd.int/
      actions/sustainability-stability-security-3s-initiative (last visited 29 May 2021).
74    *Id.*
75    *Growing a World Wonder*, THE GREAT GREEN WALL, ABOUT, https://www.greatgreenw
      all.org/about-great-green-wall (last visited 29 May 2021).
76    *The Great Green Wall Initiative*, ACTIONS, UNCCD, https://www.unccd.int/actions/great-
      green-wall-initiative (last visited 29 May 2021).

prior to its completion in 1994. The UNCCD therefore provides a unique and early example of an international, collaborative, and multilateral framework under which States aim to reduce desertification and degradation and to address the related human mobility issues. States Parties have taken an evolutive approach to UNCCD implementation by monitoring and adapting its strategic aims, undertaking collaborative research and projects, and supporting external initiatives at the local and regional levels. Under this approach, the relevance of the UNCCD to combatting desertification, land degradation, and climate change—as well as to addressing climate change mobility—has endured almost three decades.

## 2) *The United Nations Framework Convention on Climate Change*

The United Nations Framework Convention on Climate Change (UNFCCC), one of the UNCCD's sister conventions from the Rio Earth Summit, was adopted on 4 June 1992 and entered into force on 21 March 1994.[77] The UNFCCC creates a broad cooperative international framework within which States Parties can address the causes and impacts of climate change.[78] The UNFCCC was concluded two years before the UNCCD, but, unlike its sister convention, the UNFCCC did not formally acknowledge or address human mobility as an issue falling within its scope until almost two decades later, in December 2010.

The UNFCCC identifies its "ultimate objective" as the "stabilization of greenhouse gas concentrations in the atmosphere at a level that would prevent dangerous anthropogenic interference with the climate system."[79] In addition

---

77    United Nations Framework Convention on Climate Change, 9 May 1992, 1771 U.N.T.S. 107 [hereinafter 'UNFCCC'].

78    Vikram Kolmannskog & Lisetta Trebbi, *Climate Change, Natural Disasters and Displacement: A Multi-Track Approach to Filling the Protection Gaps*, 92 INT'L REV. RED CROSS 713, 721 (2010). The UNFCCC is a cooperative framework; it is also a legal framework under which States Parties have made commitments to, for example, reduce carbon emissions. Plaintiffs have relied upon the UNFCCC in national lawsuits attempting to block development projects or compel governments to take action against climate change. In such cases, plaintiffs generally rely upon the UNFCCC in conjunction with other national or international laws. For an example of one such lawsuit, see *Padam Bahadur Shrestha v. Office of the Prime Minister et al.* [2018] 074-WO-0283 (Supreme Court, 25 Dec. 2018) (Nepal), unofficial English translation, *available at* http://blogs2.law.columbia.edu/climate-change-litigation/wp-content/uploads/sites/16/non-us-case-documents/2018/20181225_074-WO-0283_judgment-1.pdf. The UNFCCC is, however, far more likely to have an impact on climate change mobility through cooperative action than as a basis for litigation. Amongst other factors, States Parties have not yet undertaken specific, binding legal commitments under the UNFCCC with respect to human mobility.

79    UNFCCC, *supra* note 77, art. 2.

to addressing mitigation of climate change, the parties to the UNFCCC committed to "[c]ooperate in preparing for adaptation to the impacts of climate change".[80] Adaptation has taken on an increasingly significant role within the UNFCCC framework since its inception.[81]

At its thirteenth session, the Conference of the Parties adopted the Bali Action Plan, which established the Ad Hoc Working Group on Long-Term Cooperative Action to enable enhanced action on adaptation.[82] The work of the Ad Hoc Working Group on Long-Term Cooperative Action contributed to the adoption of the Cancun Adaptation Framework by the Conference of the Parties in December 2010, which explicitly recognized human mobility as a form of adaptation.[83] Human mobility has also been included within the UNFCCC's loss and damage workstream, beginning with its recognition in the Doha Climate Gateway Decision and followed by its inclusion in the work of the Warsaw International Mechanism for Loss and Damage Associated with Climate Change Impacts, and the creation of a subsidiary Task Force on Displacement by the Paris Agreement.

a          Human Mobility within the UNFCCC Adaptation Paradigm

States Parties to the UNFCCC affirmed in the 2010 Cancun Adaptation Framework that "[a]daptation must be addressed with the same priority as

---

80   *Id.* art. 4(1)(e).
81   *See* Koko Warner, *Human Migration and Displacement in the Context of Adaptation to Climate Change: the Cancun Adaptation Framework and Potential for Future Action*, 30(6) ENV'T & PLAN. C: GOV'T & POL'Y 1061, 1062–63 (2012) [hereinafter 'Warner, *Cancun Adaptation Framework*']. *See also, generally,* E. Lisa F. Schipper, *Conceptual History of Adaptation in the UNFCCC Process*, 15(1) REV. EUR. COMP. & INT'L ENVTL. L. 82 (2006) (discussing the evolution of adaption in the UNFCCC process).
82   UNFCCC, Bali, 3–5 Dec. 2007, *Report of the Conference of the Parties on Its Thirteenth Session*, pt. 2, at 4–5, ¶¶ 1(c), 2, UN Doc FCCC/CP/2007/6/Add.1 (14 Mar. 2008). *See also* Koko Warner, *Climate Change Induced Displacement: Adaptation Policy in the Context of the UNFCCC Climate Negotiations* 4 (UNHCR, Legal & Protection Policy Research Series, PPLA/2011/02, May 2011), *available at* https://www.unhcr.org/protection/globalconsult/ 4df9cc309/18-climate-change-induced-displacement-adaptation-policy-context-unfccc. html [hereinafter 'Warner, *Adaptation Policy in the UNFCCC*'] (presenting a timeline for recognition of human mobility within the UNFCCC).
83   For an account of the work and negotiations leading up to adoption of the Cancun Adaptation Framework, see Warner, *Adaptation Policy in the UNFCCC, supra* note 82, at 4–12; Warner, *Cancun Adaptation Framework, supra* note 81, at 1064–70. For an analysis of the potential benefits and drawbacks to migration as adaptation as well as potential policy responses to these, see Jon Barnett & Michael Webber, *Migration as Adaptation: Opportunities and Limits, in* CLIMATE CHANGE AND DISPLACEMENT: MULTIDISCIPLINARY PERSPECTIVES 37 (Jane McAdam ed., 2010).

mitigation" within the UNFCCC.[84] This affirmation corresponded with increasing recognition by the scientific community that the effects of climate change had already begun to manifest and that mitigation measures will not be able to prevent climate change.[85] In the section entitled "[e]nhanced action on adaptation", States Parties were invited, under paragraph 14(f):

> to enhance action on adaptation under the Cancun Adaptation Framework, taking into account their common but differentiated responsibilities and respective capabilities, and specific national and regional development priorities, objectives and circumstances, by undertaking, inter alia, [...] [m]easures to enhance understanding, coordination and cooperation with regard to climate change induced displacement, migration and planned relocation, where appropriate, at the national, regional and international levels [...].[86]

The Cancun Adaptation Framework also established the "National Adaptation Plan" (referred to as "NAPs") process by which least developed countries would identify their medium to long-term adaptation needs and develop strategies to address those.[87] These National Adaptation Plans would build upon pre-existing "National Adaptation Programmes of Action" (referred to as "NAPAs") developed by least developed countries prior to the conclusion of the Cancun Adaptation Framework.[88] In the National Adaptation Programmes of Action, least developed countries aimed at identifying immediate adaptation needs.[89] A review of the National Adaptation Programmes of Action undertaken by Koko Warner and her coauthors in 2015 shows that "[a]lthough migration

---

84    UNFCCC, Cancun, Mex., 29 Nov.–10 Dec. 2010, *Report of the Conference of the Parties on Its Sixteenth Session*, pt. 2, at 3, ¶ 2(b), UN Doc. FCCC/CP/2010/7/Add.1 (15 Mar. 2011) [hereinafter 'UNFCCC, Cancun Report'].

85    Warner, *Cancun Adaptation Framework, supra* note 81, at 1062.

86    UNFCCC, Cancun Report, *supra* note 84, ¶ 14(f).

87    *Id.* ¶ 15.

88    The NAPA process was initiated further to article 4.9 of the UNFCCC (*supra* note 77), which provides that "[t]he Parties shall take full account of the specific needs and special situations of the least developed countries in their actions with regard to funding and transfer of technology." For further background on the NAPA process, *see Background Information on the NAPAs*, UNFCCC, https://unfccc.int/index.php/topics/resilience/work streams/national-adaptation-programmes-of-action/background-information (last visited 29 May 2021).

89    UNFCCC, *Technical Paper: Identification and Implementation of Medium- and Long-Term Adaptation Activities in Least Developed Countries*, at 5, ¶ 6, UN Doc. FCCC/TP/2011/7 (16 Nov. 2011) [hereinafter 'UNFCCC, *Adaptation Activities*'].

emerged as a theme in NAPAs, the documents generally provided little detail on strategies to prevent movements or to facilitate them when needed."⁹⁰ Warner and her coauthors, however, expressed optimism that the National Adaptation Plan process established by the Cancun Adaptation Framework was fertile ground for addressing human mobility, "provid[ing] an opportunity to ensure that migration, displacement and planned relocation are fully addressed, as both potential challenges and potential opportunities."⁹¹

The Task Force on Displacement, established by the 2015 Paris Agreement (and discussed subsequently), reported in September 2018 that, out of the documents submitted by 37 parties in conjunction with the National Adaptation Plan process, "81 per cent refer to human mobility".⁹² Although the overall number of adaptation policies submitted by that time could have been greater,⁹³ the high percentage of inclusion of human mobility therein reflects the growing recognition of the importance of taking human mobility into consideration in national climate change policies.⁹⁴ At the same time, the Task

---

90    Koko Warner et al., *National Adaptation Plans and Human Mobility*, 49 FORCED MIGRATION REV. 8, 8 (2015) [hereinafter 'Warner et al., *National Adaptation Plans*'] (noting, however, that "[f]ew NAPAs view the spontaneous movement of people from rural to urban areas as a positive adaptation strategy; in fact, governments have generally decried rural-to-urban migration and sought programmes to deter people from leaving home rather than facilitate their movement"). For further information on the content of NAPs in relation to human mobility, see Emily Wilkinson et al., *Climate-Induced Migration and Displacement: Closing the Policy Gap* 6 (Overseas Development Institute Briefing, Oct. 2016), *available at* https://cdn.odi.org/media/documents/10996.pdf. *See also* UNFCCC, *Adaptation Activities*, *supra* note 89, Annex III, at 42 (summarizing "[r]esettlement of communities at risk" as a commonly proposed adaptation solution in order to protect "life and property against climate extremes and disasters, including along low-lying and coastal areas").

91    Warner et al., *National Adaptation Plans*, *supra* note 90, at 8.

92    UNFCCC, Task Force on Displacement, *Report of the Task Force on Displacement*, at 10, ¶ 46 (Advanced unedited version, 17 Sept. 2018), *available at* https://unfccc.int/sites/default/files/resource/2018_TFD_report_17_Sep.pdf [hereinafter 'TFD 2018 Report'].

93    By the time the Task Force on Displacement compiled its 2018 Report, only 43 of the 197 States Parties to the UNFCCC had submitted a NAP. The Task Force on Displacement reviewed 37 of these NAPs and was unable to review the remaining 6 "[d]ue to language barriers". International Organization for Migration, *Mapping Human Mobility and Climate Change in Relevant National Policies and Institutional Frameworks* 9–10, n.40 (Analysis Report Prepared for the Second Meeting of the UNFCCC Task Force on Displacement, Aug. 2018), *available at* https://unfccc.int/sites/default/files/resource/20180917%20WIM%20TFD%20I.1%20Output%20final.pdf.

94    The Task Force on Displacement notes that the "significant awareness among national climate policy actors regarding the inclusion of human mobility dimensions takes place in a context of increased global policy attention dedicated to human mobility and climate change, notably linked to the catalytic role of the WIM Excom [Executive Committee of

Force on Displacement noted that, despite the inclusion of human mobility in national policy development, such policies had not yet been implemented at the time of its report and that they were generally unaccompanied by legislation or legal frameworks.[95]

As noted earlier, the Cancun Adaptation Framework was the first time the Conference of the Parties agreed on a text regarding migration, displacement, and planned relocation.[96] The inclusion of this language within the Cancun Adaptation Framework was welcomed by many as a significant recognition of human mobility as a legitimate issue connected with climate change.[97] Others questioned whether it would be helpful to include human mobility as an issue within the UNFCCC process at all, raising concerns about cumbersome negotiations, a lack of focus on remedies, potential detraction from mitigation efforts, and the overall limitations of the framework.[98] Some questioned whether framing human mobility as an issue of adaptation is ultimately unhelpful or even damaging.[99] Warner, on the other hand, opines that

---

the Warsaw International Mechanism] Workplan." TFD 2018 Report, *supra* note 92, at 10, ¶ 50.

95    *Id.* at 11.

96    Warner, *Cancun Adaptation Framework, supra* note 81, at 1061.

97    *See* Walter Kälin, *From the Nansen Principles to the Nansen Initiative*, 41 FORCED MIGRATION REV. 48, 48 (2012) [hereinafter 'Kälin, *Nansen Principles to the Nansen Initiative*']; Christine Gibb & James Ford, *Should the United Nations Framework Convention on Climate Change Recognize Climate Migrants?*, 7 ENVTL. RES. LETT. 1, 1 (2012); Jane McAdam, *Creating New Norms on Climate Change, Natural Disasters and Displacement: International Developments 2010–2013*, 29(2) REFUGE 11, 12–13 (2014) [hereinafter 'McAdam, *Creating New Norms*'].

98    *See* Kolmannskog & Trebbi, *supra* note 78, at 721; Gibb & Ford, *supra* note 97, at 3–4; *Position Paper for The Greens/EFA in the European Parliament: Climate Change, Refugees and Migration*, at 9 (May 2013) (*by* Hélène Flautre et al.), *available at* https://europea ngreens.eu/sites/europeangreens.eu/files/news/files/Greens%20EFA%20-%20Posit ion%20Paper%20-%20Climate%20Change%20Refugees%20and%20Migration.pdf; David Hodgkinson et al., *'The Hour When the Ship Comes In': A Convention for Persons Displaced by Climate Change*, 36(1) MONASH U. L. REV. 69, 77, 81–82 (2010); Bonnie Docherty & Tyler Giannini, *Confronting a Rising Tide: A Proposal for a Convention on Climate Change Refugees*, 33 HARV. ENVTL. L. REV. 349, 358 (2009).

99    *See* KNOMAD Symposium on Environmental Change and Migration: State of the Evidence, Washington, D.C., 28–29 May 2014, *Thematic Working Group on Environmental Change and Migration*, at 12 (*by* Wesley Wheeler), https://www.knomad.org/sites/defa ult/files/2017-03/KNOMAD_Symposium_Report_Final_TWG11%20%28final%20vers ion%29.pdf; François Gemenne, *One Good Reason to Speak of 'Climate Refugees'*, 49 FORCED MIGRATION REV. 70, 70–71 (2015); MD SHAMSUDDOHA, CLIMATE-INDUCED DISPLACEMENT AND MIGRATION: POLICY GAPS AND POLICY ALTERNATIVE: A LIKELY LEGAL INSTRUMENT FOR A RIGHTS-BASED POLITICAL SOLUTION 9 (2015), *available*

it would be "hard to imagine disadvantages of having migration and displace-
ment discussed in the UNFCCC process", while emphasizing the importance
of keeping "realistic expectations" of what could be achieved through the
UNFCCC, which she views primarily as having a "catalytic role".[100] The Cancun
Adaptation Framework's acknowledgement of the connection between cli-
mate change and human mobility paved the way for the formulation of the
Nansen Principles on climate change and displacement in June 2011 (Nansen
Principles). The Nansen Principles were followed by the Nansen Initiative on
cross-border disaster-induced displacement and its successor, the Platform on
Disaster Displacement, all of which are discussed later in this chapter.[101]

   According to Warner, the fact that the Cancun Adaptation Framework presented human mobility as an issue for nationally driven adaptation and cooperation brought it out of the realm of controversy, liability, and blame.[102] In
this respect, framing the issue in this fashion has built political momentum.
Moving away from liability also meant moving away from the issue of compensation, a source of discontent for some developing States.[103] On the other hand,
recognition of human mobility as a form of adaptation has allowed adaptation
funding to be directed to these issues.[104] Funding for research into the drivers of migration due to global climate change is of particular importance due

---

     *at* https://unfccc.int/files/adaptation/groups_committees/loss_and_damage_executive_
     committee/application/pdf/briefing_paper_climate_induced_displacement_and_migrat
     ion.pdf.

100   Warner, *Adaptation Policy in the UNFCCC, supra* note 82, at 13. For a critique of this view,
     *see* Gibb & Ford, *supra* note 97, at 3–4.

101   *See generally* 1 NANSEN INITIATIVE, AGENDA FOR THE PROTECTION OF CROSS-
     BORDER DISPLACED PERSONS IN THE CONTEXT OF DISASTERS AND CLIMATE
     CHANGE 15 (2015) [hereinafter 'NANSEN PROTECTION AGENDA'] ("The Nansen Initiative
     builds on paragraph 14(f) of the 2010 UNFCCC Cancun Agreement on climate change
     adaptation that calls for '[m]easures to enhance understanding, coordination and coop-
     eration with regard to climate change induced displacement, migration and planned relo-
     cation,' as well as the Nansen Principles that synthesize the outcomes of the 2011 Nansen
     Conference on Climate Change and Displacement." (citations omitted)); Kälin, *Nansen
     Principles to the Nansen Initiative, supra* note 97; McAdam, *Creating New Norms, supra*
     note 97, at 18, 20.

102   Warner, *Cancun Adaptation Framework, supra* note 81, at 1066.

103   *See* Benoît Mayer, *Migration in the UNFCCC Workstream on Loss and Damage: An
     Assessment of Alternative Framings and Conceivable Responses,* 6(1) TRANSNAT'L ENVTL.
     L. 107, 110 (2017) (citing to *id.*).

104   *See* Warner, *Adaptation Policy in the UNFCCC, supra* note 82, at 10, 13. On funding mecha-
     nisms that could potentially apply to climate change mobility, originating within the UNF-
     CCC process or otherwise, see Katrina Miriam Wyman, *Responses to Climate Migration,* 37
     HARV. ENVTL. L. REV. 167, 182–85 (2013).

to the amount of scientific work that needs to be done in this area, including identifying with specificity the States and regions that will be the first to require international assistance to adapt to changes in the environment affecting vulnerable populations.

The Cancun Adaptation Framework explicitly recognizes three different forms of mobility (displacement, migration, and planned relocation) that represent varying degrees of compulsion and imply a wide range of cost/benefit scenarios. The Cancun Adaptation Framework must also be read in the context of adaptation as the counterpart to mitigation within the UNFCCC, i.e., as addressing the potential consequences of climate change, in the event that mitigation efforts fail.[105] Adaptation (including human mobility) may thus equate to balancing between two undesirable outcomes, rather than something which is desirable or endorsed as a positive outcome.[106] The inclusion of human mobility within the Cancun Adaptation Framework as an issue of adaptation should therefore not be understood as a categorical endorsement of mobility (in any of its forms) as a beneficial or even acceptable outcome of climate change. The Cancun Adaptation Framework does not indicate that mobility should be promoted, but rather invites States Parties to enhance their understanding, cooperation, and coordination to address the issue. Addressing human mobility as part of adaptation measures is an attempt to responsibly come to terms with the reality of the situation and the consequences of anthropogenic effects upon the environment. It also refers to building resilience and averting undesirable mobility, as well as confronting the inevitability of some mobility, albeit unwelcome.[107] In this respect, the Cancun Adaptation

---

105    Adaptation is undefined in the UNFCCC. A factsheet on adaptation published by the UNFCCC describes adaptation as one "of the two central approaches in the international climate change process. The term refers to adjustment in natural or human systems in response to actual or expected climatic stimuli or their effects, which moderates harm or exploits beneficial opportunities." UNFCCC, Factsheet: The Need for Adaptation (undated), https://unfccc.int/files/press/backgrounders/application/pdf/press_factsh_ adaptation.pdf. The UNFCCC website further describes adaptation as referring "to adjustments in ecological, social, or economic systems in response to actual or expected climatic stimuli and their effects or impacts. It refers to changes in processes, practices, and structures to moderate potential damages or to benefit from opportunities associated with climate change." *What Do Adaptation to Climate Change and Climate Resilience Mean?*, UNITED NATIONS FRAMEWORK CONVENTION ON CLIMATE CHANGE, https:// unfccc.int/topics/adaptation-and-resilience/the-big-picture/what-do-adaptation-to- climate-change-and-climate-resilience-mean (last visited 29 May 2021).

106    For an analysis on the issue of balancing non-economic costs and values of land and places, see Petra Tschakert et al., *Climate Change and Loss, as if People Mattered: Values, Places and Experiences*, 8(5) WIRES CLIMATE CHANGE e476 (2017).

107    *See supra* note 105 on the definition of adaptation.

Framework refers not only to "migration" and "planned relocation", but also to "displacement", which is generally understood as a detrimental form of involuntary or forced movement and therefore something to be reduced or avoided when possible.[108]

b          The Intersection of Climate Change Mobility with Loss
           and Damage

In December 2012, the Conference of the Parties again recognized the connection between climate change and human mobility in the Doha Climate Gateway Decision in the context of the loss and damage workstream, acknowledging the need for "further work to advance the understanding of and expertise on loss and damage", including "[h]ow impacts of climate change are affecting patterns of migration, displacement and human mobility".[109]

According to Benoît Mayer, human mobility in the context of climate change can be understood in relation to loss and damage in three different ways: (i) as a way to reduce loss and damage arising from climate change impacts, (ii) as a source of (economic and non-economic) loss and damage for people moving, and (iii) as a source of loss and damage for "other concerned communities" (such as host communities).[110] Mayer considers that various migration scenarios tend to evoke one of the above described concepts of loss and damage.[111] For example, Mayer notes that "voluntary migration is more often depicted as a way of reducing loss and damage".[112] He acknowledges, however, that the three concepts of loss and damage "are not mutually exclusive in principle," even if they "tend to suggest distinct responses to the growing momentum for action on climate migration".[113] All of these aspects of loss and damage are interconnected. Efforts to avoid and/or reduce loss and damage will themselves give rise to other forms of loss and damage, bearing in mind that loss and damage can take on both economic and non-economic

108   For a discussion on human mobility "as an adaptive strategy and as a human tragedy", see Olivia Serdeczny, *What Does It Mean to "Address Displacement" Under the UNFCCC? An Analysis of the Negotiations Process and the Role of Research* 15–18 (German Dev. Inst., Discussion Paper 12/2017, 2017), *available at* http://climateanalytics.org/files/dp_12.2017.pdf (quotation at 15).

109   UNFCCC, Doha, Qatar, 26 Nov.–8 Dec. 2012, *Report of the Conference of the Parties on Its Eighteenth Session,* pt. 2, at 22–23, ¶ 7(a)(vi), UN Doc. FCCC/CP/2012/8/Add.1 (28 Feb. 2013).

110   Mayer, *supra* note 103, at 115–21 (quotation at 118).

111   *Id.* at 115.

112   *Id.*

113   *Id.*

dimensions, with these dimensions often taking on greater significance in developing countries.[114]

Human mobility, and particularly displacement, can itself constitute a form of non-economic loss, which could impair "security, dignity and agency".[115] In addition, mobility—where it means leaving behind one's home, family, land, community, and/or country—intersects with other forms of non-economic loss for both the persons moving and their communities, such as loss of territory, cultural identity, or indigenous knowledge.[116] As Petra Tschakert and her colleagues observe, "[p]lace 'is not just a thing in the world ... [it is] also a way of seeing, knowing and understanding the world.' Place gives meaning to people's lives and attachment to place fundamentally contributes to well-being."[117] Psychological harm may also flow from "disrupted lives, broken families, or communities, as well as a sense of despair".[118]

Mayer cautions, however, that construing mobility as a form of loss and damage "should not refute the possible benefits of migration as a normal process of social adjustment".[119] Whether mobility is ultimately more beneficial than harmful will depend upon whether the potential (economic or non-economic) loss that may be avoided by moving (e.g., loss of life, health, livelihood) outweighs the potential loss that moving will cause (e.g., loss of community, identity, livelihood, health).[120] Understanding mobility as ultimately more beneficial or harmful will often depend upon a highly subjective valuation of non-economic factors, which will not be the same for all persons concerned.[121] Understanding and addressing loss and damage in both their economic and non-economic forms is therefore extremely complex, situation-specific, and person-specific, which means that a local, bottom-up approach is essential

---

114   UNFCCC, *Technical Paper: Non-Economic Losses in the Context of the Work Programme on Loss and Damage*, ¶¶ 32–49, UN Doc. FCCC/TP/2013/2 (9 Oct. 2013) [hereinafter 'UNFCCC, *Non-Economic Losses*']; Tschakert et al., *supra* note 106.

115   UNFCCC, *Non-Economic Losses, supra* note 114, at 23, tbl.2; *see also* ¶¶ 82–86.

116   *See* Tschakert et al., *supra* note 106, at e482–83; *id.* ¶¶ 78–95.

117   Tschakert et al., *supra* note 106, at e482 (quoting from Tim Cresswell, *Introduction: Defining place, in* PLACE: A SHORT INTRODUCTION 1, 18 (Tim Cresswell ed., 2004)).

118   FANNY THORNTON, CLIMATE CHANGE AND PEOPLE ON THE MOVE: INTERNATIONAL LAW AND JUSTICE 71 (2018).

119   Mayer, *supra* note 103, at 118.

120   For a discussion on some of the non-economic losses that may be related to land and location, see Tschakert et al., *supra* note 106. For an analysis of the potential benefits and drawbacks to migration as adaptation as well as potential policy responses to these, see Barnett & Webber, *supra* note 83.

121   *See* Tschakert et al., *supra* note 106, at e479, e485–86.

for meaningful decision-making.[122] It is therefore crucial, particularly in the context of mechanisms operating within global structures like the UNFCCC, to avoid oversimplifying the relationship between human mobility and loss and damage.

c          The Warsaw International Mechanism

At its nineteenth session in November 2013, the UNFCCC Conference of the Parties established, under the Cancun Adaptation Framework, the Warsaw International Mechanism for Loss and Damage Associated with Climate Change Impacts (Warsaw International Mechanism) "to address loss and damage associated with impacts of climate change, including extreme events and slow onset events, in developing countries that are particularly vulnerable to the adverse effects of climate change."[123] The Warsaw International Mechanism would implement this task:

> by undertaking, inter alia, the following functions:
> (a)   Enhancing knowledge and understanding of comprehensive risk management approaches to address loss and damage associated with the adverse effects of climate change, including slow onset impacts [...];
> (b)   Strengthening dialogue, coordination, coherence and synergies among relevant stakeholders [...];
> (c)   Enhancing action and support, including finance, technology and capacity-building, to address loss and damage associated with the adverse effects of climate change, so as to enable countries to undertake actions [...].[124]

---

122   *See id.* at e479 ("Science-driven, top–down, end-to-end approaches rely heavily on climate and risk modelling or economic modelling; yet they tend to overlook place-specific and culturally subjective drivers of vulnerability and lived experiences on the ground. [...] Indeed, L&D is intrinsically about values and therefore is socially constructed. What level of loss is considered, is acceptable, and is fair can only be understood within place- and culture-specific contexts, taking into account various levels of power, rather than according to a universal metric of justice, especially when threatened values are incommensurable." (citations omitted)) and at e489 ("typologies of what individuals, groups, and societies deem to be of value underrepresent both the complexity and fluidity of their lived values and the likely power struggles of whose potential losses matter or matter most when dealing with climate risks.").

123   UNFCCC, Warsaw, Pol., 11–23 Nov. 2013, *Report of the Conference of the Parties on Its Nineteenth Session*, pt. 2, at 6, ¶ 1, UN Doc. FCCC/CP/2013/10/Add.1 (31 Jan. 2014).

124   *Id.* at 6–7, ¶ 5. *See also* Jessica Wentz & Michael Burger, *Designing a Climate Change Displacement Coordination Facility: Key Issues for COP 21*, at 3–4 (Columbia Law School,

The initial two-year workplan for the Warsaw International Mechanism, formulated by its Executive Committee, confirmed that the Warsaw International Mechanism would address human mobility as its "Action Area 6", from January 2015 to December 2016, in order to "[e]nhance the understanding of and expertise on how the impacts of climate change are affecting patterns of migration, displacement and human mobility" and undertake "the application of such understanding and expertise".[125] In its report of October 2016, the Executive Committee of the Warsaw International Mechanism confirmed that it had collected information from more than thirty organizations and experts on "projected migration and displacement based on projected climate and non-climate related impacts in vulnerable populations" and that it had synthesized this information and therefrom promulgated "key lessons learned and good practices".[126]

The Executive Committee proposed that the Warsaw International Mechanism would continue to focus on human mobility in its indicative workstream for a five-year rolling workplan, in which it included: "[m]igration, displacement and human mobility, including the task force on displacement".[127] The Task Force on Displacement is an entity created in accordance with the 2015 Paris Agreement, discussed in subsequent sections. At its twenty-second meeting in Marrakech in November 2016, the Conference of the Parties requested the Warsaw International Mechanism "to continue to implement activities from its initial two-year workplan" and approved its indicative workstream for a five-year rolling workplan (both of which address human mobility).[128]

In the context of its decision on the Warsaw International Mechanism in Marrakech, the Conference of the Parties also "[e]ncourage[d] Parties to

---

Sabin Center, Briefing Note, Sept. 2015), *available at* http://columbiaclimatelaw.com/files/ 2016/06/Wentz-and-Burger-2015-09-Displacement-Coordination-Facility.pdf    (opining that the stated purpose of the Warsaw International Mechanism "clearly encompasses" issues of migration and displacement, as confirmed by their subsequent inclusion in the Warsaw International Mechanism two-year workplan).

125   UNFCCC, Report of the Executive Committee of the Warsaw International Mechanism for Loss and Damage Associated with Climate Change Impacts, Annex II, at 11, UN Doc. FCCC/SB/2014/4 (24 Oct. 2014).

126   UNFCCC, Report of the Executive Committee of the Warsaw International Mechanism for Loss and Damage Associated with Climate Change Impacts, Annex III, ¶¶ 13–14, UN Doc. FCCC/SB/2016/3 (14 Oct. 2016).

127   *Id.* Annex I, at 12, tbl.2.

128   UNFCCC, Marrakech, Morocco, 7–8 Nov. 2016, *Report of the Conference of the Parties on Its Twenty–Second Session*, pt. 2, at 8, ¶¶ 2, 3, UN Doc. FCCC/CP/2016/10/Add.1 (31 Jan. 2017).

incorporate or continue to incorporate the consideration of extreme events and slow onset events, non-economic losses, *displacement, migration and human mobility*, and comprehensive risk management into relevant planning and action, as appropriate, and to encourage bilateral and multilateral entities to support such efforts".[129]

d          Human Mobility in the Paris Agreement
In the Paris Agreement adopted in December 2015, the UNFCCC Conference of the Parties requested the Executive Committee of the Warsaw International Mechanism to establish a "task force" which would:

> complement, draw upon the work of and involve, as appropriate, existing bodies and expert groups under the Convention including the Adaptation Committee and the Least Developed Countries Expert Group, as well as relevant organizations and expert bodies outside the Convention, to *develop recommendations for integrated approaches to avert, minimize and address displacement related to the adverse impacts of climate change.*[130]

The Paris Agreement indicated that this task force on displacement (the 'Task Force on Displacement') should have a particular focus on displacement as a form of mobility to be averted, minimized, or addressed.[131] The Paris Agreement did not mandate explicitly that the Task Force on Displacement address the other forms of human mobility recognized by the Cancun Adaptation Framework, i.e., migration and planned relocation. The Terms of Reference for the Task Force on Displacement, later established by the Executive Committee of the Warsaw International Mechanism, confirmed the scope of

---

129    *Id.* at 9, ¶ 9 (emphasis added).
130    UNFCCC, Paris, Fr., 30 Nov.–13 Dec. 2015, *Report of the Conference of the Parties on Its Twenty–First Session*, pt. 2, at 8, ¶ 49, UN Doc FCCC/CP/2015/10/Add.1 (29 Jan. 2016) [hereinafter 'UNFCCC, Paris Report'] (emphasis added).
131    *See* Serdeczny, *supra* note 108, at 23–24 (analyzing the meaning of the terms "to avert, minimize and address": "As the analysis above shows, the wording 'to avert, minimize and address' encompasses both positions: those who have an interest in pointing to the international responsibility of loss and damage, and those who have an interest in pointing to the national responsibility of coping with adverse situations on the ground. 'To avert' and 'to minimize' are more reflective of the latter position focusing on preventive measures and stressing the importance of country-driven approaches. 'To address' refers to positions insisting on the importance of backwardlooking measures and international loss-sharing.").

the mandate under the Paris Agreement,[132] but also provided that the work of the Task Force on Displacement later could be expanded to include assisting the Warsaw International Mechanism to fulfill its own, broader mandate.[133] The scope of the Task Force on Displacement's mandate was further clarified at the twenty-third session held in November 2017, when the Conference of the Parties invited the Task Force on Displacement "to take into consideration both cross-border and internal displacement, in accordance with its mandate, when developing recommendations".[134]

A reference to human mobility also appears in the preamble to the Paris Agreement, in which the Conference of the Parties acknowledges the responsibilities of States Parties to take into account and respect the rights of "migrants":

> Acknowledging that climate change is a common concern of humankind, Parties should, when taking action to address climate change, respect, promote and consider their respective obligations on human rights, the right to health, the rights of indigenous peoples, local communities, *migrants*, children, persons with disabilities and people in vulnerable situations and the right to development, as well as gender equality, empowerment of women and intergenerational equity [...].[135]

UNHCR has urged that, although the word "migrant" is generally used to describe voluntary movement, the term as used in the Paris Agreement preamble should not be construed narrowly and:

---

132  UNFCCC, Terms of Reference: Task Force on Displacement ¶ 5 (undated), https://unfccc.int/files/adaptation/groups_committees/loss_and_damage_executive_committee/application/pdf/tor_task_force_final.pdf.

133  *Id.* ¶ 7 ("In addition to its activities related to its mandate, the Task Force may, at the request of the Executive Committee, assist the Executive Committee in guiding the implementation of the Warsaw International Mechanism, in an advisory role. Specifically, in line with the Action area 6. of the Workplan, the task force may be requested by the Executive Committee to help it undertake activities related to 'enhancing the understanding of and expertise on how the impacts of climate change are affecting patterns of migration, displacement and human mobility; and the application of such understanding and expertise'."). For a discussion on the role of the Task Force on Displacement and its overall function in relation to the rest of the UNFCCC structure, see Serdeczny, *supra* note 108, at 18–23; Sarah Louise Nash, *The Devil's in the Detail: Policymaking on Climate Change and Human Mobility in the UNFCCC* 8–11 (IPC-Mercator Policy Brief, May 2017), *available at* https://ipc.sabanciuniv.edu.tr/wp-content/uploads/2017/04/The-Devil%e2%80%99s-in-the-Detail_Sarah-Louise-Nash1.pdf.

134  UNFCCC, Bonn, Germany, 6–18 Nov. 2017, *Report of the Conference of the Parties on Its Twenty–Third Session*, pt. 2, at 20, ¶ 8, UN Doc FCCC/CP/2017/11/Add.1 (8 Feb. 2018).

135  UNFCCC, Paris Report, *supra* note 130, at 2 (emphasis added).

should extend to the most vulnerable people on the move, including people forcibly displaced by the effects of climate change. This should also extend to all internally displaced persons, refugees and asylum-seekers situated in climate change hotspots who are doubly affected by conflicts and climate impacts.[136]

Provisions which would have established a "climate change displacement coordination facility" in the loss and damage workstream appeared in some of the draft materials leading up to the Paris Agreement.[137] For example, the "Elements for a draft negotiating text" that were annexed to the 2014 Lima Call for Climate Action included an option to establish within the loss and damage workstream a "climate change displacement coordination facility that: [p]rovides support for emergency relief; [a]ssists in providing organized migration and planned relocation; [and u]ndertakes compensation measures."[138] Ultimately no climate change displacement coordination facility was included in the Paris Agreement.

Some, such as Alexander Betts, consider the language on human mobility in the Paris Agreement to be "vague to the point of meaninglessness" and symptomatic of the issue having been overlooked.[139] Among other issues, Betts regrets that the draft proposal for a climate change displacement coordination facility was "watered down" to a "vague statement" establishing the Task Force on Displacement.[140] In this respect, the Task Force on Displacement fulfills,

---

136   UNHCR, *Policy Brief: Displacement at COP 22*, at 2 (Policy Brief for UNFCCC COP 22, Marrakech, Morocco, Nov. 2016), *available at* http://disasterdisplacement.org/wp-cont ent/uploads/2016/11/UNHCR-COP22-Policy-Brief-1.pdf.

137   For background and discussion of the role that such a climate change displacement coordination facility might play, see Wentz & Burger, *supra* note 124, at 4–18. *See also* Displacement Solutions, A Climate Change Displacement Coordination Facility in the Paris Draft Agreement: Summary of Facts (6 Nov. 2015), http://displacementsolutions. org/wp-content/uploads/2015/11/Climate-change-displacement-coordination-facility. pdf; Phillip Dane Warren, Note, *Forced Migration After Paris COP21: Evaluating the "Climate Change Displacement Coordination Facility"* 116 COLUM. L. REV. 2103, 2134–2144 (2016).

138   UNFCCC, Lima, Peru, 1–14 Dec. 2014, *Report of the Conference of the Parties on its Twentieth Session*, pt. 2, Annex, at 18, ¶ 33.3, UN Doc. FCCC/CP/2014/10/Add.1 (2 Feb. 2015) [hereinafter 'UNFCCC, Lima Report'].

139   Alexander Betts, *Global Issues Don't Live in Separate Boxes. Why No Mention in Paris of Refugees?*, THE GUARDIAN (13 Dec. 2015), https://www.theguardian.com/commentisf ree/2015/dec/13/refugee-status-extended-people-displaced-climate-change. *See also* Jane McAdam, *From the Nansen Initiative to the Platform on Disaster Displacement: Shaping International Approaches to Climate Change, Disasters and Displacement*, 39(4) UNIV. NEW S. WALES L. J. 1518, 1528–29 (2016) [hereinafter 'McAdam, *Nansen Initiative to Platform on Disaster Displacement*'] (citing the same article by Betts).

140   Betts, *supra* note 139.

under its original and current mandates, a different role from that which had been proposed for a climate change displacement coordination facility.

Others welcomed the Paris Agreement as "a milestone in terms of global commitment to move from enhancing knowledge on climate-related displacement to taking action to avert, mitigate and address such displacement".[141] In a report delivered in 2018, the Task Force on Displacement also referred to the Paris Agreement as a "milestone".[142] The report credits the Paris Agreement as having a "catalytic role" in the substantially increasing inclusion, from 2015 onwards, of human mobility and climate change in international policy and legal frameworks and processes.[143]

e          The Evolving Mandate of the Task Force on Displacement
In accordance with its mandate, the Task Force on Displacement delivered its recommendations in a report dated September 2018, along with summaries of the results of its activities (2018 Report). In particular, the Task Force on Displacement's 2018 Report summarizes its findings on human mobility and climate change in "national policies and institutional frameworks"; in workplans within UNFCCC bodies and work programs; in "international processes, policies and legal frameworks"; and within the United Nations system.[144] The 2018 Report also summarizes findings on "existing international and regional guidance and tools on averting, minimizing, addressing and facilitating durable solutions to displacement" and "systematic data collection and monitoring of displacement and its impacts".[145] In accordance with these findings, the Task Force on Displacement addresses, as appropriate, separate recommendations to the Warsaw International Mechanism, other bodies under the UNFCCC and the Paris Agreement, States Parties, UN agencies, relevant organizations, and other stakeholders.

The 2018 Report also contains a section "assessing the state of knowledge on displacement related to slow onset events",[146] an issue which has been gaining

---

141    High Commissioner's Dialogue on Protection Challenges: Understanding and Addressing Root Causes of Displacement, Geneva, Switz., 16–17 Dec. 2015, *Co-Chairs' Summary: Thematic Session 2: Addressing "New" Root Causes: Urbanization, Food Insecurity, Water Scarcity, Natural Hazards and Climate Change*, at 3 (*by* Walter Kälin & Kelly Clements) (emphasis in original omitted), *available at* http://www.unhcr.org/58be72337.pdf. *See also* McAdam, *Nansen Initiative to Platform on Disaster Displacement, supra* note 139, at 1528 (citing this passage).

142    TFD 2018 Report, *supra* note 92, at 21, ¶ 76.

143    *Id.* at 21, ¶¶ 75–76.

144    *Id.* at 9, 18, 20, 25.

145    *Id.* at 29, 32.

146    *Id.* at 13, ¶ 55.

increasing attention in recent years within the adaptive framework. In the 2018 Report, the Task Force on Displacement observes that the distinction between migration and displacement is often unclear in relation to slow onset hazard events, but that slow onset hazard impacts are usually only one factor—and often not the dominant factor—in decisions to move.[147] With respect to migration, the Task Force on Displacement observes that migration can be a form of adaptation to slow onset hazard impacts, but that adaptation policies generally do not include migration policies.[148]

With respect to "displacement", the Task Force on Displacement considers slow onset hazard events to be a risk factor and identified four ways in which slow onset hazards could become disasters and increase displacement risk:

1. Slow onset hazards can lead to scarcity of vital resources, which may in turn disrupt livelihoods. When this surpasses coping capacity, the situation can become a disaster which leads to displacement.

2. Rapid and slow onset hazards are often intertwined. Slow onset hazards may become disasters by an intervening, related rapid onset hazard event. For example, desertification may lead to a wildfire, or sea level rise may result in flooding.

3. Slow onset hazards can erode a community's or an ecosystem's resilience to slow onset or rapid onset hazard impacts, which could "trigger a cascade of hazards, prompting displacement".

4. Slow onset hazards are often a "hidden aggravating factor in many contexts, acting as a threat multiplier for other factors of crisis" that lead to displacement.[149]

In its recommendations with respect to slow onset hazards, the Task Force on Displacement recognized the importance of further research into the nexus between slow onset hazard events and displacement through, amongst other methods, improved data collection, integration, and sharing.[150] In December 2018, the Internal Displacement Monitoring Centre, referring to the same four categories of ways in which slow onset hazards could become disasters and in reference to its engagement in the Task Force on Displacement, launched a research agenda on slow onset hazard events in relation to displacement.[151]

---

147    *Id.* at 13, ¶ 58.
148    *Id.* at 15, ¶ (c).
149    *Id.* at 14–15, ¶¶ 60(d)–(g).
150    *Id.* at 16–18.
151    INTERNAL DISPLACEMENT MONITORING CENTRE, RESEARCH AGENDA AND CALL FOR PARTNERS 2–3 (Thematic Series: No Matter of Choice: Displacement in a Changing

The Internal Displacement Monitoring Centre has since issued a number of publications concerning displacement in relation to slow onset hazards.[152]

The contents of the 2018 Report demonstrate that the Task Force on Displacement interpreted its mandate broadly to include human mobility in forms other than displacement. To recall, the Paris Agreement established the Task Force on Displacement to "develop recommendations for integrated approaches to avert, minimize and address *displacement* related to the adverse impacts of climate change".[153] Notwithstanding, the 2018 Report, as a whole, takes into account, addresses, and issues recommendations more broadly on human mobility, including migration and relocation. Some sections do, however, focus more on displacement than on other forms of human mobility.[154]

Following review of the 2018 Report, the Executive Committee of the Warsaw International Mechanism extended the mandate of the Task Force on Displacement.[155] At its twenty-fourth session in December 2018, the Conference of the Parties welcomed the 2018 Report and the extension of the Task Force on Displacement's mandate[156] and encouraged the Executive

Climate, Dec. 2018), *available at* https://www.internal-displacement.org/sites/defa ult/files/publications/documents/20181213-slow-onset-intro.pdf [hereinafter 'IDMC, RESEARCH AGENDA'].

152   These publications include, *e.g.*, INTERNAL DISPLACEMENT MONITORING CENTRE, MONITORING METHODOLOGY FOR DISPLACEMENT ASSOCIATED WITH DROUGHT (Jan. 2020), *available at* https://www.internal-displacement.org/sites/default/files/publi cations/documents/202001-Drought%20displacement.pdf; ROGER GUIU, WHEN CANALS RUN DRY: DISPLACEMENT TRIGGERED BY WATER STRESS IN THE SOUTH OF IRAQ (IDMC Thematic Series: No Matter of Choice: Displacement in a Changing Climate, Feb. 2020), *available at* https://www.internal-displacement.org/sites/default/files/publicati ons/documents/202002-iraq-slow-onset-report.pdf; PABLO CORTÉS FERRÁNDEZ, 'NO LAND, NO WATER, NO PASTURE': THE URBANISATION OF DROUGHT DISPLACEMENT IN SOMALIA (IDMC Thematic Series: No Matter of Choice: Displacement in a Changing Climate, 2020), *available at* https://www.internal-displacement.org/sites/default/files/ publications/documents/202003-somalia-slow-onset.pdf.

153   UNFCCC, Paris Report, *supra* note 130, at 8, ¶ 49 (emphasis added).

154   For example, although Section IV(B) on slow onset processes refers to migration in the discussion, the recommendations refer solely to displacement and forced movement. TFD 2018 Report, *supra* note 92, at 13–18.

155   UNFCCC, Katowice, Poland, 2–5 Dec. 2018, *Report of the Executive Committee of the Warsaw International Mechanism for Loss and Damage Associated with Climate Change Impacts*, at 8, ¶ 36, UN Doc FCCC/SB/2018/1 (15 Oct. 2018).

156   UNFCCC, Katowice, Poland, 2–5 Dec. 2018, *Report of the Conference of the Parties on its Twenty–Fourth Session*, pt. 2, at 40, ¶¶ 1(c), 4, UN Doc FCCC/CP/2018/10/Add.1 (19 Mar. 2018).

Committee of the Warsaw International Mechanism to "continue its work on human mobility".[157]

The Task Force on Displacement is currently operating under a plan of action for 2019–2021,[158] which includes a broader range of activities than its original mandate and work plan. In addition to gathering, summarizing, and disseminating relevant knowledge, the Task Force on Displacement is now mandated to raise awareness on integrating climate change displacement into "national laws, policies and strategies"; provide regional capacity-building training opportunities; help States Parties to assess displacement risk; and identify funding possibilities for projects to avert, minimize, and address climate change related displacement.[159] Despite the expansion of its activities, the Task Force on Displacement still does not fulfill the role of the climate change displacement coordination facility that had been proposed prior to the Paris Agreement. Such a coordination facility, as proposed, would have undertaken activities related to the provision of assistance and support for emergency relief efforts, organized migration, and planned relation, as well as compensation measures.[160]

∴

The UNFCCC therefore provides another example of an international, collaborative, and multilateral framework addressing climate change with evolving implementation strategies. Concluded in 1992, the UNFCCC initially focused on mitigation of climate change. Since then, adaptation has taken on increasing importance within the UNFCCC. Almost two decades after its creation, human mobility was included within the scope of adaption efforts within the UNFCCC and brought within the loss and damage workstream. Since then, a designated Task Force on Displacement has taken on an increasingly broad mandate, which has included developing recommendations, raising awareness, capacity building, assisting in displacement risk assessment, and identifying funding opportunities in relation to climate change mobility.

---

157   *Id.* at 40, ¶ 5(b).
158   UNFCCC, Madrid, Spain, 2–9 Dec. 2019, *Report of the Executive Committee of the Warsaw International Mechanism for Loss and Damage Associated with Climate Change Impacts: Addendum*, at 9, Annex I, FCCC/SB/2019/5/Add.1 (15 Nov. 2019) [hereinafter 'WIM ExCom 2019 Report'].
159   *Id.* at 10, 12, 14, Activities 7, 12, 13, 20.
160   *See* UNFCCC, Lima Report, *supra* note 138, Annex, at 18, ¶ 33.3.

## B      Disaster Risk Reduction

As observed in an earlier chapter, the Internal Displacement Monitoring Centre (IDMC) reported almost 1,900 disasters worldwide in 2019, triggering new internal displacements of 24.9 million persons—three times higher than the worldwide number of displacements caused by conflict and violence in 2019.[161] This number reflects only internal displacements and therefore does not reflect cross-border displacements during that time. Almost 24 million of these internal displacements were caused by weather-related disasters, as opposed to geophysical disasters such as earthquakes and volcanic eruptions.[162] These weather-related disasters include extreme temperatures, landslides, droughts, wildfires, floods, and storms (including cyclones, hurricanes, and typhoons).[163] These disasters therefore include rapid onset hazard events that may have been caused or exacerbated by anthropogenic climate change. Climate change is expected to continue to increase the frequency and intensity of such natural disasters. Slow onset hazard events are also increasingly considered to constitute "disasters", or at least factors that may contribute to disaster risk.[164]

---

161    INTERNAL DISPLACEMENT MONITORING CENTRE, 2020 GLOBAL REPORT ON INTERNAL DISPLACEMENT, pt. 1, at 9, *available at* https://www.internal-displacement.org/global-report/grid2020/. This is an observation on worldwide figures. A regional breakdown shows that some regions, such as the Middle East and Africa, experienced far more internal displacements due to conflict and violence as compared to disasters.

162    *Id.* pt. 1, at 10.

163    *Id.*

164    The 2015 Sendai Framework includes a definition of "disasters" that explicitly includes slow onset hazards. Sendai Framework for Disaster Risk Reduction 2015–2030, G.A. Res 69/283, UN GAOR, 69th Sess., Annex II, ¶ 15, UN Doc. A/RES/69/283 (23 June 2015) [hereinafter 'Sendai Framework']. On the other hand, the United Nations Office for Disaster Risk Reduction (UNDRR) terminology suggests that the UNDRR views slow onset events as "drivers" of hazard or risk rather than as hazards themselves: "Environmental hazards may include chemical, natural and biological hazards. They can be created by environmental degradation or physical or chemical pollution in the air, water and soil. However, many of the processes and phenomena that fall into this category may be termed drivers of hazard and risk rather than hazards in themselves, such as soil degradation, deforestation, loss of biodiversity, salinization and sea-level rise". *Hazard, Terminology*, UN OFFICE FOR DISASTER RISK REDUCTION, https://www.undrr.org/terminology/hazard (last visited 9 June 2021). The UNDRR definition for "disaster" does not address the distinction between rapid onset and slow onset hazards, defining a "disaster" as "[a] serious disruption of the functioning of a community or a society at any scale due to hazardous events interacting with conditions of exposure, vulnerability and capacity, leading to one or more of the following: human, material, economic and environmental losses and impacts." *Disaster, Terminology*, UN OFFICE FOR DISASTER RISK REDUCTION,

Disaster risk reduction is the objective of managing the risks posed by disasters, including the risks relating to human mobility. The United Nations International Strategy for Disaster Reduction (UNISDR), predecessor of the United Nations Office for Disaster Risk Reduction (UNDRR), defined "disaster risk reduction" as "[t]he concept and practice of reducing disaster risks through systematic efforts to analyse and manage the causal factors of disasters, including through reduced exposure to hazards, lessened vulnerability of people and property, wise management of land and the environment, and improved preparedness for adverse events."[165]

States Parties to the UNFCCC recognized the importance of disaster risk reduction as an adaptation strategy to address climate change impacts in the Cancun Adaptation Framework, which invites States Parties to enhance:

> climate change related disaster risk reduction strategies, taking into consideration the Hyogo Framework for Action, where appropriate, early warning systems, risk assessment and management, and sharing and transfer mechanisms such as insurance, at the local, national, subregional and regional levels, as appropriate [...].[166]

The particular relevance of disaster risk reduction to human mobility in the context of climate change has also been recognized by scholars and policy makers. As Jane McAdam and her colleagues explain, disaster risk reduction can be "an important tool for building the capacity of people to remain *in situ*", acknowledging also that "[w]here *in situ* adaptation is not viable [...],

---

https://www.undrr.org/terminology/disaster (last visited 9 June 2021). The IDMC also tends to view slow onset hazards as triggers for rapid onset hazard events or disasters, as well as a factor which may erode resilience. IDMC, RESEARCH AGENDA, *supra* note 151, at 2–3.

165  The United Nations International Strategy for Disaster Reduction (UNISDR) defined "disaster risk management" as "[t]he systematic process of using administrative directives, organizations, and operational skills and capacities to implement strategies, policies and improved coping capacities in order to lessen the adverse impacts of hazards and the possibility of disaster." UNITED NATIONS INTERNATIONAL STRATEGY FOR DISASTER REDUCTION, 2009 UNISDR TERMINOLOGY ON DISASTER RISK REDUCTION 10–11 (May 2009), *available at* https://www.undrr.org/publication/2009-unisdr-terminology-disaster-risk-reduction. The updated definition by UNDRR is less descriptive: "Disaster risk reduction is aimed at preventing new and reducing existing disaster risk and managing residual risk, all of which contribute to strengthening resilience and therefore to the achievement of sustainable development." *Disaster Risk Reduction, Terminology*, UN OFFICE FOR DISASTER RISK REDUCTION, https://www.undrr.org/terminology/disaster-risk-reduction (last visited 9 June 2021).

166  UNFCCC, Cancun Report, *supra* note 84, ¶ 14(e) (citation omitted).

movement away from impacted areas may be another form of adaptation/ disaster risk reduction."[167]

The importance of disaster risk reduction to human mobility in the context of climate change was further recognized in the Nansen Principles, a set of ten broad policy recommendations formulated during the Nansen Conference on Climate Change and Displacement, hosted by Norway in June 2011 and attended by 230 delegates from governments, civil society, and representatives of the humanitarian and scientific communities.[168] The recommendations set forth in the Nansen Principles therefore relate specifically to human mobility in the context of climate change. Nansen Principle 6 states that "[b]uilding local and national capacity to prepare for and respond to disasters is fundamental" and that the "international disaster response system needs to be reinforced".[169] Nansen Principle 5 recalls the responsibility of "[i]nternational, regional, and local actors" to implement the Hyogo Framework for Action 2005–2015: Building Resilience of Nations and Communities to Disasters (Hyogo Framework).[170]

1)      *The Hyogo Framework for Action 2005–2015: Building the Resilience of Nations and Communities to Disasters*

The Hyogo Framework was adopted by 168 Governments at the Second World Conference on Disaster Reduction held in Kobe, Hyogo, Japan from 18 to 22 January 2005[171] and was thereafter endorsed by the UN General Assembly in March 2006.[172] The Hyogo Framework, as indicated by its name, provided a

---

167   Jane McAdam et al., *International Law and Sea-Level Rise: Forced Migration and Human Rights* 25, ¶¶ 62, 66 (Fridtjof Nansen Inst., FNI Report 1/2016, Jan. 2016), *available at* https:// www.fni.no/getfile.php/131711-1469868996/Filer/Publikasjoner/FNI-R0116.pdf [hereinafter 'McAdam et al., *Sea-Level Rise*']. *See also* Brookings Inst. et al., Guidance on Protecting People from Disasters and Environmental Change Through Planned Relocation, at 3 (7 Oct. 2015), https://www.brookings.edu/wp-content/uploads/2016/06/GUIDANCE_PLAN NED-RELOCATION_14-OCT-2015.pdf.

168   *See* Elisabeth Rasmusson & Pål Presterud, *Foreword* to The Nansen Conference, Oslo, Norway, 6–7 June 2011, *Climate Change and Displacement in the 21st Century* 3 (*text by* Christian Gahre), *available at* https://www.unhcr.org/4ea969729.pdf. The Nansen Principles are discussed later in this chapter.

169   The Nansen Conference, Oslo, Norway, 6–7 June 2011, *Climate Change and Displacement in the 21st Century*, *supra* note 168, at 5 [hereinafter 'Nansen Report'].

170   *Id.* World Conference on Disaster Reduction, Hyogo, Japan, 18–22 Jan. 2005, *Hyogo Framework for Action 2005–2015: Building the Resilience of Nations and Communities to Disasters*, UN Doc. A/CONF.206/6 (22 Jan. 2005) [hereinafter 'Hyogo Framework'].

171   Hyogo Framework, *supra* note 170, at 6, ¶ 1.

172   G.A. Res. 60/195, at 2, UN Doc. A/RES/60/195 (2 March 2006).

framework for international action from 2005–2015 to strengthen resilience to reduce risks associated with disasters. To this end, it comprises three main strategic goals and five priorities for action, with suggested key activities suggested for each priority for action.

The Hyogo Framework is the successor to the Yokohama Strategy and Plan of Action for a Safer World (Yokohama Strategy),[173] which was the outcome of the first World Conference on Natural Disaster Reduction, held in Yokohama, Japan in May 1994 as a part of the United Nations International Decade for Natural Disaster Reduction.[174] The Yokohama Strategy promoted disaster prevention, preparedness, and mitigation as favorable to disaster response.[175] The Hyogo Framework was designed to build upon the Yokohama Strategy and to address the gaps and challenges which were identified in the latter's implementation.[176]

The Yokohama Strategy does not explicitly acknowledge the link between natural disasters and climate change, nor does it refer to human mobility as a consequence of disaster impacts. By contrast, the Hyogo Framework explicitly acknowledges climate change as a risk factor for disasters. Amongst other references to climate change, the Hyogo Framework states—in connection with implementation of follow-up on the priorities for action—that States should endeavor to "promote the integration of risk reduction associated with existing climate variability and future climate change into strategies for the reduction of disaster risk and adaptation to climate change" and "ensure that the management of risks associated with geological hazards, such as earthquakes and landslides, are fully taken into account in disaster risk reduction programmes."[177]

The Hyogo Framework also briefly refers to a connection between disaster risk and human mobility in its fourth priority for action (reducing underlying risk factors), recommending that parties "[e]ndeavour to ensure, as appropriate, that programmes for displaced persons do not increase risk and vulnerability to hazards".[178] This provision recognizes displacement (which could

---

173   World Conference on Natural Disaster Reduction, Yokohama, Japan, 23–27 May 1994, *Yokohama Strategy and Plan of Action for a Safer World* [hereinafter 'Yokohama Strategy'].

174   The United Nations General Assembly declared the International Decade for Natural Disaster Reduction to promote international cooperation in mitigating the impact of natural disasters. *See* G.A. Res. 45/185, Doc. A/RES/45/185 (21 Dec. 1990).

175   Yokohama Strategy, *supra* note 173, at 4, ¶ 3.

176   Hyogo Framework, *supra* note 170, ¶¶ 6–9.

177   *Id.* ¶ 30(g).

178   *Id.* ¶ 19(ii)(i). *See also* Lorenzo Guadagno, *Human Mobility in the Sendai Framework for Disaster Risk Reduction*, 7 INT'L J. DISASTER RISK SCI. 30, 31 (2016); Walter Kälin, *Sendai Framework: An Important Step Forward for People Displaced by Disasters*, BROOKINGS

itself stem from disasters or from other drivers such as conflict) and related programs as a potential risk factor that could increase vulnerability to disasters.[179] The focus is therefore more on managing displacement as a pre-disaster vulnerability risk than on addressing post-disaster mobility.

Although the Hyogo Framework does not focus a great deal on human mobility in connection with disaster risk, the fifth Nansen Principle recognized the Hyogo Framework as a key tool for preventing displacement from climate change impacts and strengthening resilience:

> Prevention and resilience need to be further strengthened at all levels, particularly through adequate resources. International, regional, and local actors have a shared responsibility to implement the principles enshrined in the Hyogo Framework for Action 2005–2015: Building Resilience of Nations and Communities to Disaster.[180]

Although the Hyogo Framework did not address extensively the nexus between disaster risk reduction, climate change, and human mobility, it paved the way for future advancement on this issue in the Sendai Framework.

### 2) *The Sendai Framework for Disaster Risk Reduction*

The Sendai Framework for Disaster Risk Reduction 2015–2030 (Sendai Framework) was adopted by the Third World Convention on Disaster Risk Reduction on 18 March 2015 and endorsed by the UN General Assembly in June 2015.[181] Despite its non-binding nature, the Sendai Framework is considered "highly authoritative".[182] The Sendai Framework, building upon the work of the Hyogo Framework, sets forth a non-binding framework comprising seven targets or goals and four priorities for action, as well as thirteen guiding principles, which are aimed at building resilience to disasters and disaster risk reduction at global, regional, national, and local levels.

---

INSTITUTE (20 Mar. 2015), https://www.brookings.edu/blog/up-front/2015/03/20/sendai-framework-an-important-step-forward-for-people-displaced-by-disasters/ [hereinafter 'Kälin, *Sendai Framework*'].

179 Guadagno, *supra* note 178, at 31.

180 Nansen Report, *supra* note 169, at 5.

181 Sendai Framework, *supra* note 164; Margareta Wahlström, *New Sendai Framework Strengthens Focus on Reducing Disaster Risk*, 6 INT'L J. DISASTER RISK SCI. 200, 200 (2015) [hereinafter 'Wahlström, *New Sendai Framework*']; Guadagno, *supra* note 178, at 30.

182 Kälin, *Sendai Framework*, *supra* note 178; McAdam, *Nansen Initiative to Platform on Disaster Displacement*, *supra* note 139, at 1528.

The Sendai Framework addresses the issue of human mobility in the context of disasters in a more comprehensive manner than the Hyogo Framework.[183] The Sendai Framework proactively seeks to facilitate planned relocation, reduce disaster-related displacement risk, and promote preparedness for disaster related evacuation and displacement at global, regional, national, and local levels.[184] The significance of these provisions is underscored by the fact that their inclusion was a contentious issue that contributed to a delay in the conclusion of the Sendai Framework.[185] The inclusion of provisions explicitly addressing human mobility in the Sendai Framework is at least in part attributable to the efforts of States that were affiliated with the Nansen Initiative, a State-led consultative process.[186]

The Sendai Framework is also noteworthy for its inclusion of slow onset hazards in its broad definition of "disasters", which applies "to the risk of small-scale and large-scale, frequent and infrequent, sudden and slow-onset disasters caused by natural or man-made hazards, as well as related environmental, technological and biological hazards and risks."[187] The inclusion of slow onset as well as rapid onset hazards within the scope of "disasters" is in contrast to the way that "disasters" have been interpreted, for example, in connection with the Guiding Principles and the Kampala Convention. Although the use of this term in the Kampala Convention is often understood as being restricted to rapid onset hazards, such an interpretation is still open to debate.[188]

∵

---

183   As noted previously, the Hyogo Framework contained only a brief reference to displacement, recommending that parties "[e]ndeavour to ensure, as appropriate, that programmes for displaced persons do not increase risk and vulnerability to hazards". Hyogo Framework, *supra* note 170, ¶ 19(ii)(i). *See also* Guadagno, *supra* note 178, at 31; Kälin, *Sendai Framework*, *supra* note 178. The Sendai Framework also innovates from its predecessor by giving greater emphasis to disaster *risk* management rather than disaster management. Sendai Framework, *supra* note 164, Annex II, ¶¶ 3–15; *see also, generally*, Wahlström, *New Sendai Framework*, *supra* note 181.

184   *See, e.g.*, Sendai Framework, *supra* note 164, Annex II, ¶¶ 27(k), 28(d), 30(l), 33(h). For a background on the inclusion of human mobility issues in the Sendai Framework and an analysis of the resulting text, see Guadagno, *supra* note 178; Kälin, *Sendai Framework*, *supra* note 178.

185   *See* Kälin, *Sendai Framework*, *supra* note 178.

186   *Id.* The Nansen Initiative is discussed in detail later in this chapter.

187   Sendai Framework, *supra* note 164, Annex II, ¶ 15.

188   A discussion as to whether the term "disaster" includes rapid and/or slow onset hazard impacts is included in connection with the Kampala Convention in the previous chapter.

Climate change is expected to continue to increase the frequency and intensity of natural disasters, which cause massive human displacements every year. Disaster risk reduction frameworks have increasingly recognized the impact of climate change on natural disasters, as well as the need to address related human mobility. The recently adopted Sendai Framework reflects this growing inclination to address human mobility within disaster risk reduction frameworks, aiming to facilitate planned relocation, reduce disaster-related displacement risk, and promote preparedness for disaster related evacuation and displacement. The Sendai Framework also reflects a trend towards recognizing slow onset hazard events as "disasters" or at least factors that may contribute to disaster risk.

C        **Human Mobility Policy Frameworks**

Human mobility is increasingly recognized as a crucial aspect of frameworks addressing mitigation and adaptation to climate change impacts and disaster risk reduction. However, as those frameworks are designed to address all aspects of mitigation, adaptation, and disaster risk reduction, human mobility is only one of many essential issues addressed therein. Human mobility has therefore developed as a subtopic within those frameworks. The increasing recognition of the importance of human mobility within those frameworks has, however, led to the development of policy frameworks that address climate change mobility as their primary focus. The heightened visibility of the issue has also enabled the inclusion of climate change mobility within the 2018 Global Compacts—cooperative global policy agreements aimed at addressing challenges faced by refugees and migrants.

1)        *Frameworks Tailored to Climate Change Mobility*
a             The Nansen Principles
In June 2011, Norway hosted the Nansen Conference on Climate Change and Displacement (Nansen Conference), during which high level discussions between over 230 delegates, from governments and civil society, including from the humanitarian and scientific communities, were used to formulate broad policy recommendations on human mobility and climate change in the form of ten "Nansen Principles".[189] These Principles were named in honor of the scientifically rigorous, visionary Norwegian polar scholar and explorer,

---

189    Nansen Report, *supra* note 169, at 5.

Fridtjof Nansen, who later went on to serve as the first High Commissioner for Refugees under the League of Nations.

The Nansen Conference built on the momentum of previous events, following the recognition of human mobility within the United Nations Framework Convention on Climate Change (UNFCCC) via the Cancun Adaptation Framework, issued after the sixteenth Conference of the Parties in November and December 2010. The Nansen Conference was also preceded by the Bellagio Expert Roundtable on Climate Change and Displacement, an event organized by the United Nations High Commissioner for Refugees in February 2011 in Bellagio, Italy, to discuss human mobility and climate change.[190] At the Bellagio Roundtable, participants emphasized the need to create a "global guiding framework" on cross-border displacement relating to rapid onset hazards.[191]

The Nansen Principles focus on "displacement"—or forced movement—resulting from rapid onset hazards. Whilst acknowledging the potential difficulty in distinguishing between forced and voluntary movement, the Chairperson of the Nansen Conference summarizes that "[t]he displacement dimension is most evident today in the context of sudden-onset disasters. There is, however, a need to further explore the range of issues that could arise as a result of slow-onset disasters and longer-term climate change impacts, such as planned relocation and migration management."[192] The Nansen Principles resulting from the Nansen Conference therefore address primarily "displacement", rather than other forms of movement which are generally considered to be voluntary, such as migration.

Other aspects of human mobility were not, however, completely excluded from the Nansen Principles. The Chairperson's summary highlights the importance of recognizing and supporting migration as an adaptation strategy or development plan.[193] Nansen Principle 10 emphasizes that any planned relocations must adhere to principles of "non-discrimination, consent,

---

190   *See* UNHCR, Expert Roundtable, Bellagio, Italy, 22–25 Feb. 2011, *Summary of Deliberations on Climate Change and Displacement* (Apr. 2011), *available at* http://www.unhcr.org/4da2b5e19.pdf.

191   *Id.* at 1.

192   Margareta Wahlström, *Chairperson's Summary, in* Nansen Report, *supra* note 169, at 18, ¶ 7 [hereinafter 'Wahlström Nansen Summary']; *see also* at 18, ¶ 6.

193   Wahlström Nansen Summary, *supra* note 192 at 19, ¶ 15 ("Migration—whether within a country or across national borders—may be a natural and rational adaptation response. States—if need be, supported by the international community—should proactively anticipate and plan for migration as part of their adaptation strategies and development plans. Existing regional and sub-regional arrangements, including mechanisms already enabling free movement, could apply to climate-related migration.").

empowerment, participation and partnerships with those directly affected, with due sensitivity to age, gender and diversity aspects." Despite this reference to planned relocation and any potential ambiguity in the scope of the other Nansen Principles, the primary focus on displacement is clarified in an introductory paragraph, which states that the Nansen Principles "were recommended to guide responses to some of the urgent and complex challenges raised by *displacement* in the context of climate change and other environmental hazards."[194]

The Nansen Principles contemplate a multi-tiered approach that includes the involvement of local communities and governments, national governments, and the international community. Nansen Principle 2 recalls that sovereign States hold the primary responsibility for protection of persons who move in connection with climate change.[195] It is emphasized in Principle 3 that the involvement of "local governments and communities, civil society, and the private sector" is required "to address effectively the challenges posed by climate change, including those linked to human mobility."[196] At the same time, the Nansen Principles stress the key role of the international community in supporting national efforts and recognizes the need to address cross-border movement in Principle 9, which states that "a more coherent and consistent approach at the international level is needed to meet the protection needs of people displaced externally owing to sudden-onset disasters."[197]

As noted previously, the Nansen Principles acknowledge the criticality of disaster risk reduction to addressing climate change mobility. At the Nansen Conference, a session was held on climate change adaptation and disaster risk reduction. One noteworthy observation from that discussion highlighted the imperative to take pre-emptive action against disaster risk: "[a]ll disasters are in a sense man-made, because knowledge and resources exist to prevent a lot more than we do."[198] Nansen Principles 5 and 6 identify the need to address disaster prevention and resilience with adequate resources, including through

---

194   Nansen Report, *supra* note 169, at 5 (emphasis added).

195   *Id.* at 5, Principle II ("States have a primary duty to protect their populations and give particular attention to the special needs of the people most vulnerable to and most affected by climate change and other environmental hazards, including the displaced, hosting communities and those at risk of displacement.").

196   *Id.* at 5, Principle III.

197   *Id.* at 5, Principle IX. With respect to internal displacement, the Nansen Principles conclude that "[t]he Guiding Principles on Internal Displacement provide a sound legal framework to address protection concerns arising from climate- and other environmentally-related internal displacement." *Id.* at 5, Principle VIII.

198   *Id.* at 10.

implementation of the Hyogo Framework—now succeeded by the Sendai Framework—, as well as "[b]uilding local and national capacity to prepare for and respond to disasters".[199]

Following the Nansen Conference, and building on the momentum from the Cancun Adaptation Framework and the Bellagio Roundtable discussions, the United Nations High Commissioner for Refugees presented the issue of human mobility and climate change during a Ministerial Meeting, held in December 2011 to commemorate the 60th anniversary of the Refugee Convention and the 50th anniversary of the 1954 Convention (2011 Ministerial Meeting). In his opening statement, (then) High Commissioner António Guterres suggested the Nansen Principles as a possible tool to help the international community respond to new challenges falling outside existing frameworks.[200] States were asked for input as to whether efforts should be directed to establishing a framework or instrument, falling outside of the asylum framework, to address human mobility and particularly movement in connection with climate change and natural disasters.[201] Despite these prompts, the official *communiqué* resulting from the 2011 Ministerial Meeting did not mention human mobility and climate change, the Nansen Conference, or the Nansen Principles.[202]

---

199    *Id.* at 5, Principle VI.

200    Statement by Mr. António Guterres, UN High Commissioner for Refugees, Intergovernmental Meeting at Ministerial Level to mark the 60th anniversary of the 1951 Convention relating to the Status of Refugees and the 50th anniversary of the 1961 Convention on the Reduction of Statelessness, Geneva, Switzerland (7 Dec. 2011), https://www.unhcr.org/admin/hcspeeches/4ecd0cde9/statement-mr-antonio-guterres-united-nations-high-commissioner-refugees.html ("Other possible ways forward could be inspired by the methodology that led to the Guiding Principles on Internal Displacement. The Nansen Conference on climate change and displacement in Oslo proposed a set of principles to guide states in addressing the needs of those who cross borders owing to climate change and other environmental hazards. We are ready to work with interested states and other relevant actors to help develop such guiding frameworks.").

201    Intergovernmental Event at the Ministerial Level of Member States of the United Nations on the Occasion of the 60th Anniversary of the 1951 Convention Relating to the Status of Refugees and the 50th Anniversary of the 1961 Convention on the Reduction of Statelessness, Geneva, Switzerland, 7–8 Dec. 2011, *Background Note for the Roundtables*, at 4, ¶ 7(viii), UN Doc. HCR/MINCOMMS/2011/08 (18 Nov. 2011); *see also* McAdam, *Nansen Initiative to Platform on Disaster Displacement*, *supra* note 139, at 1521.

202    *See generally* Intergovernmental Event at the Ministerial Level of Member States of the United Nations on the Occasion of the 60th Anniversary of the 1951 Convention Relating to the Status of Refugees and the 50th Anniversary of the 1961 Convention on the Reduction of Statelessness, Geneva, Switzerland, 7–8 Dec. 2011, *Pledges 2011: Ministerial Intergovernmental Event on Refugees and Stateless Persons*, *available at* https://www.unhcr.org/4ff55a319.pdf [hereinafter 'Pledges 2011'].

This omission was, according to Professor Walter Kälin, "no accident but rather the expression of a lack of willingness by a majority of governments, whether from reasons of sovereignty, competing priorities or the lead role of UNHCR in the process."[203]

The 2011 Ministerial Meeting nevertheless sparked further action. During the meeting, Norway and Switzerland made a joint pledge, with reference to the Nansen Conference, calling "for a more coherent and consistent approach at the international level to meet the protection needs of people displaced externally owing to sudden-onset disasters, including where climate change plays a role" and pledging "to cooperate with interested states and other relevant actors, including UNHCR, with the aim of obtaining a better understanding of such cross-border movements at relevant regional and sub-regional levels, identifying best practices and developing consensus on how best to assist and protect the affected people."[204] In keeping with their pledge, Norway and Switzerland launched the Nansen Initiative.

b        The Nansen Initiative Protection Agenda

In October 2012, Norway and Switzerland launched the Nansen Initiative, "a state-led, bottom-up consultative process intended to identify effective practices and build consensus on key principles and elements to address the protection and assistance needs of persons displaced across borders in the context of disasters, including the adverse effects of climate change."[205] The Nansen Initiative's work culminated in the Agenda for the Protection of Cross-Border Displaced Persons in the Context of Disasters and Climate Change (Nansen Initiative Protection Agenda), a non-binding conceptual framework built on consultative research, whose aim is to address cross-border displacement in the context of disasters stemming from climate change impacts or otherwise.[206]

The Nansen Initiative Protection Agenda consolidates effective practices by States and regional and sub-regional organizations and presents policy options which aim at: "(1) preventing people from being displaced in the first place;

---

203   Kälin, *Nansen Principles to the Nansen Initiative, supra* note 97, at 49.

204   Pledges 2011, *supra* note 202, at 101, 117. This pledge was endorsed by Germany and Mexico during the meeting (at 77, 95). According to Jane McAdam, Costa Rica joined the pledge after the meeting. McAdam, *Nansen Initiative to Platform on Disaster Displacement, supra* note 139, at 1522, n.20.

205   NANSEN PROTECTION AGENDA, *supra* note 101, at 6.

206   Nansen Initiative, Global Consultation, Geneva, 12–13 Oct. 2015, *Conference Report*, at 9, *available at* https://www.nanseninitiative.org/global-consultations/ [hereinafter 'Nansen Initiative, Global Consultation']; NANSEN PROTECTION AGENDA, *supra* note 101, at 7.

(2) helping people move in a safe, regular, and planned manner before disasters make forced movements inevitable; and (3) providing protection when displacement cannot be avoided and people are forced to move".[207] The Nansen Initiative Protection Agenda identifies three main priority areas for future action, which address (to varying degrees) both cross-border and internal displacement:

1.  Collecting data and enhancing knowledge on cross-border disaster-displacement;
2.  Enhancing the use of humanitarian protection measures for cross-border disaster-displaced persons, including mechanisms for lasting solutions, for instance by harmonizing approaches at (sub-)regional levels;
3.  Strengthening the management of disaster displacement risk in the country of origin by:
    A.  Integrating human mobility within disaster risk reduction and climate change adaptation strategies, and other relevant development processes;
    B.  Facilitating migration with dignity as a potentially positive way to cope with the effects of natural hazards and climate change;
    C.  Improving the use of planned relocation as a preventative or responsive measure to disaster risk and displacement;
    D.  Ensuring that the needs of IDPs displaced in disaster situations are specifically addressed by relevant laws and policies on disaster risk management or internal displacement.[208]

During a Global Consultation in October 2015, delegates from 109 countries endorsed the Nansen Initiative Protection Agenda.[209] The work of the Nansen Initiative concluded in December 2015.[210] The Platform on Disaster Displacement now seeks to implement the Nansen Initiative Protection Agenda.[211] The Platform on Disaster Displacement is also a State-led process which builds on partnerships with other stakeholders to continue to develop

---

207    UNHCR, UNHCR, ENVIRONMENT & CLIMATE CHANGE 10 (Volker Türk et al. eds., updated version, 2015) [hereinafter 'UNHCR, ENVIRONMENT & CLIMATE CHANGE'].
208    NANSEN PROTECTION AGENDA, *supra* note 101, at 44, ¶ 107 (emphasis in original omitted).
209    Nansen Initiative, Global Consultation, *supra* note 206, at 8; *Our Response*, PLATFORM ON DISASTER DISPLACEMENT, https://disasterdisplacement.org/the-platform/our-response (last visited 30 May 2021) [hereinafter 'PDD, *Our Response*'].
210    McAdam, *Nansen Initiative to Platform on Disaster Displacement*, *supra* note 139, at 1520.
211    PDD, *Our Response*, *supra* note 209.

the knowledge base and policy responses to address cross-border displacement in the context of disasters.[212] To carry out its work, the Platform on Disaster Displacement has identified four strategic priorities:

1. Addressing "knowledge and data gaps";
2. Enhancing "the use of identified effective practices" through cooperative action to prevent and address cross-border displacement resulting from disasters;
3. Promoting "policy coherence and mainstreaming of human mobility challenges in, and across, relevant policy and action areas" by coordinating efforts with existing initiatives and organizations;
4. Promoting "policy and normative development" to address legal gaps through standard-setting initiatives at domestic and regional levels (but without seeking "to develop new global legal standards or normative frameworks").[213]

The Nansen Initiative's mandate addressed human mobility in the context of "disasters" and not broader "climate change" impacts specifically, although earlier drafts of the mandate had referred to "disasters 'particularly in the context of climate change' ".[214] According to Professor Jane McAdam, the choice to focus the Nansen Initiative's work on disasters, rather than climate change impacts specifically, was fundamental to obtaining the support of some States, but does not prevent the Nansen Initiative from addressing disasters with anthropogenic roots.[215] In any event, there is little reason to distinguish between the impacts of disasters that stem from climate change and those that occur "naturally".[216] The full title of the Nansen Initiative Protection Agenda indicates that its scope is even more expansive, specifically stating that it is an agenda for the protection of persons displaced "in the Context of Disasters *and* Climate Change".[217]

---

212  *Id.*
213  PLATFORM ON DISASTER DISPLACEMENT, ADDRESSING THE PROTECTION NEEDS OF PEOPLE DISPLACED ACROSS BORDERS IN THE CONTEXT OF DISASTERS AND CLIMATE CHANGE 3 (2016), *available at* http://disasterdisplacement.org/wp-content/uploads/2016/11/PDD-Leaflet-11-2016-screen.pdf; *see also* McAdam, *Nansen Initiative to Platform on Disaster Displacement, supra* note 139, at 1533.
214  McAdam, *Creating New Norms, supra* note 97, at 19.
215  *Id.*
216  *See* Nansen Report, *supra* note 169, at 5 ("From a protection perspective, there is no compelling reason to distinguish between displacement due to climate-related and other disasters.") (cited by *id.*).
217  *See* NANSEN PROTECTION AGENDA, *supra* note 101, title page & *passim* (emphasis added).

Although much of the impetus for creating the Nansen Initiative arose from concerns relating to rapid onset hazards, the Nansen Initiative Protection Agenda conceptualizes disasters as including both rapid onset and slow onset hazards, noting that "[t]he relevant distinction is not the character of the disaster, but rather whether it triggers displacement, understood as the (primarily) forced movement of persons".[218] Recognizing that distinguishing voluntary from involuntary movement can be challenging in the context of slow onset hazards, the Nansen Initiative Protection Agenda considers that slow onset hazards may reach an "emergency phase" or otherwise erode resilience against other hazards, ultimately leading to displacement.[219]

Although the Nansen Initiative Protection Agenda is primarily aimed at addressing cross-border movement, it recognizes this as being interrelated with internal displacement, given that "it has been observed that cross-border disaster-displacement could potentially be avoided or reduced if IDPs [internally displaced persons] received adequate protection and assistance following disasters. In particular, a lack of durable solutions is one reason why internally displaced persons may subsequently move abroad."[220] The Nansen Initiative Protection Agenda therefore also contains a section on effective practices and gaps in relation to internal displacement.[221]

The Nansen Initiative Protection Agenda is a cooperative framework that combines adaptation and protection; it constitutes neither a hard law nor a soft law instrument.[222] However, its wide endorsement by State delegations and the State-driven efforts of the Platform on Disaster Displacement to implement its recommendations make the Nansen Initiative Protection Agenda an influential framework.[223]

---

218    *Id.* at 16, ¶ 11. *See also* McAdam, *Creating New Norms, supra* note 97, at 19.
219    NANSEN PROTECTION AGENDA, *supra* note 101, at 24, ¶ 36. *See also* McAdam, *Creating New Norms, supra* note 97, at 19.
220    NANSEN PROTECTION AGENDA, *supra* note 101, at 39, ¶ 99.
221    *Id.* at 39–41, ¶¶ 99–105.
222    Kälin, *Nansen Principles to the Nansen Initiative, supra* note 97, at 48; *see also* McAdam et al., *Sea-Level Rise, supra* note 167, at 39, ¶ 98 ("The agenda is a roadmap, not a soft law instrument. Indeed, legal experts engaged with the process considered it premature to develop any formal legal instrument at this point in time."); François Gemenne & Pauline Brücker, *From the Guiding Principles on Internal Displacement to the Nansen Initiative: What the Governance of Environmental Migration Can Learn from the Governance of Internal Displacement*, 27(2) INT'L J. REFUGEE L. 245, 259 (describing the Nansen Initiative as "a pre-soft law initiative, which seeks to build political consensus and open the way to greater legal achievements.") (cited by McAdam, *Nansen Initiative to Platform on Disaster Displacement, supra* note 139, at 1525).
223    *See* UNHCR, ENVIRONMENT & CLIMATE CHANGE, *supra* note 207, at 10.

c    The Peninsula Principles

Displacement Solutions, a non-governmental organization, has developed the Peninsula Principles on Climate Displacement within States, concluded on 18 August 2013 (Peninsula Principles). Formulated by legal experts following consultations with stakeholders, the Peninsula Principles aim to provide a normative framework on internal displacement in the context of climate change that reflects existing international legal guidelines and imperatives.[224]

Seeking to build upon the Guiding Principles on Internal Displacement, the Peninsula Principles apply to internal displacement, noting in the preamble that, "while climate displacement can involve both internal and cross-border displacement, most climate displacement will likely occur within State borders".[225] The preamble to the Peninsula Principles further references the "work of the Nansen Initiative on disaster-induced cross-border displacement", reflecting the decision of the drafters to build a framework which would be complementary to the work of the Nansen Initiative and its successor, the Platform on Disaster Displacement.[226] The choice to focus on the development of a framework in the form of non-binding principles also reflects, in part, a recognition of the political barriers to creating, in the short- to mid-term, a binding international treaty or new State obligations.[227]

In addition to reflecting the Guiding Principles, the Peninsula Principles clarify and consolidate legal norms from a number of international fields, such as human rights law; humanitarian law; and housing, land, and property rights protection.[228] The Peninsula Principles seek to repackage the

---

224    DISPLACEMENT SOLUTIONS, PENINSULA PRINCIPLES ON CLIMATE DISPLACEMENT WITHIN STATES 16, Principle 1 (19 Aug. 2015), *available at* http://displacementsoluti ons.org/wp-content/uploads/2014/12/Peninsula-Principles.pdf [hereinafter 'Peninsula Principles']. *See also* Bruce Burson, *The Preamble*, *in* REPAIRING DOMESTIC CLIMATE DISPLACEMENT: THE PENINSULA PRINCIPLES 36, 47 (Scott Leckie & Chris Huggins eds., 2016); Khaled Hassine, *A Rights-Based Approach to Climate Displacement*, *in* REPAIRING DOMESTIC CLIMATE DISPLACEMENT: THE PENINSULA PRINCIPLES 153, 153 (Scott Leckie & Chris Huggins eds., 2016); Ezekiel Simperingham, *The Responsibilities of States to Protect Climate-Displaced Persons*, *in* REPAIRING DOMESTIC CLIMATE DISPLACEMENT: THE PENINSULA PRINCIPLES 111, 130 (Scott Leckie & Chris Huggins eds., 2016).

225    Peninsula Principles, *supra* note 224, at 8; *see also* at 16, Principle 1(b) ("These Peninsula Principles [...] set out protection and assistance principles, consistent with the UN Guiding Principles on Internal Displacement, to be applied to climate displaced persons."); Burson, *supra* note 224, at 50–52; Hassine, *supra* note 224, at 156–57.

226    Peninsula Principles, *supra* note 224, at 13; Hassine, *supra* note 224, at 156.

227    *See* Hassine, *supra* note 224, at 155–56.

228    *Id.* at 154.

principles derived from these varied legal fields to provide practical guidelines to governments, communities at risk, and other implicated actors to manage the risk of climate change displacement and, as a last resort, to prepare for and/or respond to what the Peninsula Principles define as "climate displacement".

Principle 2(b) of the Peninsula Principles, contained in an opening "Introduction" section, defines "climate displacement" as "the movement of people within a State due to the effects of climate change, including sudden and slow-onset environmental events and processes, occurring either alone or in combination with other factors."[229] With this definition, the drafters of the Peninsula Principles sought to encompass anticipatory movement within their scope by including explicit language on their applicability to human mobility in connection with slow onset hazard events.[230] As Bruce Burson, one of the drafters, explains, those who move in connection to slow onset hazard events often seek to avoid the worst impacts that culminate in the future; this anticipatory movement tends to be viewed as a process of voluntary migration, despite the element of compulsion.[231] The explicit inclusion of slow onset hazard events thus seeks to overcome any potential protection gaps for anticipatory movement that might otherwise be viewed as voluntary. On a policy level, the Peninsula Principles embody the concept that, when *in situ* adaptation is insufficient and moving becomes inevitable, moving in anticipation of and to avoid climate change impacts is preferable to moving in response to climate change impacts after they have already struck.[232]

The Peninsula Principles also broadly define "climate displaced persons" as "individuals, households or communities who are facing or experiencing climate displacement."[233] According to Scott Leckie, founder of Displacement Solutions, this definition is "wholly inclusive" by its reference not only to individuals, but also to households and communities, thus ensuring that all relevant

229   Peninsula Principles, *supra* note 224, at 16, Principle 2(b).
230   Burson, *supra* note 224, at 50–51. According to Khaled Hassine, one of the drafters, the Peninsula Principles apply to slow onset, as well as rapid onset, hazard impacts and address one of the "major lacunae" in the Guiding Principles, which Hassine opines "do not apply to internal displacement as a result of slow-onset disasters, but are limited to internally displaced persons (IDPs) uprooted by sudden-onset disasters." Hassine, *supra* note 224, at 157.
231   Burson, *supra* note 224, at 51.
232   *Id.* at 58 (noting that "*ex-ante* internal relocation of individuals, households and communities vulnerable to the negative impacts of climate change is preferable to their *ex-post* displacement").
233   Peninsula Principles, *supra* note 224, at 16, Principle 2(c).

persons will be included in the category of protected persons.[234] In addition, the definition incorporates those "experiencing" displacement as well as those who are "facing" displacement, thus encompassing those who have already moved, as well as those who have not yet moved but whose displacement is imminent.[235] This definition, like the definition for "climate displacement", seeks to include persons moving in anticipation of climate change impacts in addition to those moving after such impacts have already occurred.[236]

As the Peninsula Principles do not create or codify law, these definitions do not themselves bestow any rights on those falling within their ambit. Instead, their value lies in the attempt to consolidate and contextualize existing norms to complement existing frameworks.[237] Insofar as the drafters of the Peninsula Principles sought to root them in existing international law, they are intended to reflect existing rights.[238] Khaled Hassine, another participant in the drafting, considers the Peninsula Principles to "constitute the global *minimum proprium*" and, consequently, their implementation to be "imperative".[239] In this respect, the Peninsula Principles include, under Principle 7, detailed national implementation procedures, a feature intended to reflect the responsibility of States to ensure the protection and assistance of persons within their borders and

234  Scott Leckie, *Using Human Rights to Resolve the Climate Displacement Problem: The Promise of the Peninsula Principles*, *in* REPAIRING DOMESTIC CLIMATE DISPLACEMENT: THE PENINSULA PRINCIPLES, *supra* note 224, at 1, 8.

235  *Id.* at 8–9.

236  Burson, *supra* note 224, at 47 ("This captures a key concern that steps taken to protect the lives and livelihoods of persons and groups impacted by the negative effects of climate change should not be left until after the event when the damage has been done. Rather an *ex-ante* approach is called for, which minimises the risk of future harm by undertaking preventive measures including planned and voluntary relocation to alternative locations.").

237  *See id.* at 47–48.

238  *Id.* at 48; *see also* Simperingham, *supra* note 224, at 130 ("In general, rather than requiring the development of considerable new normative standards for the protection of climate-displaced persons within States, Section IV of the Peninsula Principles demonstrates that a broad range of relevant human rights standards already exist and apply throughout all phases of the displacement cycle. Climate-displaced persons are already the holders of all these rights and States already have the duty and primary responsibility to respect, protect and fulfil all of these rights.").

239  Hassine, *supra* note 224, at 156; *see also* at 153 ("When considering the very nature of the [Peninsula] Principles, which are derived from existing laws and standards for the purpose of addressing situations of climate displacement, implementation becomes not only a possible option, but rather an imperative that is further corroborated by the flagrant need for international guidance on how to address the effects of climate change.").

promote the application of the Peninsula Principles by State governments.[240] The asserted obligation for States to implement the Peninsula Principles is echoed in Principle 18, situated in the final section entitled "Implementation", which declares that States must implement and disseminate the Principles in cooperation with other stakeholders.[241]

Following the "Introduction" section, containing the definitions of "climate displacement" and "climate displaced persons", the Peninsula Principles are organized into five separate sections: General Obligations, Climate Displacement Preparation and Planning, Displacement, Post-Displacement and Return, and Implementation (comprising exclusively Principle 18 discussed above).

The section entitled "General Obligations" includes provisions on the responsibility of States to take measures to prevent conditions that might lead to climate displacement. Principle 13—which falls under the section on "Climate Displacement Preparation and Planning" and which mainly addresses relocation planning—refers to an obligation to develop institutional frameworks that would assist in the prevention of climate displacement.[242]

Principles 9 through 13, on "Climate Displacement Preparation and Planning", contain extensive, detailed provisions on relocation planning and implementation, including risk management measures to anticipate relocation needs; participation and consent of persons impacted by displacement or relocation, including host communities; identifying, acquiring, and/or setting aside habitable land for displaced/relocated persons; development of laws that address loss and damage incurred in connection with climate displacement; and development of institutional frameworks to provide assistance and protection to displaced persons. These detailed provisions have been described as "arguably the clearest example to date of guidance which promotes comprehensive vulnerability reduction through climate change resettlement."[243]

---

240  Peninsula Principles, *supra* note 224, at 18, Principle 7; Bonnie Docherty, *General Obligations, in* REPAIRING DOMESTIC CLIMATE DISPLACEMENT: THE PENINSULA PRINCIPLES, *supra* note 224, at 66, 73–74.

241  Peninsula Principles, *supra* note 224, at 28, Principle 18.

242  Peninsula Principles, *supra* note 224, at 24, Principle 13(b)(i) ("States should take all appropriate administrative, legislative and judicial measures, including the creation of adequately funded Ministries, departments, offices and/or agencies at the local (in particular), regional and national levels empowered to develop, establish and implement an institutional framework to: (i) enable government technical assistance and funding to *prevent*, prepare for and respond to climate displacement [...]" (emphasis added)).

243  Brent Doberstein & Anne Tadgell, *Guidance for 'Managed' Relocation*, 49 FORCED MIGRATION REV. 27, 28 (2015).

As noted above, the Peninsula Principles provide a singular definition for "climate displaced persons" that encompasses both anticipatory relocation and post-disaster relocation. The decision to encompass both under one definition is consistent with the drafters' aim to avoid any possible interpretation of preemptive relocation as a voluntary movement to be distinguished from reactionary "displacement". However, the drafters distinguish between "relocation" and unplanned "displacement" in the substantive provisions. Principles 14 through 16, comprising the section entitled "Displacement", specifically apply to "persons experiencing displacement but who have not been relocated".[244] According to these provisions, States must assist persons who have moved in the wake of sudden onset hazard impacts by arranging adequate housing, ensuring the livelihood of such displaced persons, and providing remedies and compensation when displaced persons have suffered a violation of their rights. Section IV on "Post-Displacement and Return" comprises Principle 17, which provides that States should enable climate displaced persons to decide whether to return to their homes, allow them to do so when there is not an overriding risk to life or livelihood, facilitate such return, and provide transitional assistance to returning persons.[245]

The Peninsula Principles have not yet been formally endorsed by an international body, but have been used as a point of reference in assorted contexts. The Government of Bangladesh, in its "National Strategy on the Management of Disaster and Climate Induced Internal Displacement", referenced the Peninsula Principles as part of the key literature and discussed the definition of "climate displaced persons" therein.[246] A 2016 report issued for the United Nations Human Rights Council Advisory Committee proposed that the Peninsula Principles, along with the Guiding Principles on Internal Displacement, be used as the basis for the Advisory Committee to develop guidelines on climate change displacement and human rights.[247] A complaint

---

244  Peninsula Principles, *supra* note 224, at 25–27, Principles 14, 15(a), 16.

245  *Id.* at 28, Principle 17.

246  Bangladesh, *Comprehensive Disaster Management Program & Ministry of Disaster Management and Relief, National Strategy on the Management of Disaster and Climate Induced Internal Displacement*, at 5–6, 31 (Revised Draft Version, Jan. 2020), *available at* http://www.rmmru.org/newsite/wp-content/uploads/2020/02/NSMDCIID.pdf; *see also* Bangladesh, *Comprehensive Disaster Management Program & Ministry of Disaster Management and Relief, National Strategy on the Management of Disaster and Climate Induced Internal Displacement*, at 7–8, 29 (13 Sept. 2015), *available at* https://www.refworld.org/docid/5b2b99f74.html.

247  Human Rights Council, *Report of the Advisory Committee on its Seventeenth Session*, at 22–24, ¶¶ 32–42, UN Doc. A/HRC/AC/17/2 (7 Sept. 2016).

concerning the "Rights of Indigenous People in Addressing Climate-Forced Displacement", submitted by the Alaska Institute for Justice to a number of United Nations Special Rapporteurs (including on the Human Rights of Internally Displaced Persons and on the Rights of Indigenous Peoples), relies on the Peninsula Principles as part of the relevant "[i]nternational legal doctrine".[248] The complaint, discussed in the previous chapter, was submitted on 15 January 2020 on behalf of five different Tribes located in Louisiana and Alaska, alleging human rights violations by the government of the United States of America in connection with climate change impacts. The complaint states that the Peninsula Principles draw "on established human rights declarations and covenants" and "outline the human rights principles that must be adhered [to] when individuals and communities are forcibly displaced internally because of climate change."[249] In addition, Displacement Solutions, the non-governmental organization that compiled the Peninsula Principles, refers to this framework when working with governments and affected communities on relocation projects.[250]

Like the Guiding Principles, the Peninsula Principles were written by legal experts without the pressures and influences of intergovernmental negotiations. The Peninsula Principles relate substantively to the Guiding Principles and illustrate a similar approach in drawing from existing international treaties, principles, and obligations. However, the Guiding Principles are mainly intended as an overarching and high-level legal framework for protecting the human rights of internally displaced persons; they arguably are not intended to provide specific guidelines or detailed practical considerations for managing displacements.[251] In this way, the Guiding Principles are more consistent with a treaty-based approach, as discussed above. By contrast, the detailed provisions

---

248    Rights of Indigenous People in Addressing Climate Forced Displacement, Complaint submitted by the Alaska Institute for Justice on behalf of Tribes of Alaska and Louisiana to the UN Special Rapporteur on the Human Rights of Internally Displaced Persons et al., at 12, 48 (15 Jan. 2020).

249    *Id.* at 12.

250    *See, e.g.*, DISPLACEMENT SOLUTIONS, CLIMATE DISPLACEMENT AND PLANNED RELOCATION IN COLOMBIA: THE CASE OF GRAMALOTE 47–59 (2015), *available at* http://displacementsolutions.org/wp-content/uploads/2015/08/Colombia-final-Redux1.pdf; DISPLACEMENT SOLUTIONS, ONE STEP AT A TIME: THE RELOCATION PROCESS OF THE GARDI SUGDUB COMMUNITY IN GUNAYALA, PANAMA 19–22 (2015), *available at* http://displacementsolutions.org/wp-content/uploads/2015/07/One-Step-at-a-Time-the-Relocation-Process-of-the-Gardi-Sugdub-Community-In-Gunayala-Panama.pdf.

251    *See* Gemenne & Brücker, *supra* note 222, at 249 (observing that the Guiding Principles are "exclusively concerned with human rights, and only marginally addresses aspects related to migration management or financial compensation for the displacement.").

of the Peninsula Principles contribute a roadmap to anticipating, planning, and managing displacement and relocation. The Peninsula Principles therefore reflect an adaptive approach through their focus on risk management, advance planning, practical implementation and in their refusal to distinguish between "reactive" or "anticipatory"—i.e., "involuntary" or "voluntary"—movement, which might otherwise be treated with differing approaches.

## 2)    *The 2018 Global Compacts*

In September 2016, 193 United Nations Member States unanimously adopted the New York Declaration for Refugees and Migrants (New York Declaration), an expression of political commitment to cooperate globally to address the difficulties faced by refugees and migrants, as well as the root causes of these movements.[252] The New York Declaration recognizes in its introductory paragraph that climate change impacts drive human movement.[253] Addressing both refugees and migrants in the same document, the New York Declaration acknowledges that, "[t]hough their treatment is governed by separate legal frameworks, refugees and migrants have the same universal human rights and fundamental freedoms."[254] The New York Declaration goes on to present joint commitments to both migrants and refugees, as well as separate commitments to each.[255]

In Annex II to the New York Declaration, States Parties commit to launch negotiations for "a global compact for safe, orderly, and regular migration."[256] These negotiations began in April 2017 and concluded in December 2018 in Marrakech, Morocco, with the adoption by 164 Member States of the Global Compact for Safe, Orderly and Regular Migration (Migration Compact). The United Nations General Assembly endorsed the Migration Compact later that month.[257] The New York Declaration also initiated, in consultation with States and other relevant United Nations entities, the development by the United Nations High Commissioner for Refugees of a "comprehensive refugee response framework".[258] The United Nations High Commissioner for Refugees

252   New York Declaration for Refugees and Migrants, G.A. Res. 71/1, UN Doc. A/RES/71/1 (3 Oct. 2016) [hereinafter 'New York Declaration'].
253   *Id.* ¶ 1.
254   *Id.* ¶ 6.
255   Section II of the New York Declaration contains "Commitments that apply to both refugees and migrants"; Section III contains "Commitments for migrants;" and Section IV contains "Commitments for refugees."
256   New York Declaration, *supra* note 252, Annex II, ¶ 1.
257   Global Compact for Safe, Orderly and Regular Migration, UN Doc. A/RES/73/195 (11 Jan. 2019) [hereinafter 'Migration Compact'].
258   New York Declaration, *supra* note 252, Annex I, ¶¶ 1–2.

presented a Global Compact on Refugees, containing a comprehensive refugee response framework, in its annual report to the United Nations General Assembly on 17 December 2018 (Refugee Compact).[259] The General Assembly, at the same time that it endorsed the Migration Compact, affirmed the Refugee Compact, with 181 Member States in favor.[260]

Neither the Refugee Compact nor the Migration Compact is binding. Each addresses, to differing degrees, human mobility in connection with climate change.

a          The Global Compact on Refugees
As discussed in detail in the previous chapter, climate change mobility is widely understood as falling outside the scope of refugee movements in most cases. The Refugee Compact takes a nuanced approach, acknowledging the potential connection between refugee flows and climate change impacts and human movements. The Refugee Compact further acknowledges the need for international protection solutions for forced movement stemming from "disasters", leaving the door open for international cooperation on this issue, albeit at each State's discretion. In a section addressing prevention and root causes, the Refugee Compact acknowledges the potential impact of climate change on refugee movements, even if it is not considered to be a trigger that gives rise to refugee protection: "While not in themselves causes of refugee movements, climate, environmental degradation and natural disasters increasingly interact with the drivers of refugee movements."[261] This section also calls upon the international community to "reduce disaster risks", amongst other prevention measures in line with the United Nations' 2030 Agenda for Sustainable Development, the Sendai Framework for Disaster Risk Reduction, and Agenda 2063.[262] As discussed previously, weather-related disasters may be caused or

---

259    Report of the UN High Commissioner for Refugees, *Global Compact on Refugees,* UN Doc. A/73/12 (Part II) (13 Sept. 2018); GAOR, 73rd Sess., Supp. No. 12 (2018) [hereinafter 'Refugee Compact'].

260    G.A. Res. 73/151, ¶ 23, UN Doc. A/RES/73/151 (10 Jan. 2019); Meetings Coverage, General Assembly, General Assembly Endorses Landmark Global Compact on Refugees, Adopting 53 Third Committee Resolutions, 6 Decisions Covering Range of Human Rights, UN Meetings Coverage GA/12107 (17 Dec. 2018), https://www.un.org/press/en/2018/ga12107. doc.htm.

261    Refugee Compact, *supra* note 259, at 2, ¶ 8.

262    *Id.* at 3, ¶ 9. The Sendai Framework and disaster risk reduction more generally are discussed *supra*. The Agenda for Sustainable Development 2030 is a 15-year plan, adopted in 2015 by United Nations Member States, to achieve seventeen goals aimed at protecting the planet, ending poverty and promoting global prosperity. 2030 Agenda for Sustainable Development, *supra* note 54. Agenda 2063 is a strategic framework by the African Union

aggravated by anthropogenic climate change; reducing disaster risks therefore means reducing the risks brought about by climate change—as well as so-called "natural"—hazard events.

An introduction to the "programme of action" for the comprehensive refugee response framework (contained within and forming an integral part of the Refugee Compact) acknowledges that, in addition to refugee movements, "external forced displacement may result from sudden-onset natural disasters and environmental degradation."[263] States may therefore "seek support from the international community" to address such movements, with support building "on the operational partnerships between relevant actors, including UNHCR and the International Organization for Migration".[264] According to the United Nations High Commissioner for Refugees, this paragraph was "carefully crafted to ensure that the GCR [Refugee Compact] applies not only to large refugee situations, but also to countries affected by environmental degradation and natural disasters. It allows such countries to draw on the arrangements for burden- and responsibility-sharing laid out in the GCR [Refugee Compact]".[265]

Finally, the Refugee Compact's comprehensive refugee response framework contains a section on areas in need of support, including international protection needs. In this section, it is observed that relevant stakeholders "will provide guidance and support for measures to address other protection and humanitarian challenges", which "could include measures to assist those forcibly displaced by natural disasters".[266] Although disasters can be caused or exacerbated by climate change, specific reference to climate change is conspicuously absent from this language.[267] A preceding paragraph encourages States to interpret and fulfill their protection obligations in a way that avoids protection gaps: "[m]echanisms for the fair and efficient determination of individual international protection claims provide an opportunity for States to duly determine the status of those on their territory in accordance with their

---

which seeks to advance, among other aspirations, sustainable development, unity and prosperity. AFRICAN UNION COMMISSION, AGENDA 2063: THE AFRICA WE WANT (Apr. 2015).

263    Refugee Compact, *supra* note 259, at 3, ¶ 12.

264    *Id.*

265    UNHCR, *Climate Change and Disaster Displacement in the Global Compact on Refugees*, at 1 (undated), *available at* https://www.unhcr.org/protection/environment/5c9e13297/clim ate-change-disaster-displacement-global-compact-refugees.html [hereinafter 'UNHCR Note on Refugee Compact'].

266    Refugee Compact, *supra* note 259, at 12, ¶ 63.

267    *See* T Alexander Aleinikoff, *The Unfinished Work of the Global Compact on Refugees*, 30(4) INT'L J. REFUGEE L. 611, 615 (2018).

applicable international and regional obligations, in a way which avoids protection gaps and enables all those in need of international protection to find and enjoy it."[268] The United Nations High Commissioner for Refugees considers that these two paragraphs, read in conjunction, avoid any gaps for persons in need of protection in connection with climate change impacts, including disasters.[269] Professor Alexander Aleinikoff considers this formulation to be problematic, as it leaves discretion to States to determine when and how to provide protection in accordance with their own laws, despite offering a "'hook' for advocacy on behalf of 'all those in need of international protection'."[270] Aleinikoff considers the biggest gap in the Refugee Compact (and in the Migration Compact), however, to be the choice not to include internally displaced persons, which receive only the "barest mention" in the Refugee Compact and are not mentioned at all in the Migration Compact.[271]

The United Nations High Commissioner for Refugees considers that the Refugee Compact "effectively acknowledges and addresses the reality of increasing displacement in the context of disasters, environmental degradation and climate change, and provides a basis for measures to tackle the many challenges arising in this area."[272] Professor Walter Kälin, on the other hand, is disappointed that the Refugee Compact did not go further and acknowledge that persons displaced by natural disasters could, in some situations, qualify for protection under the Refugee Convention or other regional asylum instruments.[273]

The limitations of the Refugee Compact reflect the disinclination of States to address climate change mobility within the refugee framework.[274] Notwithstanding the limitations of the Refugee Compact, Aleinikoff considers that it may provide "a springboard for meaningful action".[275] In this respect, he considers that both the Refugee Compact and the Migration Compact will have

---

268    Refugee Compact, *supra* note 259, at 11, ¶ 61.
269    UNHCR Note on Refugee Compact, *supra* note 265, at 1.
270    Aleinikoff, *supra* note 267, at 614.
271    *Id.* at 615.
272    UNHCR Note on Refugee Compact, *supra* note 265, at 1.
273    Walter Kälin, *The Global Compact on Migration: A Ray of Hope for Disaster-Displaced Persons*, 30(4) INT'L J. REFUGEE L. 664, 667 (2018) [hereinafter 'Kälin, *Global Compact on Migration*'].
274    *Id.* at 667; Aleinikoff, *supra* note 267, at 615.
275    Aleinikoff, *supra* note 267, at 616. Alexander Betts also accepts that the Refugee Compact "could not realistically have addressed all aspects of the refugee system". Alexander Betts, *The Global Compact on Refugees: Towards a Theory of Change?*, 30(4) INT'L J. REFUGEE L. 623, 626 (2018).

to be "read together to develop approaches for climate change-related migration"—with the New York Declaration serving as an "interpretive guide".[276]

b        The Global Compact for Safe, Orderly and Regular Migration

Given the limitations for addressing human mobility and climate change in the Refugee Compact, advocates focused their efforts on the inclusion of these issues in the Migration Compact.[277] The Migration Compact reflects these efforts in its explicit acknowledgement of the connection between climate change, disasters, and migration. Professor Walter Kälin considers the recognition of the "disaster-migration nexus" and the commitment to address mobility in relation to disasters and climate change to be "[o]ne of the most innovative elements" of the Migration Compact.[278] According to migration specialist François Gemenne, the Migration Compact is the first major migration policy to address climate change.[279]

The Migration Compact aims to provide "enhanced cooperation on international migration in all its dimensions".[280] To this end, it comprises twenty three objectives and sets forth 187 actions, upon which States commit to draw in support of these objectives.[281] Actions to address the drivers and impacts of climate change are included under several objectives and targeted by specific action points. Amongst these, Objectives 2 and 5 address climate change and environmental drivers directly.

Under Objective 2, States endeavor to mitigate the drivers of migration. The actions supporting this objective include a subsection on "[n]atural disasters, the adverse effects of climate change, and environmental degradation".[282] As Kälin observes, this is the only thematic subsection in the document, and the Parties agreed to insert it "at the very last moment into the final version of the Compact as a symbolic recognition of the particular importance of the topic."[283] In connection with movements resulting from sudden and slow onset

---

276    Aleinikoff, *supra* note 267, at 616, n.3.

277    *Id.* at 615.

278    Kälin, *Global Compact on Migration, supra* note 273, at 664.

279    Carolyn Beeler, *UN Compact Recognizes Climate Change as Driver of Migration for First Time*, THE WORLD (11 Dec. 2018), https://www.pri.org/stories/2018-12-11/un-compact-recognizes-climate-change-driver-migration-first-time.

280    Migration Compact, *supra* note 257, at 2.

281    Lex Rieffel, *The Global Compact on Migration: Dead on Arrival?*, BROOKINGS UP FRONT BLOG (12 Dec. 2018), https://www.brookings.edu/blog/up-front/2018/12/12/the-global-compact-on-migration-dead-on-arrival/.

282    Migration Compact, *supra* note 257, at 10.

283    Kälin, *Global Compact on Migration, supra* note 273, at 665.

hazard events (both referred to as "disasters"), climate change impacts, and environmental degradation, five paragraphs promote taking steps to advance:

1.  information sharing and cooperative analysis, in order to understand and predict such movements;
2.  the development of adaptation and resilience strategies (whilst prioritizing adaptation in the country of origin);
3.  the integration of "displacement considerations into disaster preparedness strategies";
4.  the development and harmonization at the regional and sub-regional levels of approaches to address vulnerabilities of persons affected by sudden onset and slow onset hazard events; and
5.  the development of "coherent approaches to address the challenges of migration movements in the context of sudden-onset and slow-onset natural disasters," taking into account the recommendations from the Platform on Disaster Displacement and other State-led consultative processes. [284]

Under Objective 5, States commit to enhance the availability and flexibility of pathways for regular migration. Action 5(g) includes developing or building upon existing practices to admit and allow the stay of migrants who have been compelled to leave their country of origin because of "sudden onset disasters". With respect to slow onset disasters and other climate change impacts, States, under action 5(h), should:

> cooperate to identify, develop and strengthen solutions for migrants compelled to leave their countries of origin owing to slow-onset natural disasters, the adverse effects of climate change, and environmental degradation, such as desertification, land degradation, drought and sea level rise, including by devising planned relocation and visa options, in cases where adaptation in or return to their country of origin is not possible [...].

These provisions under Objective 5 are noteworthy not only because they recognize the connection between climate change impacts and migration, but also because they express an intention to create pathways that might accommodate this kind of migration.

---

284   Migration Compact, *supra* note 257, at 10, Objective 2(h)–(l).

Although sudden onset hazard events are distinguished from slow onset hazard events within the Migration Compact, both are referred to as "disasters". As discussed in previous chapters, slow onset hazard events are not always considered to fall within the scope of "disasters". The recognition of slow onset hazard events as "disasters" within the Migration Compact is part of a trend within the adaptive framework by which slow onset hazard events are increasingly recognized as constituting or contributing to "disasters" and, as such, can be a factor that compels people to move.

The non-binding nature of the Migration Compact is confirmed in paragraph 15(b), with paragraph 15(c) affirming "the sovereign right of States to determine their national migration policy and their prerogative to govern migration within their jurisdiction, in conformity with international law." The effectiveness of the Migration Compact will therefore depend upon what governments do to implement and follow this cooperative framework.[285]

The fact that so many States were able to conclude a Migration Compact with an ambitious agenda is encouraging,[286] particularly given the controversy leading up to the completion of the Migration Compact and its renunciation, in the last hour, by several countries that had participated in the negotiations.[287] Kälin calls the Migration Compact a "breakthrough" and a "ray of hope" for persons displaced by disasters.[288] The UNFCCC's Task Force on Displacement also views the Migration Compact with optimism, noting that it "could trigger a review of existing national human mobility policy frameworks in line with GCM [Global Compact for Migration] provisions. New mobility policy

---

285    As Gemenne observes, "It will all depend on what the governments will do." Beeler, *supra* note 279.

286    Gemenne considers it "remarkable" that States could agree on a common policy basis for cooperation on migration. Beeler, *supra* note 279. Kathleen Newland used the same word, stating that the most "remarkable thing about the [...] (Migration Compact) is that it exists at all." Kathleen Newland, *The Global Compact for Safe, Orderly and Regular Migration: An Unlikely Achievement*, 30(4) INT'L J. REFUGEE L. 657, 657 (2018).

287    The United States was the only United Nations Member State that refused to participate in the negotiation of the Migration Compact. Rick Gladstone, *U.S. Quits Migration Pact, Saying It Infringes on Sovereignty*, NEW YORK TIMES (3 Dec. 2017), https://www.nytimes.com/2017/12/03/world/americas/united-nations-migration-pact.html. Hungary joined the United States in actively voting against the Migration Compact. After the text had been finalized in July 2018 but before its formal adoption in December 2018, a number of other States renounced the Migration Compact. For an account of this development, see Kathleen Newland, *An Overheated Narrative Unanswered: How the Global Compact for Migration Became Controversial*, MIGRATION POLICY INSTITUTE, COMMENTARIES (DEC. 2018), https://www.migrationpolicy.org/news/overheated-narrative-unanswered-how-global-compact-became-controversial.

288    Kälin, *Global Compact on Migration, supra* note 273, at 664, 665.

frameworks could also be developed on the basis of this Compact, opening the possibility to further mainstream climate and environmental dimensions."[289]

Others are less optimistic that the Migration Compact will lead to meaningful change in the way that States deal with migration. Policy advisor Lex Rieffel opines that both the Migration and Refugee Compacts are "likely to be ignored more than respected."[290] Regarding the ambitious policy agenda set forth in the Migration Compact, he considers the 23 Objectives and their accompanying 187 actions to be "overload" and "wishful thinking".[291]

To encourage State action, implementation measures have been incorporated into the Migration Compact. Amongst others, the Global Compact for Safe, Orderly and Regular Migration establishes an "International Migration Review Forum" to take place every fourth United Nations General Assembly to serve as a platform for discussions on implementation.[292] Even to the extent that States advance implementation of the Migration Compact, Kälin cautions that keeping disaster and climate-related human mobility on the agenda amongst other important migration issues will require concerted action by States and advocates.[293]

∴

Non-binding frameworks specifically tailored to human mobility in the context of disasters and climate change have emerged within the past decade. Increasing attention to climate change mobility in other frameworks catalyzed State-driven efforts to formulate and implement the 2015 Nansen Initiative Protection Agenda, a non-binding cooperative framework targeted at cross-border disaster displacement. The 2013 Peninsula Principles are a complementary normative framework aimed at internal climate change mobility, designed to reflect existing international legal guidelines and imperatives. By contrast, the Peninsula Principles were not created by State-driven initiatives, but by legal experts. They have yet to receive widespread endorsement by States or an international body, but have been identified as part of the key legal doctrine on climate change mobility in various contexts. Their influence in the international sphere may therefore still expand. The political

---

289   TFD 2018 Report, *supra* note 92, at 11, ¶ 54.

290   Rieffel, *supra* note 281.

291   *Id.*

292   Migration Compact, *supra* note 257, ¶ 49. *See also* Kälin, *Global Compact on Migration, supra* note 273, at 667.

293   Kälin, *Global Compact on Migration, supra* note 273, at 667.

momentum that catalyzed the creation of the Nansen Initiative Protection Agenda and the Platform on Disaster Displacement has not since subsided. Growing urgency to address climate change mobility led to its inclusion in the 2018 Global Refugee and Migrant Compacts—both of which were either formulated or endorsed by United Nations Member States. None of these frameworks imposes binding obligations, reflecting the desire of States to address the issue on a cooperative basis and to maintain control over the extent of their commitments for the time being. Like the Sendai Framework for disaster risk reduction, these human mobility frameworks reflect a trend towards recognizing slow onset hazard events as "disasters" or at least factors that may contribute to disasters.

## D        Assessing the Adaptive Framework

As explored above, climate change mobility is addressed in the adaptive framework as a component of mitigation and adaptation to climate change, as a factor to be addressed in the context of disaster risk reduction, and as a component (or sometimes the focus) of human mobility policy frameworks. The current adaptive framework demonstrates a shifting focus towards the development of cooperative multilateral agreements, non-binding frameworks, and initiatives that attempt to coordinate across sectors and at local, national, regional, and international levels. At the international level, the progression towards a collaborative, adaptive approach reflects the desire of States to maintain control over the specifics of the problem-solving process and the extent of their commitments vis-à-vis climate change mitigation and adaption, including with respect to human mobility.[294] This phenomenon is a natural result of the inherent uncertainty associated with and potential magnitude and breadth of human mobility scenarios in the context of climate change. States have therefore eschewed, at least for now, the pursuit of hard law instruments on human mobility in connection with climate change in favor of an approach that leaves liminal space to adapt to the evolving scientific and political landscapes. This adaptive approach is a cautious one, but one that has the potential to allow States to adopt a proactive role, while leaving room for local input into the process, an essential component of successful adaptation. Whether those who move in relation to climate change consider

---

294   *See* JANE MCADAM, CLIMATE CHANGE, FORCED MIGRATION, AND INTERNATIONAL LAW 197–99 (2012); McAdam, *Creating New Norms, supra* note 97, at 12.

their decisions to be an empowered adaptive strategy or a result of victimization may in part depend upon the amount of input they had into the process and related frameworks.[295]

Ensuring that ongoing local input is properly incorporated in any adaptation process and policy or legal decisions is particularly essential in the context of massive global frameworks like the UNFCCC. Coordinating internal UNFCCC processes with local and regional needs, values, and perspectives and with other entities engaging at this level, such as the Platform on Disaster Displacement, could help to ensure that information and policy decisions flowing from the UNFCCC do not become top-down decisions driven by the least common denominator principle. Given that States appear increasingly prepared to address human mobility within the UNFCCC process, the further expansion of the mandate of the Task Force on Displacement may eventually help to coordinate work (and funding) in this area.

To recall, the mandate of the Task Force on Displacement was recently expanded to include interacting with States on the development of national laws, policies, and strategies that address climate change displacement; capacity-building training; assessing displacement risk; and identifying funding possibilities for projects to avert, minimize, and address climate change-related displacement.[296] This expanded mandate still does not transform the Task Force on Displacement into the kind of climate change displacement coordination facility that was proposed prior to the Paris Agreement. Such a coordination facility, as proposed, would have undertaken activities related to the provision of assistance and support for emergency relief efforts, organized migration, planned relocation, and compensation measures. It does, however, give the Task Force on Displacement a significant role in cooperating and coordinating with States. In this way, the Task Force on Displacement is in a position to help ensure that efforts within the UNFCCC to address human mobility remain consistent with other efforts and with local, national, and regional considerations. The Task Force on Displacement is also now in a position to coordinate and develop funding efforts aimed at human mobility adaptation within the UNFCCC, which will be vital to the ability of some developing States to undertake adaptive measures. For the moment and in anticipation of obtaining funding, such States have the possibility of developing tailored adaptation strategies vis-à-vis human mobility through the UNCCD National Action

---

295   *See* Jane McAdam & Elizabeth Ferris, *Planned Relocations in the Context of Climate Change: Unpacking the Legal and Conceptual Issues*, 4 CAMBRIDGE J. INT'L & COMP. L. 137, 144–45 (2015).

296   *See* WIM ExCom 2019 Report, *supra* note 158, at 10, 12, 14, Activities 7, 12, 13, 20.

Programme (NAP) or UNFCCC National Adaptation Plan (NAP) process. How the Task Force on Displacement will interpret and act in this expanded role remains to be seen and may depend in part on cooperation of States Parties.

The decision of States Parties to address human mobility within the UNFCCC has acted as a catalyst for consensus building in other forums for dealing with climate change mobility. Examples include the Nansen Initiative and its successor, the Platform on Disaster Displacement, which coordinates scientific research, awareness raising, and policy development and implementation to address human mobility, including *in situ* adaptation and protective measures, at local, regional, and international levels and across disciplines. Such efforts epitomize the adaptive approach and even leave the door open for future legally binding rights-based approaches. Importantly, the inclusion of human mobility within the UNFCCC process has qualified scientific research, projects, and initiatives connected with human mobility adaptation for funding through the UNFCCC. This is of critical importance due to the amount of research that needs to be done in this area to more fully understand this crescive global problem and to find tailored, neoteric solutions.

Many of the initiatives described above are recently initiated or still in progress. The adaptive approach does not aim to produce a specific legal instrument or short-term outcome, but rather to cultivate "climate foresight"[297] through stable trajectories for societal transformations over a long-term time horizon. The effectiveness of the adaptive approach therefore remains to be gauged and is, by necessity, a work in progress.

297   *See* Warner, *Cancun Adaptation Framework, supra* note 81, at 1073 ("It will be important to incorporate long-term time horizons (or 'climate foresight') as opposed to simple 'impact/vulnerability' mapping (that results in providing short-term 'coping' strategies) in adaptation planning.").

# CHAPTER 6

# The Application of Complexity Theory to Large-Scale Desertification and Land Degradation in Sahelo-Saharan Africa

> The one who plants trees, knowing that he will never sit in their shade, has at least started to understand the meaning of life.
>
> – RABINDRANATH TAGORE

∴

> [W]e ought to follow Nature as our guide, to contribute to the general good by an interchange of acts of kindness, by giving and receiving, and thus by our skill, our industry, and our talents to cement human society more closely together.
>
> – MARCUS TULLIUS CICERO

∵

## A     Complexity Theory and the Great Green Wall

The Sahel is an ecoclimatic and biogeographic transition zone situated in between the Sahara Desert to the north and the woody savannah of the Sudanean zone to the south.[1] The slow onset of desertification in Sahelo-Saharan Africa is destroying entire cultures as tens of millions of people are forced to migrate to surrounding areas for their survival. In response, the

---

[1]  Cheikh Mbow, *The Great Green Wall in the Sahel*, CLIMATE SCIENCE, OXFORD RESEARCH ENCYCLOPEDIA 1–2 (2017), https://oxfordre.com/climatescience/view/10.1093/acrefore/9780190228620.001.0001/acrefore-9780190228620-e-559 ("*Sahel* is an Arabic word that refers to the fringe between the Sahara and the woodlands of the southern part."). The present chapter is based upon a paper delivered in 2017 at an international conference organized in Rome by Loyola University Chicago School of Law's Program on Rule of Law for Development (PROLAW) and entitled "Conference on Complexity, Legal and Institutional Change, and Rule of Law".

ambitious project to construct a Great Green Wall was conceived to halt and reverse land degradation and desertification. This project is an excellent example of how international adaptive frameworks, including the UNCCD and the UNFCCC, can influence changes on the ground. It also provides the opportunity to explore how other legal frameworks could be adapted to complement and advance adaptive projects. The harmonization between relevant legal frameworks (international, regional, and domestic) could create synergy amongst the efforts of stakeholders in this area and thus help to achieve "critical mass" for achieving land restoration along the Great Green Wall corridor. The fashioning of mutually reinforcing legal norms could promote the rule of law and thus foster the compatibility of complexity-based development programs with the Sustainable Development Goals.

Toward this end, complexity theory can be employed to investigate the Daedalean web of governments; international, regional, and local organizations; civil society; scientists; local populations; and private companies engaged in the construction of the Great Green Wall. International organizations, in particular, may need to undergo internal and external governance reforms in order to marshal more climacteric action than States are willing and/or able to take.

The relatively recent advent of complexity theory and its application to international environmental law has been an important development. It has allowed scholars and scientists to more accurately analyze the complex web of systems that impact the relationship between humans and their environment. Complexity theory and its application to public international law has been the subject of much academic debate; scholars have defined complexity theory through a multitude of profoundly divergent conceptual lenses.[2] The purpose

---

2   *See, e.g.*, Gerald Andrews Emison, *The Potential for Unconventional Progress: Complex Adaptive Systems and Environmental Quality Policy*, 7 DUKE ENVTL. L. & POL'Y F. 167 (1996); Eric Kades, *The Laws of Complexity & the Complexity of Laws: The Implications of Computational Complexity Theory for the Law*, 49 RUTGERS L. REV. 403 (1997); Lynn M. LoPucki, *The Systems Approach to Law*, 82(3) CORNELL L. REV. 479 (1997); Randal C. Picker, *Simple Games in a Complex World: A Generative Approach to the Adoption of Norms*, 64 U. CHI. L. REV. 1225 (1997); David G. Post & David R. Johnson, *"Chaos Prevailing on Every Continent": Towards A New Theory of Decentralized Decision-Making in Complex Systems*, 73(4) CHI.-KENT L. REV. 1055 (1998); Andrea Bianchi, *Ad-hocism and the Rule of Law*, 13 EUR. J. INT'L L. 263 (2002); Daniel A. Farber, *Probabilities Behaving Badly: Complexity Theory and Environmental Uncertainty*, 37 U.C. DAVIS L. REV. 145 (2003); Erika de Wet, *The Prohibition of Torture as an International Norm of* Jus Cogens *and Its Implications for National and Customary Law*, 15 EUR. J. INT'L L. 97 (2004); Nico Krisch, *International Law in Times of Hegemony: Unequal Power and the Shaping of the International Legal Order*, 16(3) EUR J. INT'L L. 369 (2005); Julian Webb, *Law, Ethics and Complexity: Complexity Theory and the Normative Reconstruction of Law*, 52 CLEV. ST. L. REV. 227 (2005); Ole Spiermann, *Twentieth Century Internationalism in Law*, 18(5) EUR

of the present chapter is not to attempt to arrive at one, unified theory of complex systems, but rather to apply one ingemination of the theory to the problem of desertification in Sahelo-Saharan Africa in a non-reductionist manner. The particular iteration chosen in the present chapter is one that has doctrinal coherence and practical application.

Professor Graham Room—in his 2011 book, entitled *Complexity, Institutions and Public Policy: Agile Decision-Making in a Turbulent World*—develops a conceptual and methodological framework, drawing upon and integrating complexity science and institutionalism, in order to answer the following question: to what extent "is it possible to provide analytical tools for policymakers in a world of non-linearity and path dependence".[3] Proceeding from the premise that the world is not only complex, but also turbulent, he argues that complexity science needs to take into account the actions of institutions and that institutionalism requires the formal dynamic modelling of complexity science.[4] Room's institutionally grounded complexity perspective "directs our attention to the local novelties that emerge 'bottom up' and then are variously adopted by the population, in turn abrading and co-evolving with the larger technological and institutional 'eco-system'." Order then emerges in this complex adaptive system, as it self-organizes across dynamic fitness landscapes (deepen-widen-warp).[5]

The Great Green Wall for the Sahara and the Sahel Initiative (GGWSSI, Great Green Wall Initiative, or Initiative) is a classic project for the application

J. INT'L L. 785 (2007); Hanqin Xue, *Chinese Observations on International Law*, 6(1) CHINESE J. INT'L L. 83 (2007); Giuseppe Martinico, *Complexity and Cultural Sources of Law in the EU Context: From the Multilevel Constitutionalism to the Constitutional Synallagma*, 8(3) GERMAN L. J 205 (2007); Gregory Todd Jones, *Dynamical Jurisprudence: Law as a Complex System*, 24(4) GA. ST. U. L. REV. 873 (2008); J.B. Ruhl, *Law's Complexity: A Primer*, 24(4) GA. ST. U. L. REV. 885 (2008); Peter Hilpold, *What Role for Academic Writers in Interpreting International Law? A Rejoinder to Orakhelashvili*, 8(2) CHINESE J. INT'L L. 291 (2009); Bing Bing Jia, *The Relations between Treaties and Custom*, 9 CHINESE J. INT'L L. 81 (2010); Yannick Radi, *Standardization: A Dynamic and Procedural Conceptualization of International Law-Making*, 25(2) LEIDEN J. INT'L L. 283 (2012); Aoife O'Donoghue, *International Constitutionalism and the State*, 11(4) INT'L J. CONST. L. 1021 (2013); Marcelo Dias Varella, *Central Aspects of the Debate on the Complexity of International Law*, 27 EMORY INT'L L. REV. 1 (2013); DAVID BYRNE & GILL CALLAGHAN, COMPLEXITY THEORY AND THE SOCIAL SCIENCES: THE STATE OF THE ART (2014).

3  GRAHAM ROOM, COMPLEXITY, INSTITUTIONS AND PUBLIC POLICY: AGILE DECISION-MAKING IN A TURBULENT WORLD 8–9 (2011); *see also* David Turner, *Book Review, Complexity, Institutions and Public Policy: Agile Decision-Making in a Turbulent World*, 90(1) PUB. ADMIN. 276, 288 (2012).

4  ROOM, *supra* note 3, at 10–11.

5  *Id.* at 303–05.

of complexity theory. A conceptual application of Room's theory of adaptation of fitness landscapes to large-scale land degradation in Sahelo-Saharan Africa reveals that the process of "deepening" has already commenced with governments, non-governmental organizations, scientists, and local communities ("first movers") making the initial forays into holistic restoration and reforestation initiatives in the region. Next, international and regional stakeholders are augmenting the work of the first movers by coordinating on-going international, regional, and national efforts and by establishing and managing a centralized voluntary trust fund (the Global Environment Facility) to support domestic and regional remediation programs and continued scientific research. This process is considered "widening" by "second movers" under Room's theoretical model. Finally, this coalition of States, non-State actors, and international institutions could create critical mass for construction of the Great Green Wall by harmonizing national, regional, and international law, which could be regarded as Room's "warping" principle—which could, in turn, tip the scales in favor of long-term and durable solutions to land degradation in Sahelo-Saharan Africa.

B        Deepening by First Movers: The Origins of the Great Green Wall

Room's agile first mover strives for positional advantage, pushes social systems out of equilibrium, and attempts to shape their self-organization. The turbulence of the environment provides opportunities, and the first mover seeks new combinations of technologies and institutions. First movers use knowledge of the present and the past to imagine future possibilities[6] where—as Aristotle would have phrased it—the whole is greater than the sum of its parts.[7] In the context of desertification, the international community itself can be described as a "first mover". As discussed previously, following the 1977 United Nations Conference on Desertification (which led to the United Nations Plan of Action to Combat Desertification—the PACD),[8] the United Nations Convention to

---

6   *Id.* at 103–04.
7   ARISTOTLE, METAPHYSICS: BOOK H 1045a 8–10 ("The totality is not, as it were, a mere heap, but the whole is something besides the parts. [πάντων γὰρ ὅσα πλείω μέρη ἔχει καὶ μὴ ἔστιν οἷον σωρὸς τὸ πᾶν]"); *see also* EUCLID, ELEMENTS: BOOK I, Common Notion 5 ("The whole is greater than the part. [τὸ ὅλον τοῦ μέρους μεῖζον]").
8   United Nations Conference on Desertification, Nairobi, Kenya, 29 Aug.–9 Sep. 1977, *Report of the United Nations Conference on Desertification*, at 2-63, UN Doc. A/CONF.74/36 (7 Sept. 1977).

Combat Desertification in Those Countries Experiencing Serious Drought and/or Desertification, Particularly in Africa (UNCCD) was adopted on 17 June 1994 and entered into force on 26 December 1996.

Some States of the region, such as Nigeria, have decided to implement their obligations under the UNCCD in the context of the Great Green Wall Project, as part of a concerted, synergetic implementation of relevant multilateral environmental agreements, such as the three Rio Conventions: the UNCCD, UNFCCC, and United Nations Convention on Biological Diversity (UNCBD).[9] The Great Green Wall Initiative is a project of cyclopean size and labyrinthine complexity. In 2005, the former President of Nigeria, Olusegun Obasanjo,[10] proposed to the African Union the creation of a corridor of trees and other vegetation almost 8,000 kilometers long and 15 kilometers wide stretching from Dakar (Senegal) to Djibouti along the southern border of the Sahara Desert and through several States of the Sahel. In 2007, the Assembly of the African Union adopted the "Decision on the Implementation of the Green Wall for the Sahara Initiative", which endorsed the Great Green Wall Initiative;[11] and, in 2010, several States signed a convention in Ndjamena, Chad to create the Great Green Wall Agency.[12]

The Great Green Wall Initiative is taking place in a region that has faced much turbulence in its recent history, caused in part by conflicts over dwindling resources. Due to the complexity and turbulent landscape in which the project is being implemented, it is well suited for an application of complexity theory. Inspired by the Great Wall of China that was constructed to check the advance of nomadic groups of the Eurasian Steppe, the Great Green Wall is an aspirational symbol intended to inspire different, individual projects across the region. With respect to integrated ecosystem management, the massive

---

9    FEDERAL REPUBLIC OF NIGERIA, MINISTRY OF ENVIRONMENT, GREAT GREEN WALL
     FOR THE SAHARA AND SAHEL INITIATIVE, NATIONAL STRATEGIC ACTION PLAN
     12 (Oct. 2012). *See also, generally,* Luca Montanarella et al., *Potential Synergies Between
     Existing Multilateral Environmental Agreements in the Implementation of Land Use, Land-
     Use Change and Forestry Activities,* 10 ENVTL. SCI. & POL'Y 335 (2007).

10   Some also credit the former Head of State of Burkina Faso, Thomas Sankara, with pro-
     posing the project in the 1980s. *See* FEDERAL REPUBLIC OF NIGERIA, *supra* note 9, at 12.
     The former President of Senegal, Abdoulaye Wade, also supported Obasanjo's proposal.
     *See* Global Environment Facility, GEF 40th Council Meeting (23–26 May 2011), LDCF/SCCF
     10th Council Meeting (26 May 2011), *Note for Information to Council Members: Sahel and
     West Africa WB/GEF Program in Support of the Great Green Wall Initiative,* at 8 (20 May
     2011) [hereinafter 'GEF Great Green Wall Note'].

11   African Union, 8th Ordinary Sess., 29–30 Jan. 2007, *Decision on the Implementation of the
     Green Wall for the Sahara Initiative,* AU Doc. Assembly/AU/Dec.137(VIII).

12   *See* GEF Great Green Wall Note, *supra* note 10, at 8.

project to construct the Great Green Wall is not just a re-forestation initiative, but rather a highly complex and inter-disciplinary mosaic of diverse initiatives to create climate resilient infrastructure. Trans-boundary water course management, food security, tree planting, and sustainable agricultural development are all part of the complicated and delicate web of measures being employed toward the overall goal of creating an environmental barrier against desertification and land degradation. As described by Cheikh Mbow, "[t]he initiative has specific goals that include contributing to halting desertification and land degradation in the Sahelian zone, improving the lives and livelihoods of smallholder farmers and pastoralists in this area, and helping these vulnerable populations to adapt to and mitigate climate change through the tree-based development program."[13]

There are a number of indigenous peoples in Sahelo-Saharan Africa. The rights of indigenous people are set forth in the United Nations Convention on Biological Diversity (UNCBD), the United Nations Declaration on the Rights of Indigenous Peoples, and the International Labour Organisation's Convention No. 169. Economic, social, and cultural rights are a necessary part of not only the means, but also the ends of reversing the spread of the desert and remedying the failure of the land in vulnerable ecosystems. Local knowledge and experience—including from indigenous populations—are vital resources for restoration of the land, as has been demonstrated through initiatives for holistic planned grazing and the timing of harvests of wild fruit. Sustainable land management does not always have to be controlled by governments and can often be accomplished more effectively and efficiently by local communities.[14]

C     **Widening by Second Movers: The Proliferation of Local Projects Supported and Funded by International and Regional Stakeholders**

Room's second movers utilize the work of the first movers to proliferate the vision and innovation of the first movers across the fitness landscape in variegated ways, called "secondary adaptations" that widen the field and application of the first movers.[15] Since the adoption of the Great Green Wall Initiative

---

13     Mbow, *supra* note 1, at 3.
14     *See* JONATHAN DAVIES, BIODIVERSITY AND THE GREAT GREEN WALL: MANAGING NATURE FOR SUSTAINABLE DEVELOPMENT IN THE SAHEL 41–42, 48 (2017); CLIMATE CHANGE AND INDIGENOUS PEOPLES, THE SEARCH FOR LEGAL REMEDIES (Randall Abate & Elizabeth Warner eds., 2015).
15     ROOM, *supra* note 3, at 42, 55, 159.

by the African Union in 2007, there has been a proliferation of international
and regional actors that have striven to support the project. Some of these
include the following: the Global Environment Facility (GEF), which is the
financial mechanism of the UNCCD; the United Nations Food and Agricultural
Organization (FAO); the United Nations Development Programme: Drylands,
Development Center (UNDP-DDC); United Nations Environment, World
Conservation Monitoring Center (UNEP-WCMC); the Global Mechanism of
the United Nations Convention to Combat Desertification (GM-UNCCD);
the World Agroforestry Centre (ICRAF); the World Overview of Conservation
Approaches and Technologies (WOCAT); the World Bank; the Panafrican
Agency of the Great Green Wall (PAGGW); the African Forest Forum (AFF); the
Permanent Inter-State Committee for Drought Control in the Sahel (CILSS);
the European Union; the West and Central Africa Office of the International
Union for the Conservation of Nature (IUCN-PACO); and the Sahara and Sahel
Observatory (OSS). The goal of the Great Green Wall Initiative is by 2030 "to
restore 100 million hectares of currently degraded land, sequester 250 million
tonnes of carbon and create 10 million jobs in rural areas."[16]

The work of the foregoing organizations (and the prodigious amount of literature they have produced) is difficult to encompass within this brief case
study. Thus far, the Great Green Wall Initiative has yielded some tangible
results, which can be summarized as follows: in Ethiopia, 15 million hectares
of degraded land have been restored; in Senegal, 18 million drought resistant
trees have been planted, and 850,000 hectares of degraded land have been
restored; in Nigeria, five million hectares of degraded land have been restored;
in Sudan, 2,000 hectares of land have been restored; and in Burkina Faso, Mali,
and Niger, 120 communities have been involved in restoring 2,500 hectares of
degraded land.[17] However, this summary cannot adequately describe the vast
efforts and the results that have been achieved in hundreds of communities
across the Sahel. To take a bird's eye view of the situation is inherently to dis-
tort the reality on the ground. Ultimately, the success of the Great Green Wall
Initiative is to be measured one community at a time. Many of the financial

16    *2030 Ambition*, GREAT GREEN WALL, https://www.greatgreenwall.org/2030ambition (last
      visited 30 May 2021); *see also The Great Green Wall Initiative*, UNCCD, http://www2.unccd.
      int/actions/great-green-wall-initiative (last visited 30 May 2021).
17    *The Great Green Wall Initiative*, UNCCD, http://www2.unccd.int/actions/great-green-wall-
      initiative (last visited 30 May 2021); *Results*, GREAT GREEN WALL https://www.greatgr
      eenwall.org/results (last visited 30 May 2021); *African Union and FAO Expand Great Green
      Wall Partnership*, IISD, SDG KNOWLEDGE HUB, (11 Feb. 2016), http://sdg.iisd.org/news/
      african-union-and-fao-expand-great-green-wall-partnership/.

resources that have been utilized in order to achieve the gains thus far have been channeled through international organizations and actors. International organizations thus arose and/or adapted themselves to serve as the interme- diaries between the donors and local communities where the land restoration projects were being conducted. In doing so, these organizations were not func- tioning as mere servants of States that formed them, but have assumed more independent legal persona.

## D    The Warping Principle: Achieving Critical Mass

The first movers began the Great Green Wall Initiative, and the second movers have expanded its scope and impact; however, it seems as though the proj- ect is still to achieve the critical mass necessary to transform the region con- sistent with the Sustainable Development Goals, specifically Goal 15 (Life on Land: Sustainably manage forests, combat desertification, halt and reverse land degradation, halt biodiversity loss).[18] The fitness landscape is being shaped, but has not yet reached a tipping point—or, as systems theorist Fritjof Capra would call it, a "turning point".[19] Following the adaptation of a fitness land- scape by, initially, the first movers and, subsequently, the second movers, Room applies complexity science's concept of co-evolution to social and economic structures. In doing so, he argues that the actions of individuals and institu- tions within the system, in fact, change the system by their actions—called "warping" by Room. This can be a destructive change or a positive one, either generally or in respect of different strata of society. In either case, the change is one of significance, whereby the system reaches critical mass, thereby causing a cascade effect (for either good or ill).[20] Applying these principles to the Great Green Wall Initiative, there could be merit in exploring a macro-level approach to the laws of the States across the Sahel in order to stimulate long-term public and private investment on the micro-level in the affected communities.

As mentioned above, the Sahel faces security challenges and can be a turbulent region for the implementation of projects. In 2016, Mohamed Ibn Chambas, the United Nations Representative of the Secretary-General for West

---

18    Transforming Our World: the 2030 Agenda for Sustainable Development, G.A. Res. 70/1, at 24, UN Doc. A/RES/70/1 (21 Oct. 2015).

19    FRITJOF CAPRA, THE TURNING POINT: SCIENCE, SOCIETY, AND THE RISING CULTURE (1988).

20    ROOM, *supra* note 3, at 44–46, 56, 86–87, 109, 296–298.

Africa and the Sahel, addressed the United Nations Security Council, stating that West Africa and the Sahel:

> experience various unresolved conflicts ranging from the renewed insurgency in the Niger Delta, deadly clashes between farmers and herders over scarce, and dwindling, agricultural resources, to terrorist activities in Northern Mali and North East of Nigeria, which have spilled over to neighboring countries of Cameroon, Chad and Niger. These threats come hand in hand with organized crime, trafficking and violent extremism, and are exacerbated by recurring droughts that climate change, by all accounts, has rendered more frequent and hazardous. The landlocked character of the area and poor transport links is yet another strain, preventing regional trade that could provide employment and stimulate economies. [...]
>
> [T]he issues cited above have been thoroughly reviewed over the years. Problems are identified, so are the set of actions to be taken to address those problems. A number of sound initiatives exist and yet, there is a feeling of frustration because results are not as tangible as one would have wished them to be. Pulling efforts together to rationalize the implementation of the existing plans would go a long way in achieving our common goal.[21]

Keeping these comments in mind, a review of the existing literature reveals an abundance of attention to the scientific, policy, social, and financial efforts to combat land degradation in the Sahel, which are essential; however, there is a dearth of study devoted to the issue of whether reform of legal institutions and legislation is required. In a region where terrorism and conflicts over resources exist, attention to the rule of law would seem to also be an essential component of a holistic strategy for the restoration of peace and prosperity to the communities of the region. Specifically, *a trans-boundary harmonization of the laws* of the communities and States across the Sahel could lead to tangible benefits in the mid- to long term. For example, a uniform approach to labor, tax, energy, land tenure, education, and environmental laws throughout the countries of the Sahel could provide legal predictability for the individuals in the States where the Great Green Wall is located, for the States sharing the region, and

---

21    Special Representative Mohamed Ibn Chambas, Security Council Briefing on the Impact of Climate Change and Desertification on Peace and Security of the Sahel (26 May 2016), https://dppa.un.org/en/security-council-briefing-impact-of-climate-change-and-desertification-peace-and-security-sahel.

for potential investors both inside and outside the Sahel. Harmonization of national laws in the region could have an even greater benefit on activities that are conducted not only in a single State, but also across several States wherein the Great Green Wall is situated, such as projects aimed at improving the livelihoods of people in the Lake Chad Area and the Niger River basin.

New laws could expressly require the exclusive employment of citizens of the region in which a project is being conducted and could set minimum standards for their employment (e.g., remuneration and other benefits), in order to encourage the employment of locals and discourage the importation of foreign labor. Moreover, regional labor laws favoring local workers in a uniform manner, including the creation of transboundary labor unions, could give workers protection on a broad scale and leverage vis-à-vis multi-national companies, such as collective bargaining on a regional scale, minimum wages, and reasonable working hours—while at the same time providing predictability and reliability in the work force available for projects. Land rights and tenure in Africa is a complex topic; each State and each community has unique cultural and historical traditions that may not be amenable to a one-size-fits-all and top-down approach. One scholar has proposed the creation of an expert international institution to establish fair market values in land and to oversee land deals in order to ensure their fairness.[22] In areas where there is legal uncertainty regarding land rights, a uniform, minimum approach that guarantees local ownership and participation in land transactions may be beneficial to combatting external exploitation and ensuring that local communities are in control of their own land. Moreover, strict implementation of the laws already in force is essential.[23]

One resource that the Sahara and the Sahel indisputably possess in abundance—and that has hardly even begun to be harnessed—is a practically inexhaustible and reliable supply of solar radiation. In this regard, harnessing solar energy from the Sun is not a new discovery. One-hundred and eighty-two years ago, the French physicist Edmond Becquerel uncovered the photovoltaic effect in the course of an experiment with metal electrodes in a conducting solution. In the 1860s, a French mathematician, Augustin Mouchot, built upon Becquerel's work and constructed a solar powered engine. In the coming decades, the consumption of fossil fuels will begin to plateau and sustainable energy will rise; the International Energy Agency (IEA) has estimated that, according to one scenario, by 2040 nearly 60 percent of the power generated

---

22    *See generally* Jared Wigginton, *Large-Scale Land Investment in Africa: An Issue of Self-Help and Self-Determination*, 20 U.C. DAVIS J. INT'L L. & POL'Y 105 (2013).

23    *See* DAVIES, *supra* note 14, at 49.

in the world will come from renewable sources.[24] This valuable resource could be exploited by local economies working together in partnership with other communities outside the Sahel or even with companies that could export the energy outside the Sahel to places with less predictable sunshine.[25] On a shady day in Western Europe, Sahelian energy could take the place of coal.[26] Government subsidies to stabilize local wages could be funded by the tax revenues generated by solar extraction projects.

The study of the laws of the States of the Sahel and discussions on how they could be harmonized to form a solid basis for increased activity in the region could be conducted at an international conference, attended by lawyers, parliamentarians, and academics from the region. Such a conference could be held within the legal framework of the 2007 decision of the Assembly of the African Union, which endorsed the Great Green Wall Initiative; called upon the African Union Commission to fast track implementation of the Great Green Wall Initiative through the development of a master plan in collaboration with the concerned Member States, regional economic communities, the private sector, civil society organizations, and non-governmental organizations; called upon Member States to put in place necessary institutional arrangements that are required at national, sub-regional, and regional levels to guide the program implementation process; mandated the Commission to facilitate and coordinate the implementation of the Great Green Wall Initiative by Member States and regional economic communities; and called upon the development partners to support the affected Member States, regional economic communities, and the Commission to ensure the effective implementation of the Great Green Wall Initiative at national, regional, and continental levels. This legislative conference could utilize the momentum generated by the first international conference on the Great Green Wall for the Sahara and the Sahel Initiative, held from 5–7 May 2016 in Dakar, Senegal, and that issued the Dakar Declaration, which focused on deepening the commitment of participating States and organizations for "transformational actions" in the area of reversing land degradation and improving economic opportunities for

---

24    *See* INTERNATIONAL ENERGY AGENCY, WORLD ENERGY OUTLOOK 2016, at 24 (2016),
      *available at* https://iea.blob.core.windows.net/assets/680c05c8-1d6e-42ae-b953-68e04
      20d46d5/WEO2016.pdf.

25    *See generally* MICHAEL BLOOMBERG & CARL POPE, CLIMATE OF HOPE: HOW CITIES,
      BUSINESSES, AND CITIZENS CAN SAVE THE PLANET (2017).

26    DAVID MACKAY, SUSTAINABLE ENERGY—WITHOUT THE HOT AIR 177–185 (2009) (cal-
      culating how to concentrate solar power in the Sahara Desert and then transport it to
      Europe for consumption).

the people of the Sahel.[27] These "transformational actions" are precisely what Room describes as "warping" of the fitness landscape. The contemplated conference would provide bottom-up implementation of the top-down impetus of the African Union Assembly's decision and could be organized by legislative topics, such as labor, tax, energy, land tenure, education, and the environment. Working groups of the conference could discuss each topic, and the findings of each group could then be vetted by country experts from the States of the Sahel. Any major disagreements could be further discussed and refined. In the end, model legislation could be agreed upon in a plenary session of the conference, after which the national legislatures of each State could enact the legislative changes in their national codes. A neoteric review of the laws of the region could also provide an opportunity to ensure that they are sufficiently flexible to adapt to the complex and volatile socio-economic environment of the Sahel. As stated by two scholars, the "[c]ontinued operation of laws that fail to consider fluctuations or changing dynamics in ecological conditions can present barriers to actions necessary for long term adaptation".[28]

In 2016, the (then) Executive Secretary of the UNCCD, Monique Barbut, addressed the United Nations Security Council on the issue of the peace and security challenges in the Sahel region. She urged the Member States of the Council to invest in land rehabilitation for each of the "frontline" villages and communities of the Sahel, estimating that an investment of 250 US dollars per hectare for an average of 5,000 villages per country was needed to stimulate a new economy; she stressed that such an investment "would definitely be

---

27    See First International Conference on the Great Green Wall for the Sahara and the Sahel Initiative (GGWSSI), Theme: Restoring Africa's Landscapes—The Way Forward, AFRICAN UNION, MEDIA ADVISORY (2 May 2016) https://au.int/en/newsevents/30271/first-intern ational-conference-great-green-wall-sahara-and-sahel-initiative-ggwssi; First Great Green Wall Global Conference Reaffirms Commitments to Restore Africa's Drylands, IISD, SDG KNOWLEDGE HUB (23 May 2016), http://sdg.iisd.org/news/first-great-green-wall-global-conference-reaffirms-commitments-to-restore-africas-drylands/ ("The discussions drew on experiences from several Great Green Wall projects, including: the World Bank and Global Environment Facility (GEF) supported Sahel and West Africa Program (SAWAP); the Action Against Desertification (AAD) programme, which is implemented by the Food and Agriculture Organization of the UN (FAO) and funded by the partnership programme between the EU and Africa, Caribbean and Pacific countries (ACP-EU); and the Front Local Environnemental pour une Union Verte (FLEUVE), an EU-funded Great Green Wall project coordinated by the Global Mechanism of the UN Convention to Combat Desertification (UNCCD).").

28    Daniel Schramm & Carl Bruch, Adapting Laws and Institutions to a Changing Climate, 9 INT'L ENVTL LAW-MAKING & DIPL. REV. 65, 69 (2009); see also at 65–87.

cheaper and more effective than investing in walls, wars and relief".[29] Aligning
the laws of the region in these various areas could *both* attract large-scale
multi-national development (where appropriate and sustainable) *and* inner-
vate small- or single-scale projects led and owned by local communities. It is
therefore not a choice between top-down and bottom-up strategies, but rather
a combination of both: complexity perspectives can incorporate systems theory into rule of law development programming and thus aid legislative reform
and enhance rule of law development strategies.

In a 2017 study, an international team of scientists calculated that land management, including restoration, could by 2030 yield 37 percent (11.3 billion metric tons) of the carbon mitigation called for by the Paris Agreement.[30] A restoration of the land along the Great Green Wall corridor—in Benin, Burkina
Faso, Chad, Djibouti, Eritrea, Ethiopia, Ghana, Mali, Mauritania, Niger, Nigeria,
Senegal, Sudan, and Togo—would not only serve as an *in situ* adaptation measure against the effects of global climate change that are being experienced
there, but also could re-forest the region and increase carbon capture, thus
serving as an actual climate change mitigation measure.[31] Approaching this

---

29   UN Security Council, New York, USA, 26 May 2016, 7699th Meeting, *Peace and Security in
     Africa: Challenges in the Sahel Region*, at 9, UN Doc. S/PV.7699. *See also At Security Council,
     Climate Change Cited Among Factors Impacting Stability in Sahel*, UN NEWS (26 May 2016),
     https://news.un.org/en/story/2016/05/530512-security-council-climate-change-citied-
     among-factors-impacting-stability-sahel#.VofokfRXenM%22%3Ehere%3C/a%3E.

30   Tim Radford, *Land Use Can Achieve 30% of Carbon Cuts by 2030*, CLIMATE NEWS
     NETWORK (1 Nov. 2017), http://climatenewsnetwork.net/23280-2; UNFCCC, Paris, Fr., 30
     Nov.–13 Dec. 2015, *Report of the Conference of the Parties on Its Twenty–First Session*, pt.
     2, Annex, art. 2(1)(a), UN Doc. FCCC/CP/2015/10/Add.1 (29 Jan. 2016) ("This Agreement,
     in enhancing the implementation of the Convention [UNFCCC], including its objective,
     aims to strengthen the global response to the threat of climate change, in the context
     of sustainable development and efforts to eradicate poverty, including by: [...] Holding
     the increase in the global average temperature to well below 2° C above pre-industrial
     levels and pursuing efforts to limit the temperature increase to 1.5° C above pre-indus-
     trial levels, recognizing that this would significantly reduce the risks and impacts of cli-
     mate change"). *See also, generally,* Max Collett, *In the REDD: A Conservative Approach to
     Reducing Emissions from Deforestation and Forest Degradation*, 3(3) CARBON & CLIMATE
     L. REV. 324 (2009); Lee Godden et al., *Reducing Emissions from Deforestation and Forest
     Degradation in Developing Countries (REDD): Implementation Issues*, 36 MONASH U. L.
     REV. 139 (2010); PETER LAWRENCE, JUSTICE FOR FUTURE GENERATIONS: CLIMATE
     CHANGE AND INTERNATIONAL LAW 200 (2014) (noting the inherently multi-disci-
     plinary nature of the problem of climate change).

31   According to Lynn Scarlett, climate change scientists estimate that States could "achieve
     about one-third of their carbon reduction goals by halting the destruction of forests,
     grasslands, and other critical ecosystems, and by restoring degraded lands to boost their
     capacity" to absorb carbon dioxide from the atmosphere and store it. Lynn Scarlett,

endeavor in a non-linear manner and through the conceptual lens of complexity theory could be the key to ameliorating—and even reversing—the adverse effects of land degradation and anthropomorphic climate change in Sahelo-Saharan Africa and beyond.

*Climate Solutions for the 21st Century: Creating Low-Carbon Economies May Be One of the Most Difficult Tasks Humanity Has Ever Tackled—But the Benefits of Success Will Be Profound,* NATURE CONSERVANCY 28, 30 (Oct./Nov. 2016).

# Conclusion

Like the birds that gather in the treetops at night
　And scatter in all directions at the coming of dawn,
　Phenomena are impermanent.
－ SHABKAR TSOKDRUK RANGDROL

∙ ∙ ∙

[T]he gradual accretion of baby steps can take us long distances.
－ DAVID LUBAN

∙ ∙
∙

The significant gaps in the existing legal framework with respect to climate change mobility and the lack of appetite for a new binding international instrument have given impetus to the shift in focus from a rights-based approach to an adaptive approach. Addressing human mobility in the context of climate change is a herculean challenge, and our understanding of this emerging phenomenon is constantly evolving. Additional research and innovative thinking are needed to analyze emerging findings and create transformational adaptation strategies, such as supporting affected populations to remain where they live (i.e., *in situ* adaptation measures). The Great Green Wall for the Sahara and the Sahel Initiative is an example of a large-scale, transformational adaptive strategy—which can be analyzed through the lens of complexity theory. A restoration of the land along the Great Green Wall corridor could also create a positive feedback loop by serving as a climate change mitigation measure. Other transformational adaptation strategies include strengthening the resilience of communities that must move or are already displaced (as well as the communities that host them) and planning for consent-based relocation as a last resort adaptation option.

The current adaptive framework has the potential to further these transformational adaptation strategies. Climate change mobility is increasingly addressed within existing and emerging legal and policy instruments, as well as intergovernmental and civil society initiatives and institutions. Increased coordination, consultation, data sharing, and funding distribution will be crucial to building a complementary approach across institutions and policy fields. Amongst other developments, the inclusion of human mobility within the UNFCCC process has qualified scientific research, projects, and initiatives connected with human mobility adaptation for funding through the UNFCCC. Continued expansion of the mandate of the Task Force on Displacement would help to ensure the development and utilization of resources towards these aims, foster the harmonization of efforts within the UNFCCC and with external entities (e.g., with the Platform on Disaster Displacement), and help to ensure that any policy advancements reflect regional, national, and local considerations.

Protecting the rights of persons who are vulnerable to displacement and/ or who move must remain a vital part of efforts in this area. Litigation in domestic, regional, and international *fora* has an important role to play in enforcing the rights of individuals and groups in relation to climate change adaptation and mobility. Progressive judicial rulings are critical threads in the rich tapestry of measures that can be pursued, but should not be woven in isolation. Rather, litigation in courts should complement adaptive strategies, which can encourage legally binding rights-based approaches that may yet play a further complementary role in the future. Bilateral and regional agreements have been considered by some as preferable to, and a more politically feasible entry point than, one overarching international agreement; bilateral and regional agreements can be tailored to address local and regional concerns and needs with the bottom-up participation of affected populations. It has also been suggested that guiding principles on climate-induced mobility could be developed to guide decision making of governments in the short-to mid-term, drawing upon existing literature such as the Guiding Principles on Internal Displacement and the Nansen Principles. Political will is at present scarce for either creating new binding treaty commitments or creating a soft law instrument; significant conceptual and doctrinal hurdles would also need to be overcome to conceive an effective instrument. At the same time, climate change mobility is receiving increased recognition within the adaptive framework, and this momentum may eventually lead to a shift in perspective.

At the same time, as climate change impacts evolve, the very notion of statehood and nationality as a defining characteristic of legal identity may also be called into question, as populations shift by the tens or hundreds of millions and the habitable territory of entire States disappears under the oceans. In some respect and notwithstanding the state of the legal framework, the sheer scope of the human movement we may face in the future and the scale of human suffering that may result call for an approach that is beyond the classical, post-enlightenment rights-based approach to legal theory.

Due to our brief lifespans and the relative vastness of geological time, it is difficult for human beings to witness—much less intellectually understand and emotionally internalize—the changes that are continually happening all around us. The changes to the climate are poignant examples of this anthropocentric perspective of time and the transformations that occur over longer time horizons. We are currently between ice ages, otherwise known as an "interglacial period". The next ice age may not arrive for tens of thousands of years. One of the human phenomena that occurred the last time the great bastions of ice receded was that there was more of an opportunity for humans to cease, for a time, their wanderings, develop agriculture, and settle down in communities. The concept of owning a piece of the Earth developed, i.e., property law. There is a fair bit of delusional hubris in the concept of a person, who generally lives less than a century, owning a piece of the planet that has been in existence for four-and-a-half billion years and that will be around for a long time after the molecules of our bodies have been reintegrated into the ecosystem—and perhaps even into the sliver of land we once used to "own". Humans may have evolved on Earth, but if our species is to endure, we must adapt to the ever-changing environment of our origin and even venture beyond it. Quite simply, the Earth has a finite lifetime, but the human species does not. We might even be able, in millions of years hence when stars have died and been reborn and then died again, to outlast the great entropic heat death of the universe.

In any case, in about five billion years, the Sun, as it runs out of hydrogen and starts to fuse helium, will expand into a red giant star and engulf the Earth. Unless we develop a technological solution to this inevitability, humans will be forced to migrate away from Earth to another place in the Solar System or beyond. Moreover, an asteroid impact of sufficient size could alter the climate to such an extent that life on Earth for humans (and many other inhabitants) may become difficult or even impossible. The Earth has been impacted by asteroids many times before, and it will happen again. It is just a matter of time. Such eventualities are the ultimate climate changing events that our species will have to face in the future. Scientists have unequivocally proved that the carbon we have poured into the atmosphere has altered the environment and is causing the climate to change. This is a painstaking empirical measurement, not a theory. Moreover, the tireless scientific work of many in civil society have documented the movement of people due to changes in the environment. It is time for governments, businesses, and everyone on the planet to apply themselves to these movements and manage them in a responsible and compassionate manner. As Carl Sagan exquisitely observed,

> We were wanderers from the beginning. [...] When the climate was congenial, though, when the food was plentiful, we were willing to stay put. [...] Long summers, mild winters, rich harvests, plentiful game— none of them lasts forever. It is beyond our powers to predict the future. Catastrophic events have a way of sneaking up on us, of catching us unaware.[1]

With the advent of the burning of fossil fuels, instead of renewable resources, we have, ourselves, created the conditions that are now, and in the coming decades and centuries, causing us to move again. We need to become wanderers once again and embrace a self-image of our species as temporary denizens of the planet, who must care for those around us who are on the move because, in the not so distant future, it may not be isolated pockets of humanity that must move to ensure their livelihoods, but rather all of us who need to resume the life of wanderers in order to survive. Right now, we have an opportunity to make the wise and mature choices to deal with climate change mobility. We can already put the legal, policy, technological, and cultural frameworks into place in order to avoid a chaotic scramble as mass migrations intensify, so that those of us who will have to move can do so with skill, dignity, and grace. It is as if we are being presented with a grand dress rehearsal for the epic migrations of those who will come after us, when it comes time for humanity to leave the cradle of our planetary birthplace and travel to other worlds as the very means of the survival of our species. And once we get our own houses in order, perhaps then we can even begin to take more seriously our responsibility to the other species on Earth (both plant and animal) and treat them with the respect for which they are sorely overdue. For, if we ever make it to the stars, it would be quite a lonely existence if we humans were there all alone.[2]

---

1   CARL SAGAN, *Wanderers, An Introduction, in* PALE BLUE DOT: A VISION OF THE HUMAN FUTURE IN SPACE (1994).
2   LOREN EISELEY, *Magic, in* NOTES OF AN ALCHEMIST (1978); LOREN EISELEY, *The Long Loneliness, in* THE STAR THROWER (1978).

# Index